CW00505247

MY ANCESTC
LEATHER WORKER

by Ian H Waller FSG

SOCIETY OF GENEALOGISTS ENTERPRISES LTD.

Published by
Society of Genealogists Enterprises Limited
14 Charterhouse Buildings, Goswell Road
London EC1M 7BA.

© Ian Waller and Society of Genealogists 2015.

ISBN: 978-1-907199-31-8

British Library Cataloguing in Publication Data.
A CIP Catalogue record for this book is available from the British Library.

The Society of Genealogists Enterprises Limited is a wholly owned
subsidiary of the Society of Genealogists, a registered charity, no 233701.

About the Author

Ian Waller is a Fellow of the Society of Genealogists and a retired professional genealogist with over 30 years of experience in researching British ancestry. He is currently Chairman of AGRA (The Association of Genealogists and Researchers in Archives). He has taught family history to various U3A groups and at adult education centres in both Bedfordshire and Hertfordshire as well as lecturing widely at the Society and to family and local history groups around the home counties. He has written many articles for the family history press and is author of other Society publications in the 'My Ancestor' series.

Cover Images - Foreground: *The cobbler*, by O Pirsi, oil on canvas from 19th century. Public domain image (Wikimedia). Right: *The Shoemaker*, by Henrik van Oort, 1800-1830. Public domain image (Wikimedia). Background: Apprenticeship under the Poor Law (shoemaking).

CONTENTS

List of illustrations

INTRODUCTION

From prehistoric times man has used the skins of animals to help satisfy a basic clothing and footwear need. Leather dating from 1300 BC has been found in Egypt. Since then leather has played an essential role in most civilisations. Roman soldiers used leather as their principal item of armour. The Greeks used leather garments as early as 1200 BC and the use of leather spread throughout the Roman Empire. During the middle-ages, the Chinese perfected the art of manufacturing leather as had the North America Indians. Throughout the civilised world particularly Europe, Asia and America the technique of turning animal skins into leather goods has been perfected over time, albeit independently of each other.

Hides have been and still are used to make clothing, shelter, floor coverings and even decorative items. From raw leather man has, over time, produced boots and shoes, belts, clothing, saddles and harnesses, books, containers for liquids, balls and even boats particularly in the form of coracles.

Almost by accident methods of preserving and softening animal skins have evolved using smoke, grease and bark extracts. The original art of tanning leather using the bark of trees is thought to have originated in the Middle East or Mediterranean areas and was, for generations, a closely guarded secret frequently passed down from father to son. In England one of the earliest medieval trade guilds to be established was for tanners and leather workers when charters and licences were issued permitting people to practice leather tanning. In the 19th century, a chemical tanning process was invented to run alongside vegetable tanning. Today the chrome tanning process using chemicals accounts for about around 85% of all tanning undertaken. However the chemical tanning process is not used to make leather used in the soles of footwear and tooling leathers.

It seems pretty clear therefore that our ancestors, over many generations, could well have been involved in occupations dealing with leather. Many were skilled craftsmen who would have served apprenticeships but there were equally as many involved in the physical and manual labouring jobs associated with its production. Our ancestors will more than likely have been involved in more than one aspect of the leather trade particularly those who lived and worked in the rural areas or small towns and in the period before factories took over production. It was not unusual for cordwainers (shoemakers) to also be glovers and for leather tanners to be saddlers etc.

The majority of us, as did our ancestors, have leather shoes, leather clothing and furniture, leather wallets, belts, purses, gloves and cases, and those of us who ride horses may have leather saddles. Leather workers are the individuals who created all those items sometimes employed in mass production, sometimes working as individual craftsmen.

The object of this book is to examine the history, processes, working conditions and records available for research of the various trades and occupations associated with leather work from the earliest times right through to today.

1. Hides and skins of all types are used for leather goods.

Amongst our ancestors we will inevitably find family members who were leather tanners, curriers, merchants, shoemakers, saddlers and harness makers, leather bottle makers, cricket ball makers, sporran makers and bookbinders to mention a few. The leather trade generally was at its height in the early to mid-1800s gradually declining with the advent of cheaper imports of leather (often of equally good quality to English leather) and the use of more modern synthetic materials.

To put the leather working industries in context the following is a summary of the number of workers in England and Wales appearing in the various census returns around the height of the industry:

Boot and Shoe Makers	1851	274,451
	1861	250,581
	1871	223,365
Glove Makers	1851	29,882
	1861	25,300
	1871	16,811
Saddlers and Harness Makers	1851	17,583
	1861	18,229

	1871	23,011
Curriers	1851	12,920
	1861	13,109
	1871	14,710
Tanners	1851	28,330
	1861	21,938
	1871	18,348

Similar statistics are available for other census returns but the above tables emphasise that a fair number of our ancestors would have been involved in the leather trades.

Many of the archival records referred to are common to some, if not all, of the occupations including apprenticeship records, fire insurance records and general business records. There are also a large number of artefacts to be found in museums specific to the leather trades, for example Walsall Museum and Northampton Museum have sections relating to leather working, shoes etc.

First things first

Do not ignore basic sources

As always with family history research there are certain sources which form the skeleton of our research and many of these will have provided the first clues relating to leather workers.

Firstly make sure you have thoroughly researched and extracted as much information from civil registration certificates, the census returns, trade directories and parish registers as well as the following sources:

Wills and administrations - as tradesmen, many working for themselves, there is a strong likelihood that they left a will. Use the National Probate Calendars from 1858 or before then the records of the various ecclesiastical courts many of which are indexed and available on-line.

Fire insurance records - Because many workers would have had their own premises and would have been using inflammable materials in manufacture it is more than probable that they had their premises (and their homes) insured with one of the major insurance companies.

The first fire insurance company was founded in 1680 and the survival rate of records is fairly good, the most prolific being the Sun Fire Office, founded in 1710. Records, particularly policy registers, are held by the City of London Joint Archive Service. Policy registers, some of which are indexed, include the names of the policy holders and describe the property insured with its value, and give the names of tenants, if any. Registers kept by local agents may survive and may have been deposited in county record offices. Some plans and drawings of an individual's premises may exist showing the layout of buildings insured.

Claims for loss by fire are often recorded separately and can also to be found recorded in the insurance companies' minutes. The fire policy registers normally provide policy number; name and location of the agent; name, status, occupation and address of the policy holder; names, occupations and addresses of tenants; location, type, nature of construction and value of property insured; premium paid; renewal date; and may also contain some indication of previous claims or special circumstances. This may well be true of leather workers because they often kept glues and other inflammable materials in their workshops.

The Bankruptcy Act, 1869.

In the County Court of Lancashire, holden at Preston.
In the Matter of Joseph Stewardson, of No. 29, Borrowdale-road and Horse Shoe Corner, in Lancaster, in the county of Lancaster, and at Pedder-street, in Morecambe, in the said county of Lancaster, Boot and Shoe Maker, a Bankrupt.

William Hoyle, of No. 121, Moor-lane, Lancaster, Currier and Leather Merchant, has been appointed Trustee of the property of the bankrupt. The Court has appointed the Public Examination of the bankrupt to take place at the Sessions-hall, Preston, in the said county of Lancaster, on the 16th day of January, 1883, at eleven o'clock in the forenoon. All persons having in their possession any of the effects of the bankrupt must deliver them to the trustee, and all debts due to the bankrupt must be paid to the trustee. Creditors who have not yet proved their debts must forward their proofs of debts to the trustee. — Dated this 18th day of December, 1882.

2. Notices of all bankruptcies were given in the Government Gazettes.

Bankruptcy and insolvency records - Those who ran their own businesses were subject to economic fluctuations and may have fallen upon hard times. You should as a matter of course research the bankruptcy records, debtors' prisons and insolvency resources. Many such records are held by the National Archives at Kew with local record offices holding county gaol records in which many insolvent debtors were incarcerated. Useful information to confirm dates etc. can be obtained from the on-line records of the Government Gazettes at **www.thegazette.co.uk**. Examples of bankruptcies are given within the text of the book.

The Registers of Petitions for Bankruptcy for 1870-1883, held at The National Archives are arranged alphabetically by the initial letter of the surname. Although only brief information is given it enables a person to be identified from the case number, bankrupt's name, occupation and address. There are also registers of bankrupts, in both the London Bankruptcy Court and the county courts, for 1870-1886 which give dates of discharge. For cases at the London Court of Bankruptcy, the

Registers of Creditors' Petitions are the most valuable records although they are arranged chronologically and in alphabetical order of the first letter of the bankrupt's surname. They provide name, address, occupation and details of the bankruptcy as well as the date of advertisement in the *London Gazette*, the names of any trustees appointed, the amount of any dividend paid, and the date when proceedings closed.

Indexes to Declarations of Inability to Pay which were one means of becoming bankrupt, give the date of the case and name, address and occupation of the debtor and name of his solicitor. They run from 1825-1925, with separate registers of London bankruptcies and County Court bankruptcies.

Perry's Bankrupt and Insolvency Office for protection against fraud and swindling was established in London in 1810 and published the *Perry's Bankrupt and Insolvent Gazette*, monthly from 1828. The Gazette included lists of dissolutions of partnerships gazetted in England and Wales. The names of the partners were given in full, with surnames recorded in capitals, followed by their trade and address, as well as the date the partnership ended.

CERTIFICATES.—*Continued from Col. 526.*

Gazette—July 3, 1855.

BIGHAM John, of Liverpool, ship owner—2d class
CUTTER Daniel and Thomas James HUNTER, of Regent-st, tailors —1st class
DODDINGTON Frederick Thomas, of Aldersgate-st, manufacturer of lace falls and fancy goods—2d class
GRAVE Joseph, of Manchester, warehouseman—2d class
HAMMOND James, of Chancery-la. furniture dealer—2d class
JESSOP George, of Cliftonville Hove, builder—3d class
LOGSDON Edward, of Hatfield, baker—2d class suspended
MAIDLOW Charles, of Adelaide-ter, Westbourne-grove, builder and auctioneer—2d class
MORGAN George Hargrave, of Hereford, builder—1st class
NORTIMER James, of Grosvenor-rd, Saint John's-wood, builder— 2d class
RANDALL Samuel, of Wellingborough, shoe manufacturer—2d class
RILEY William, James LUPTON, Robert HALSTEAD, and John HAWORTH, of Burnley, cloth manufacturers—3d class
SAMPSON Paul, of Hythe, boot and shoe maker—3d class
SNIBSON Josiah, Thomas SNIBSON, and William SNIBSON, of Manchester, wholesale grocers and drysalters—2d class
UNDERWOOD James, of Epsom, victualler—3d class suspended
WALKER Stair, of Boundary-rd, Saint John's-wood, builder—2d class
WEBSTER Gabriel, of Dewsbury, plumber and glazier—3d class
WEST John Richard, of Sun Saw Mills, Canal-rd, Kingsland, saw mill proprietor—3d class

Gazette—July 6, 1855.

EDAKEY John and George, of Keighley, grocers—2d class
EROWETT Louisa, of Bradford, innkeeper—1st class
COXON John, of Macclesfield, butcher, victualler, & coach proprietor —2d class suspended
HARGREAVES Charles & Michael HARGREAVES, of Bradford, whitesmiths and bolt makers—1st class
MORGAN William, of Bristol and Bath, potatoe dealer and coal merchant—2d class

3. Example from Perry's Gazette showing shoe maker bankruptcies.

To declare yourself bankrupt, you had to be a trader, owe more than £100 (reduced to £50 from 1842), and petition the court. Creditors could also petition for a bankruptcy order to be made against an individual. All creditors would have a claim to any assets and the court would order how these were to be distributed among them.

A trader was anyone who made a living by buying and selling, and by the late 18th century this covered anyone who bought materials, worked on them and then re-sold them - in other words, most skilled leather craftsmen.

Insolvent debtors were people who were unable to pay their debts. They could be kept indefinitely in a debtors' prison if their creditors so wished. From 1861 insolvent debtors were allowed to apply for bankruptcy.

Friendly societies - Friendly Societies have existed since Roman times. They grew on a very simple philosophy that if a group of people contributed to a mutual fund, then they received benefits in times of need. Most meetings were of a social nature and as part of the meeting subscriptions would be collected. Friendly Societies were essentially mutual insurance clubs providing cash benefits.

The Government encouraged membership of such societies and in 1875 an act of Parliament legislated for a system of auditing and registration. Leather workers throughout the country whether based in town or village, along with many other people, joined Friendly Societies in large numbers. By the late 1800s there were around 27,000 registered Friendly Societies.

Prior to the introduction of the 20th century Welfare State they were often the only way a working person could receive help in times of ill health, old age or death of a family member. When the Welfare State was introduced during the last century the staff within the Friendly Societies already had the expertise to run the scheme and they were frequently instrumental in administering the welfare state.

Societies were usually independent, or could be affiliated to larger organisations. Many independent societies catered for particular groups of workers. Affiliated societies came to the fore in the 1820s, and were popular because they had financial security as a result of being part of a large organisation. Some trade unions were originally registered as Friendly Societies (see class FS at the National Archives for details).

Social activity was another important reason for joining and societies often had their own rituals and regalia which gave their members a feeling of belonging. The main social event of the year in most societies was a parade to the parish church for a service followed by dinner.

National Insurance from 1911 and the Welfare State and the National Health Service in the late 1940s saw the demise of many societies, as the financial relief was then provided by the state. As such the social events lost their impetus. A small number of Friendly Societies still survive today offering good value financial services.

As many of the societies met in the local hostelry detecting evidence of the existence of these societies, is sometimes problematic although a few built their own halls and club houses.

It is also thought that only a small percentage of records of Friendly Societies have been deposited in local record offices and these generally relate to local branches of national friendly societies. Deposited records often comprise society rulebooks, (which give an idea of how the societies were run) and local minute and subscription books. The annual reports produced by the official Registrar of Friendly Societies from 1852 onwards are also available and these contain detailed accounts of their work, including details of cases dealt with and various statistics. Copies are amongst Parliamentary Papers which also contain other material relating to friendly societies: the most interesting of which are reports and evidence presented to the various investigative commissions and select committees, and surveys. The most complete is a survey undertaken in 1910 listing every society or branch, county by county, with details of membership, assets, income and other information, which is impossible to find elsewhere.

Some of the surviving societies hold their own records. The National Register of Archives provides information about records of around 1700 different Friendly Societies or branches kept by record offices. Local newspapers often carried reports of meetings etc. so these should also be searched.

Apprenticeship records - Look for apprenticeship indentures amongst family papers, records of the workhouse and poor law authorities as well as the Premium Tax records 1710-1811 held in class IR1 at the National Archives which can be searched using Ancestry.co.uk.

Apprenticeships in the leather industry usually started around the age of 12 or 14 years and lasted for a period of seven years. There would have been a signed indenture, one copy for the parents of the apprentice, the other for the master. These were personal contracts. Under the Statute of Apprentices 1583 anyone practicing a trade without having served an apprenticeship could have been fined. In London, particularly if a master died, the apprentice could continue his indentures with the master's widow provided she carried on the same trade but it was not unusual for another master to take the apprentice on for the remaining term of the indenture. This was fairly common amongst the livery companies.

Business records of individuals and companies may well contain apprenticeship details and in most cases the records of the craft guilds and livery companies will provide essential information particularly in regard to freedoms (made free at the end of the apprenticeship).

4. Apprenticeship under the Poor Law - shoemaking.

Trade and Craft Guilds - The primary purpose of the craft guilds was to establish a complete system of control over all who were associated in the pursuit of a common calling. The merchant guilds, working usually in the smaller towns, organised a whole industry; the craft guilds, springing up everywhere, from London to most provincial towns (even larger villages in some cases), organised each separate part of every industry as an independent entity. Where the merchant guild had organised the leather business as a whole, craft guilds broke it up into specialties, so that tanners, saddle makers, harness makers, bridle makers, shoe makers, slipper makers, boot makers, glovers etc., each had their own fraternity. This degree of specialisation was also extended to the social interests, education and religion of its members.

Progression within the guild commenced once the indenture was completed, the apprentice graduated into the ranks of the journeymen, becoming thereby a fellow of the craft, entitled to its liberties and privileges on equal terms with all others. This passing to a higher grade was obtained by proof of his skill through a 'masterpiece' or in some cases by an examination before the wardens. (In Scotland the equivalent of a warden was a 'Deacon'). A journeyman hired himself out to some masters for two or three years at wages and then, with a little money of his own, set up in his own shop, hired journeymen, indentured apprentices and became a master.

An apprenticeship indenture was a legal document whereby a master, in exchange for a premium, agreed to instruct the apprentice in his or her trade for a set term of years which for most leather trades was between four and seven years depending upon the speciality. The provision of food, clothing and lodging was part of the agreement.

An Act of Parliament in Queen Anne's reign ruled that from 1 May 1710 a tax was to be paid on all apprenticeship indentures excepting those where the fee was less than one shilling or those arranged by parish or public charities. Trades which had not existed in 1563 when the Statute of Apprentices became law were not liable to the tax. The tax was abolished in 1804 but payments continued to trickle in until January 1811.

The tax, paid by the master not more than one year after the end of the apprenticeship, was at the rate of 6d. in the pound on agreements of £50 or less, plus one shilling for every pound above that sum. The payment of tax was entered on the reverse of the indenture, which was deemed void without this payment. Evasion, however, was common. The records are held at The National Archives in class IR1 and indexed on Ancestry and by the Society of Genealogists.

These records have significant genealogical value particularly where the indenture cannot be located or if the records of the appropriate guild have not survived. They cover a span of nearly 100 years roughly corresponding to the 18th century. Up to about 1760, the name, occupation and place of origin of the father (designated 'deceased' where appropriate), guardian or widowed mother of the apprentice is usually given. The name, occupation and place of work of the master are given throughout the series.

The Leather Trades Directory - Since around 1880 Kelly's have published a yearly directory specific to the leather trades. The directories rose to prominence in the second half of the 19th century peaking in the period up to the First World War and were published for England, Wales, Scotland and Ireland and organised by county.

Each directory lists merchants and tradesmen specific to the trades associated with leather including: Hide and Skin Merchants, Curriers, Tanners, Leather Factors, Leather Merchants, Leather Glove Manufacturers, Boot and Shoe Thread Makers, Belting Manufacturers, Boot and Shoe Makers, Portmanteau and Leather Bag

Makers, Furriers, Saddlers and Harness Makers, Leather Goods Manufacturers (Fancy), Leather Cutters and Sellers, Whip Manufacturers, Clog Makers, Legging and Gaiter Manufacturers, Grindery Merchants, Sewing Machine Manufacturers and Dealers, Golf and Cricket Ball Makers.

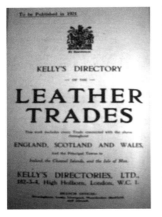  

5. *Trade directories provide information about individuals and companies involved in the leather trades.*

The ordinary Kelly and Post Office directories will also list those carrying on leather business within a particular town or locality but the listings may not be complete.
In any case please be aware that all directories no matter how comprehensive will be 'out of date' by the time they are published as information was usually collected six months or so before publication.

Provincial newspapers - newspapers particularly those published for provincial areas frequently contain a wealth of information for those involved in the leather industry. Advertisements for the individuals or companies are a valuable source to trace the existence of a company and just exactly what they offered or produced, reports covering court cases, fires, trade union meetings, awards of contracts to firms etc. can all help you to put the flesh on the bones of your ancestor's life.

It is worth keeping track of the ever increasing editions which are becoming available online through the British Newspapers Archive and also remembering that local record offices usually have a collection (usually on microfilm) some of which are supported by separate card indexes.

The monthly meeting of the Higham, Rushden, Irthlingborough, and Irchester Branch was held at the Trade Union Club, Higham-road, Rushden, on Monday evening. The chair was taken by the branch president Mr. W. Bazeley, at 8 p.m. There was a good attendance of members. After the ordinary business, nominations for Union officers were taken as follows :—General president, Mr. C. Freak; general secretary, Mr. W. B Hornidge; District Council member, Mr. D. Stanton; Parliamentary representative, Mr. T. F. Richards; Union treasurer, Mr. W. H. Lowe; Union trustees, Messrs. Wm. Ward, L. E. Bradley, and S. Adams. The conference delegate (Mr. W. Bazeley) then gave his report of the Leeds Conference, and explained to the members the most vital resolutions that would govern the future policy of the National Union —namely, labour representation in the House of Commons, affiliation of Union to Chas. Booth's League for old age pensions for all persons, it being considered by the conference that the present poor law system was a disgrace to a civilised country, and that pensions should be provided by the State. He also stated that the conference had decided by a unanimous vote to admit boys and youths under the age of 18 years at the same contributions and benefits as females, after 18 years of age to pay full contributions. This will come into operation forthwith. It was also decided to pay 5s. 3d. per day dispute pay in future instead of 3s. A resolution was also carried, as follows : "That this conference, being desirous of testifying its appreciation of the valuable services rendered to our Union, and to the labour cause in general, by Mr. Wm. Inskip, late general secretary, decides that a sum of £250 (equivalent to one year's salary) be taken from the Union funds and placed at the discretion of the Council to be employed for the benefit of his widow and children."—A vote of thanks to the president for his report was passed, to which he suitably replied.

SERIOUS CHARGES AGAINST A SHOE MAKER. William Wood, shoe maker, of Harpole, a man of about sixty, with grey hairs and whiskers, was charged with indecently assaulting two tiny girls, Ellen Richardson, aged eight, and Violet Winifred Cory, aged eight, at Harpole, on January 14th.—The cases were taken separately. In each case the evidence showed that while the children were in prisoner's house prisoner assaulted them. They were fetched out of the house by Mrs. Williams, a neighbour, and were subsequently examined by Mr. E. F. Jones, surgeon, who said that each of the children bore signs of having been interfered with.—Prisoner who said that he tried to get rid of the girls but could not, was committed for trial at the ensuing Assizes. Bail was allowed, prisoner in £50 and two sureties of £25 each.

DREADFUL FIRE AT POPLAR AND LOSS OF LIFE.—On Monday, at an early hour, there was a fire in the neighbourhood of Penny-fields, Poplar, which was attended with the loss of one life and serious, if not fatal consequences, to two other persons—one a man between 60 and 70 years of age, the other a girl about six or seven years old. The premises in which the disaster originated were situate at 41; the lower part of the building being in the occupation of a boot and shoe maker named D. J. Donovan, and the upper floor was in the occupation of another family named Donovan, but not related to the other. Fortunately, the proprietor of the shoe shop and his family were not at home when the fire commenced. The premises of Mr. Quin, proprietor of the Silver Lion Tavern, and it was owing to a little girl who was in the house that the fire was first discovered. She, it appeared, while proceeding to her bedroom, had her attention directed to a loud crackling noise in the next house. This being accompanied with dense volumes of smoke at once convinced her that the place was on fire, and she called Mr. Quin, who succeeded in making the inmates, who were asleep, &c. sible of their danger. There had been sleeping in the same room three children, their father and mother, and the servant girl, aged 13 years, named Esther Donovan. The three children and the father and mother were got out of the blazing building, but how is not precisely known, only that the father seized hold of two of his children, whom he carried under his arms through the flames, but in so doing the unfortunate man and his daughter Mary were both seriously burnt, and were removed to they hospital, where the remain in a very precarious state. The last persons who left, it is believed, were the mother and one of her children. It was at first expected that the servant girl had also been rescued and had taken shelter in the house of a neighbour, as she could not be heard of during the fire. Unfortunately, the poor creature was burnt to death in the flames. The fireman were enabled to get the flames at length extinguished, but not until the premises were totally destroyed. Further inquiries having been made for the girl, the ruins were searched, and she was found burnt in a frightful manner from head to foot. Life was quite extinct.

HIGHAM FERRERS

POLICE COURT, MONDAY —Before the Mayor (Alderman W. Spong), Mr. Owen Parker, and Mr. E. B. Randall —George Loveridge, shoe maker, no fixed abode, admitted being drunk and disorderly at Higham Ferrers on Saturday, and was sent to gaol for 14 days in default of paying a fine of 10s. and costs. — Several vaccination exemption certificates were granted.

6. A wealth of information about all aspects of leather workers can be found in provincial newspapers.

Surnames derived from the leather trade

Barker	A tanner
Boot	A maker of boots
Bracegirdle	A belt maker
Burrell	A harness maker
Butler	A maker or seller of leather bottles

Chaucer	A maker of shoes or leggings
Curres or Currier	One who applies techniques of dressing, finishing or colouring to the leather after tanning
Gant	A maker or seller of gloves
Glover	A maker or seller of gloves
Purser	A maker of purses or bags
Sadler/Saddler	A saddle maker
Sellers	A maker of saddles
Tanner	One who tans animal hides and skins to produce leather
Spurrier	A maker of spurs
Buckler	A maker of buckles
Loriner	A maker of lorinery or saddlers' ironmonger

CHAPTER ONE
Tanners, Curriers and Leather Merchants

Tanning was one of the most noxious and hazardous industries, thus was not welcome in the cities, towns or most villages. Urine and animal faeces are all associated with the treatment of leather. Many tannery workers also suffered from diseases through working within the industry thus cutting their lives short.

Homer went a long way to describe the process in the 7th century BC:

'The ox hide, which is soaked in fat, is pulled to and fro by men standing in a circle, thus stretching the skin and causing the fat to penetrate into the pores'.

Our earlier ancestors would have been involved in a very basic method of treating animal skins. Two principles applied - one was to hang the skins over the smoke from a camp fire, the other was by greasing, smoking and then stretching them. The use of traditional vegetable tanning materials is prehistoric. From the middle ages in England, oak bark was used frequently and as such, tanneries began to be established near large forest and woodland areas. In about 1780 valonia (a type of bubble algae), was often used alongside the oak bark and continued to be for the following hundred years or so. By the 1880s chrome tanning was introduced which involved various chemical processes. Different processes and materials were used to prepare different types of leather.

The worst job in history

Some time ago Channel Four television produced a series of programmes hosted by Tony Robinson which included an edition showing how early tanning was undertaken. The trailer asked - 'Are you the special person we are looking for? Is your idea of a day at work one that involves standing in a pit of rotting flesh, dog poo and chicken dung? - Then tanning, the conversion of cattle and sheep hides into leather, is just the job for you'. Not a particularly awe inspiring description but maybe this is the type of advertisement which would have been seen by our ancestors who replied and became tannery workers. The entrepreneurs amongst our ancestry who owned the businesses had no shortage of applicants for such jobs.

The tanning process

Skins (from smaller animals such as calves, lambs, goats etc.) and hides (from the larger animals such as cows, deer and horses), as living organisms, could be made resistant to bacteriological decay by steeping them in tannin for which the prime source in this country was oak bark. In 1805, Sir Humphrey Davy discovered that materials from other trees such as chestnut and ash had the same properties and could also be used. Leather was processed essentially for the main trades of shoemaking and saddle/harness making, both of which figured amongst the village trades which were essential for the local economy. Tan yards were a familiar sight and smell in virtually every village in the country, usually located by a river or stream. Hence, in early periods it was essentially a village trade conveniently located to be supplied with cattle hides by local farmers. Tanners who operated in the towns invariably bought their skins from the abattoirs or local butchers who slaughtered their own animals. The quality of the finished leather goods not only depended upon the type of skin or hide used but also on the skill of both the tanner and currier which today are essentially one process. Our ancestors would either have been the owners or operators of tannery businesses or the individuals who were employed by them and did not mind doing the 'worst job in history'.

7. Early tanning and currier processes.

There were regular advertisements appearing in provincial newspapers for 'Bark Peelers', those who prepared the oak bark for processing literally stripping the bark from the trees and grinding it to a powder for use, and also for the sales of tanneries or tan yards. In 1796 such an advertisement existed for the sale of Sattersfield tan yard in Derbyshire. It boasted 43 pits, 44 handlers, 6 lime pits, 3 drying rooms, 2 bark mills and was located near a plentiful supply of water and a neighbourhood well stocked with oak timber. This was by no means large scale.

So how did our ancestors treat the leather? All leather was treated in much the same way. It was traditionally done by the initial salting down to prevent putrification after the animals had been killed. In some urban areas this was actually instigated at the abattoir or slaughterhouse. As well as preserving, salting also began to loosen and dissolve dirt and grease, followed by a soaking in water to remove the residue salt and dirt. In areas where lime was readily available, the hides were laid in lime pits to start the process of loosening hairs. In other localities they were dusted with ground up oak tree bark. Whichever process was used the treated skins were after a period of time, immersed in a shallow pit or vat containing the fermenting solution of organic matter (urine, dog excrement and chicken dung), commonly known as enzymatic 'bate'. The bacteria which grew as a result of this soaking were sufficient to fully loosen the hair and fat from the skins. These were sold off as a by-product to make glue - another noxious business! At this stage further tanning material, usually more oak bark, was skilfully added until the solution fully penetrated the skin. The extent of this penetration affected the quality of the finished product. This process could take up to a year or so depending upon the thickness and type of the hide. Following this any remaining hair or fat was removed with a blunt stone or wooden scrapper and the leather was then hung in open sheds for several days to dry and cure.

The later introduction of earth salts, which were alum based, produced a fine white leather, considered to be the best for the growing fashion industry for gloves, bags etc. The industrial revolution saw a great demand for leather and as such, the process of tanning changed. Chemicals like hydrochloric and sulphuric acid signalled the end of traditional processes. By the end of the 19th century many smaller traditional tanneries closed because the demand from the fashion houses made leather treated with vegetable based materials unworkable because it was too thick or too brittle.

8. Medieval tanning process (Bate).

An alternative method involved using a brain soup to coat the hide with. Tanning breaks down the glycerin and loosens the fibres of the skin. The agent used in this method is found in the brain of the animal that provided the hide.

Two new processes were introduced into the tanneries in the 1800s and these changed the tanning industry forever. These were replacement of the vats with drums and the use of chromium as the tanning agent both of which reduced the time taken in process of tanning from a few months to a few days.

Although certain changes have been brought about in the leather production process over time, most of the tools used have remained fundamentally the same, thus proving that the craft has remained intact.

At the dawn of the Industrial Revolution, the demand for softer leather rose exponentially. Not only for apparel; a great many of the machines invented used leather belts to drive the mechanisms that automated much of what was formally manual labour.

9. 1960s tannery.

This fundamental change in the process became known as Chrome Tanning, the name being derived from using the salts of the metal Chromium (known in the trade as 'liquor'). This process is still used today. To accommodate the change and demand, tanneries became larger and mainly town-based employing a significant number of men. Now for the science: in 1897 the appropriate 'liquor' was made by adding sugar to an acidified potassium bi-chromate solution. A remarkable number of other obscure chemical solutions were also tried. Scientific advances later gave rise to the use of synthetic tanning solutions including formaldehyde. The tanning process had become much more advanced in the 20th century and as such, many different qualities of leather, all for different finished products, had been produced using the large variety of processes.

Today's process includes a finishing step, which includes treatments such as dyes, polishing or sanding and these are carried out by a currier after tanning is complete.

Regulation within the leather processing industry was never easy to achieve but an attempt was made as early as 1663 to try and regulate the industry which at best resulted in a 'code of conduct' for tanners. An example of regulation taken from the records of the Northamptonshire leather industry is given below:

Tanners' Regulations 1663
Northamptonshire County Records Office NRO/G2982

'Whereas by severall good statutes heretofore made and yet in force diverse Penalties and Forfeitures are provided sett & ordayned for & upon Offenders & offences against the said Statutes: The maine Drift & End thereof being to prevent the great Damadge dayly ariseing to us by bringing in & conveying away out of this our Kingdom of England, Dominion of Wales & Towne of Berwicke upon Tweed, Divers great quantities of severall forreigne Goods & Native Commodities, as of Tanned & Curried Leather & Wooll &c. And whereas in the first & fourth yeares of the Reigne of our Royall Grandfather King James and in the fowerteenth year of our Reigne severall good lawes & Statutes have bin made for Redresse of the said Griefs & the better preventing such frauds & violences for the time to come. And likewise for the true & just Tanning, Currying & workeing of Leather & for the redressing of such Deceipts and abuses which have bin & are commonly practiced by Butchers, Tanners, Curriers & workers of leather. It is amongst other things enacted that no Butcher by himslfe or any other person shall gash, slaughter or cutt any hide of Oxe, Bull, Steer or Cow in slaying thereof, or otherwayes whereby the same shall be impaired or hurt; Nor shall offer or put to sale any Hide being putrified or rotten: Nor shall kill any Calfe to sell being under five weeks old. And that no person or persons professing the Art & Mistery of Tanning of Leather shall overhasten the Tanning of Leather by indirect meanes, crafty & subtle practices by which they make their Leather to seeme both faire well & sufficiently tanned within a very shorte space: nor offer or put to Sale any Leather that shall not be well & sufficiently tanned and thoroughly dried. Nor shall cutt or make their upper leather hides, backs, butts or calveskins. And that no tanned Leather be bought or sold any place but in the open & publick faire or markett: And against unlawfull Buyers & Sellers against forestalling of Marketts & that no leather be sold before the same be searched & sealed: And against Sealers & searchers who doe not faithfully perform their dutys. And that no currier shall carry any kind of Leather except it be well & perfectly tanned & well & thoroughly dried, not shall burn or scald any hide nor leather in the currying, nor shall gash or hurt any Leather in the shaving, nor shall seale any leather except it be well & sufficiently tanned: and diverse other branches & clauses forfeitures & penalties mentioned in the said Statutes. Nowithstanding the strictness of the said lawes those & divers other great abuses & fraudulent practices mentioned therein are now more committed then ever to the great prejudice of all our good

Subjects of this our Realme of England &c. And whereas it manifestly appeareth to us that by the neglect of the due Execution of those & other good lawes many great inconveniences & mischiefs are dayly received & growing up (equalling if not exceeding those mentioned in the preambles of the said Statutes, being the ground & Ocassion thereof) which tend much to the damadge of us and the empoverishment of our good subjects of this our kingdome: For prevention whereof in the future our Will & pleasure is that the said Lawes be duly & strictly put in Execution. And we having in our princely care the Prosperity & Welfare of all our good people of this our Kingdome of England & Dominion of Wales: And holding ourselves bound in a matter of so great an Abuse to make it our Worke to put the same in such Execution as the Law requires. Wee doe therefore for us & in our behalfe nominate, appoint, impower, authorize our Trusty & Welbeloved John Croke Esq, Gent in ordinary of our most honourable privy Chamber and his sufficient Deputy & Deputyes so far as in us lyes for that service: for & in the name and to & for the use of Us our heires & Successors by all just & lawfull wayes & meanes to enquire into search for & discover all offenders & offences acted, committed, done or suffered, or that at any time hereafter shall be acted, committed, done or suffered within this our Kingdom of England & Dominion of Wales or either of them, or in our said Towne of Berwick or any parts thereunto belonging, contrary to the Tenure Forme & Effect of the said Statutes. And also in the Name and to & for the use of Us our heirs & Successors as well by land as by water to search for, seize, detaine & carry away any forfeited leather or hides wrought or unwrought, cutt or uncutt, packt or unpackt, intended or purposed to be transported by any person & persons into any of the parts beyond the Seas, and likewise all unlawfull wares made of leather & any other prohibited & uncustomed Commodities that now are or hereafter at any time shall be forfeited, seizable, comeing or accrueing to us our heires & Successors by force & tenure of the same Statutes or any of them. And also to endeavour & see that due prosecution be had & made against all such offenders for all & every such offence according to Law. And also that notwithstanding the known way & course of Officers purposely constituted to attend & act therein, yet dayly experience shewes that through neglect of their duty or some secret practizes or combinations betweene owners of goods & persons intrusted in this behalfe; or other indirect dealings great quantities of leather & Calveskins Wool & other native commodities are commonly exported contrary to the said lawes & Statutes, without any seizures made or punishment inflicted for the same. And we being carefull & desirous to prevent the said Mischiefs for the future & to that end to make tryall of such probable wayes & meanes as hath bin manifested unto us. Our further Will & Pleasure is that all the said lawes be duely observed & strictly executed for the time to come, And therefore do nominate, appoint, impower, give Licence unto & authorize our said Trustee & Welbeloved John Croke Esq & his sufficient Deputy or Deputies to be deputed by writeing under his hand & Seale & for whom he shall & will answer: to have, hold, use, exercise & enjoy all & every the said Liberties Licences, Powers & Authorities to the end & in the manner aforesaid. And our Will & pleasure is that he the said John Croke Esq his Deputy or Deputyes within tenn dayes or other convenient time after any seizure or discovery made shall give notice thereof in writing to the remembrances of our Exchequer, or to such other publick officer there as to them shall seem fitting in this behalfe to the end that such due course and proceedings may be had & taken therein as the case shall require. And the said John Croke Esq his deputy or deputyes are not for any cause to favour connive at nor conceale or mitigate any offender or offences whatsoever happening within their search commission or knowledg.

And this our Licence power & Authority granted as aforesaid is not to restraine or barre any others in what they justly may or ought to doe in or relateing to any [of] the premises. And our further will & pleasure is that it shall & maybe lawfull to & for the said John Croke Esq or his sufficient Deputy or Deputyes their under officers & servants or any of them, Authorized by writt of Assistance under the seale of our Court of Exchequer (which said Writt the Barons of our said Court are hereby willed & required to grant & issue forth unto them to take a Constable, Headborough or any other publique Officer inhabiting near unto the place, whivh said Officer or Officers shall not refuse to aid countenance & assist him the said John Croke Esq his deputy or deputees at his or their perills: To enter into at Will & Pleasure & goe into any vessel, boat, house, shop, sellar, Warehouse, Tanners house or yard, roome or other place whatsoever where they shall suspect or receive information that such unlawfull & prohibited goods are, And in case of resistance break open doores, chests, truncks & other packadge, there to seize & from thence to bring & carry away all forfeited leather & Wooll & all other prohibited & uncustomed goods whatsoever: And put & secure the same in some safe place or Warehouse near unto the place where such seizures shall be made, hereby requiring the no deputy or deputyes, under officers or servants of ours belonging to the said John Croke Esq shall in any wise or at any time be molested troubled arrested imprisoned or detained in the Execution of their office aforesaid. And further our Will & pleasure is that all Majors, Sheriffs, Viceadmiralls, Governours of Garrisons & forts, Justices of the peace, bailiffs, constables & all other officers & persons whatsoever shall be aiding & assisting unto him the said John Croke Esq his deputy or deputyes under Officers & servants in all things wherein they or any of them shall require their aid & assistance in the due execution of their duty & place of this our service & in secureing the persons of all such offenders untill by order & Courte of Law such further course may be taken with them & every of them as the Law in that case doth require. Given at our court at Whitehall —- day of —- in the fifteenth yeare of our Raigne Anno Doni 1663.'

There were often law suits and court cases in relation to the regulation of the trades of both tanner and currier and even Parliament became involved in the early 1700s.

Growth of the tanning and leather dressing industry

The 1951 Census showed 35,878 people employed at that time in the tanning and leather dressing industry in England and Wales. Northamptonshire, which by then was considered the centre of the industry, employed 2,557. The tanning and leather dressing industry at the time was scattered throughout the country but there were three geographical concentrations of production. In north-western England from Merseyside to Leeds, second in the south-east Midlands, particularly on the Northamptonshire, Bedfordshire and Buckinghamshire borders; and, third around London. In 1951 2,168 Londoners were still employed in tanning and leather dressing centred on Bermondsey.

10. The state of the tanning industry in England in 1951.

Leather dressing establishments were frequently smaller than the tanneries and employed fewer people. The premises were smaller and the demand for water less than for tanning. Most leather dressers were not dependant on local tanneries for their supplies as the railways easily transported leather from further afield. In the mid 1950s Northamptonshire provided employment for around 1,800 people in about seventy leather dressing/currying businesses some employing around 25-30 staff. By the start of the 21st century only seven existed including the only known supplier of bookbinding leathers.

Most large tanneries employed fewer than 150 workers but required large premises, large amounts of water for the process and specialist plant to dispose of resultant effluents. The characteristic smell associated with tanneries made them unpopular amongst town residents. Out of town semi-rural sites were preferred by the planners but to some extent this presented a challenge for employment of a labour force. It was however the leather dressers who were important to the local economy because of their role in preparing and providing upper leathers for the footwear industry which was so prevalent in Northamptonshire.

11. Hand tanning processes

There was total interdependency between the tanning, leather dressing and footwear industry in Northamptonshire. The leather production and processing industries have been subject to a constantly changing environment. Changes in production techniques and manning levels over three centuries have affected output. The wide variations and volatility of international hide prices have been beyond industry control. Availability of capital for the purchase of hides when prices were reasonably low was an important factor of survival. However this policy also resulted in the increased need for warehousing or on-site storage space and the need to maintain those hides in good condition. The suppliers of raw and semi-processed hides from other countries such as India became competitors and still are today.

Leather tanners in India

Leather tanning is one of the oldest manufacturing industries in India. The British introduced industrial scale modern processes and the first tanning and leather factory was set up in 1857 at Kanpur. Several other large tanneries were subsequently opened by British businessmen. Despite this, leather tanning, even today, is a traditional Indian craft and the primitive methods used for leather-making are still alive in many of the more remote areas of the country.

By 1912 the tanning and leather dressing business in India was extensive. Many tanneries in all three Presidencies were owned and operated by British industrialists who used leather merchants with established markets in London. Most of the India tanneries had active London agents. The British were very much involved in the ownership, management and technical side of the business but most of the operatives were native or Anglo-Indian. 30% of the tannery workforce was women.

12. Early Chrome Tanning factory in India.

The British owned tanneries, most of whom had head offices in London and operating in India by 1912 were:

Bengal Tannery Co.
Cuthbertson & Harper
James Monteth & Co.
Morrison & Cottle
John Teil & Co, (owned by Mrs N E M Barlow)
Watts & Co
Young & Co

All of the above companies operated out of Kolkata (formerly Calcutta).

Chambers & Co.
Indian Grove Leathers
Mysore Tannery
Government Boot & Army Equipment Factory, Cawnpore
King leathers
James Shearing & Co.
John Forstner

All of the above companies operated from Chennai (formerly Madras).

The following merchants representing the Indian tanneries had London based headquarters:

S. Deb & Co
Don Watson & Co
James Monteith
Watts & Co
David and Sassoon

In the early 20th century nearly 40% of all leather used in the United Kingdom was imported from India.

There were some other key developments as a result of British involvement:

1880: A boot factory was established by the British India Corporation in Kanpur.

1890: The British set up sixty more tanneries in Bengal, Bombay, Odisha (formerly Orissa) and Central India.

1895: Chrome tanning was introduced at tanneries in Pallavaram, Chennai, Bangalore, Cuttack and slightly later in Kolkata.

1913: By 1913, 22 large chrome tanneries were operating throughout India.

The effects of the two world wars lead to the establishment of even more tanneries and product manufacturing factories in Kanpur, Agra, Chennai and other places.

1947: At Independence the British still controlled all the major tanneries but soon relinquished that control as the Indian government wanted to return the industry to the small sector which is still the case today.

1951: Independent India banned the export of raw hides and skins and the British rapidly withdrew from the industry.

Records of tannery workers and owners in India can be located using local directories such as Thacker's Indian Directory (the 1895 edition is online on Ancestry and others are available at on Digital Library of India website) or by searching records held in the British Library for wills, details of government contracts etc. There is some useful background information in the various area gazetteers for India. Most records relating to individual operations are held as company archives and for this the researcher will need to pursue the locations of the company archives some of which are held in England and some still with successor companies in India.

London tanners

Tanners and curriers were well represented in the major cities despite the many objections on the grounds of smell. In London for example the 'Tanners Directory of England', published in 1869, records fifty five such establishments out of a total of five hundred and seven around England. This does not include all the small 'cottage industry tanneries' found in many villages at the time. The centre of the leather trade in London had long been the areas around Farringdon, where many curriers traded and Bermondsey where the Leather Market and Exchange was established on the corner of Weston Street and Leathermarket Street.

Skins came from the many London butchers around Smithfield and were processed using local water supplies and oak bark before being sold on the London Markets. The industry in Bermondsey from the middle/late 1700s employed many immigrant workers who originated from the Low Countries particularly Belgium and Holland. Most of these were housed locally in both hostels and in multiple occupation houses. In 1745 there were also tanneries along Long Lane. A search of the many historical maps will show clearly their locations.

So prevalent was the trade that twenty ninth in succession of London Livery Companies is that of the Worshipful Company of Curriers, granted arms in 1583. The original charter for the company is dated 1605 and is still preserved at the Guildhall Library. The records are fairly extensive and many individuals are named. There are very few references to tanners except where both processes were carried out together.

Today tanning industries still exist as leather still needs to be treated. This is now very much a single machine based process except where the finished product is of high value and quality where both the tanning and currying processes may still be carried out by hand.

In 1738 a petition was made to Parliament by the tanner and leather worker journeymen of London and Westminster in respect of laws about tanned leather, particularly the encroachment of curriers on other trades as they sold cut leather. It was subsequently decided that a bill should be passed allowing curriers to sell small pieces of leather!

Bermondsey - a centre for leather

By the late 1790s / early 1800s nearly one half of all Britain's finished leather originated in Bermondsey. As a centre for leather manufacture Bermondsey was full of establishments both on the riverfront and in the central area. The River Thames supplied water for the tanning pits and was a source of power within the industry both for tanners and leather-dressers. There was also access to a large supply of oak bark for tanning from the managed woodlands in nearby rural Surrey.

In 1703 a trade guild known as the Leather Hide and Wool Exchange was established and thereafter a charter of incorporation was granted to all persons who had served as apprentices in the tanning industry for seven years and who subsequently practiced as tanners or curriers in the parish. The Guild was required have a minimum of fourteen members out of which they had to elect a master and two wardens each year.

By the mid-1700s there were numerous tanners in business and numerically these were more extensive than in any other part of the country. The spin off was for the establishment of allied trades in the area. A large number of the population in the parish carried on the business of fellmongers (a dealer in animal skins), curriers, leather-dressers and parchment makers and dyers and needle and pin makers were also represented.

During 1832-1833 the Bermondsey Leather Market was constructed by the principal tanners in the parish. From as early as 1488 and up until this time, all the leather produced in Bermondsey (along with that from other areas of London) had been sold exclusively at Leadenhall Market. The Bermondsey Market was extended in 1879 to include a leather exchange. The later complex was divided in two; the market and the exchange. Parts of the market, including a grand clock tower, slaughterhouses and animal pens, were destroyed during World War Two. There are five carved reliefs on the building depicting various processes of leatherworking: the buying and selling of hides; the un-hairing and de-fleshing of hides; hide being agitated in a pit; tanned hide being rolled by hand; hides being hung up to dry.

13. Artists impression of the original Leather Exchange, Bermondsey.

Just ten years later and Bermondsey had undergone virtually a complete population change. Wealthier residents, apart from the tannery owners had left the parish. A densely populated area along the Thames was occupied by those whose income was irregular such as porters, labourers and jobbers, costermongers, watermen, lightermen and seamen. The remainder of the population, who occupied overcrowded accommodation verging on 'slums', were the leather workers mainly the tanners, fellmongers, leather-dressers and tannery labourers. On average four to five persons slept in one room, standards of cleanliness and temperance were virtually non-existent and the population barely subsisted on a diet of bread and potatoes. One of the tannery buildings was taken over by Hartley's to make jam!

London's leather trade continued to decline not helped by the effects of two world wars. Many of Bermondsey's tanneries had been destroyed, and demand for the heavy leather they produced was falling.

14. Tanning Pits at Bevington's Tannery in Bermondsey.

Companies and individuals worked in Bermondsey within the leather trades as tanners, curriers and leather dressers. Some of the more established were:

Hepburns
S A Keyser
Richard King Watts & Co
Bevington & Sons Ltd
James Ashworth & Son
William Axtell & Son
Learmouth & Tickner
Ross & Co
DeClermont & Donner

along with individuals including:

Thomas Dakeyne,
Joshua Butterworth,
William Ursell,
Jacob Tout,
James Macrae,

William Undy,
Susannah Ash,
Caleb Crookenden,
William Kent
and Alexander Lamb.

For many of these archive material is available at various London repositories but the fire insurance records held by Sun Fire Office give an insight into the premises they occupied and their extent.

Bacon's Free School

When local leather merchant Josiah Bacon died in 1703 he left £700 in his will for the purchase of land with which to endow a free school. Poor children, whose parents were unable to provide for their education, were taught to read English and do enough arithmetic to keep merchants' books so that they could be prepared for jobs in trade. The local minister and churchwardens were to be governors of the school. Provision was also made for accommodation for the school-master. The school was constructed on Grange Road by 1718.

In 1849 the school was amalgamated with another charity school in the area, which had been founded in 1612 to provide education for the sons of seamen.

The Topographical Directory of London and its Environs describes the school thus:

'BACON'S FREE SCHOOL, Bermondsey, situated in Grange Road is a charitable institution founded by Mr Josiah Bacon who by his will charged his real and personal estates, with raising such a sum of money as should be requisite for building a free school within the parish of Bermondsey in which he was born, and also a dwelling house for the master, limiting the purchase to £700 and his trustees were to settle £150 a year for the maintenance of the school and the payment of the master and ushers. The scholars are to be poor children of inhabitants and they are taught English, writing and arithmetic to fit them for trades or to keep merchants' books as clerks. There are always to be forty and never more than sixty. The Trustees are always to be six or eight of the principal inhabitants of the parish who are nominated by the minister and churchwardens for the time being. The Minister, churchwardens and other chief officers of the parish for the time being are governors of the school and visit it as such from time to time.

This charity was, for some time after the school-house etc. were erected involved in a Chancery suit but in 1732 Thomas Bacon esq. in pursuance of the decree granted to the trustees a clear annuity for ever, charged upon the estates at Midloe and Little Paxton in the county of Huntingdon. Further particulars of this school may be found in Highmore's 'Pietas Londinensis'.'

Surviving records of Bacon's Free School, Bermondsey, include Josiah Bacon's will; Chancery orders relating to the school; articles of agreement for building the school; various leases, releases and assignments of annuities relating to school property; the administrative records of the school including Governors' and Trustees minutes; financial records; reports; and school log-books. The records are held by the London Metropolitan Archives as follows:

Reports, regulations and probate;
Property records;
Probate records;
Minutes and agendas;
Finance;
Miscellaneous;
Logbooks.

The logbooks which are particularly interesting are as follows:

Log Book of Bacon Free School Sep 1880 - Jul 1890.
Log Book, with index, marked 'Star Corner' Jan 1863 - Jun 1886.
Log Book of Bermondsey Church Boys' School, Griggs Place Jun 1886 - Jan 1909.
Log Book of Bacon Free School. Jan 1909 - Apr 1913.

The following is a report taken from a local newspaper in regard to the extent of involvement of the church in the administration of the school upon the failure of a trustee to attend a meeting. The date and the title of the newspaper are unknown but it is believed to be around the time that the newer school building was commissioned in 1891:

'Sir,
- At a meeting of the Vestry of this parish on October 5th, a remark was made by one of the Vestry, and echoed by our friend the Jackdaw in your last week's impression, which I think is calculated to mislead many of your readers with regard to the management of the above school. He there stated 'that there is practically only one trustee, for no one knows where the others are, as they may be at Halifax, New York, or anywhere else.' This is incorrect; the present trustees are - Messrs' Alfred Bevington, Charles Fauntleroy, John Cox, Edward M'Murdo, and Thomas Maskew. The first three gentlemen have, for years, been at almost every meeting for the transaction of business, unless through illness unable to attend. The following is an extract from the minutes relating to the election of trustees of the Free School, Bermondsey, bearing date 17th September, 1804:

'Whenever the trustees are reduced to four, it is the duty of the minister, churchwardens, and overseers, to nominate proper persons (being vestrymen) to fill up the number to six or eight, and it will be for the convenience of the Governors if they are nominated out of their body.'

I may here remark that a new trust deed would entail an expense which should, if possible, be avoided. Besides these trustees, who we may call the Tory element in the direction of the school, the churchwardens, sidesmen, and overseers for the time being are, by right of office, governors, consequently every year fresh blood is infused into the government of the school, and, indeed, they being in the proportion of eight to the five trustees, the majority must always rest with those annually chosen, independent of which the churchwarden is chairman of the Governors, and, therefore, entitled to a double vote. The practical working of the school is, I think, best shown by the results of the education, one of our late churchwardens being brought up in the school. Several scholars now hold good appointments under the parish; a late scholar is now a partner in one of the largest firms in the City; others are receiving as much as £1,000 a year and very many are holding responsible situations in South London. These have all been pupils of the present respected master since he has for the last thirty-eight years occupied the post.'

The Currier

15. Shaving leather.

Today the process of currying is very much a part of the tanning process. In history however they were two very distinct but complementary trades. When the tanning process was completed the currier took over for the final stages of preparation. These were skilled craftsmen who usually ran their own businesses. Currying was the process of stretching and finishing tanned leather rendering it supple and strong for the use of a saddler or cobbler.

Currier originates from the Latin term 'corium' which interpreted is the skin layer between the outer epidermis and the flesh underneath. In animals it is made up of a complex series of fibres and this determines the difference in texture between leathers.

The process of the currier was to pare or shave the leather to a level and uniform thickness, then to dye or colour it, treat it with oils or greases and then drying and treating the grainy surface with a wax dubbing (cod liver oil and beef tallow) or shellac finish.

Curriers existed in many villages and often the currier was also the local shoemaker or involved in other leather work. Currying leather was hard manual labour, needing skills which most gained having served at least a seven year apprenticeship. The apprentice currier was bound to a master currier or was taught by the family as the trade was often continued generation after generation in the same family. It also required specialist tools. The Currier worked on a many different hides as opposed to skins, including ox, cow, calf, goat, sheep, pig and deer. The hide was first stretched on a variety of different frames, depending on the type of leather to be curried. The Currier would gradually tighten the frame from every direction until the hide was as taut as possible. Another method of stretching the hide was by using an implement resembling a mangle where a handle was turned, gradually tightening the material.

Once the hide had been stretched sufficiently the tanned leather was washed and scrubbed to soften the hide which demanded more physical labour, The currier then went to work with a 'sleeker', a specialist tool resembling a short bladed knife. This process forced any remaining tanning fluid from the hide. The hide was then ready to be dressed, to make it smooth, waterproof, strong and flexible.

16. Splitting leather.

Next a currying knife, referred to as a 'shave', was used on the inner side of the hide to make it more even. The tool was worked like a woodworkers plane, shaving the surface of the leather and was perhaps the most skilful part of the process. If the process was not carried out correctly then it would mean the hide was worthless. It is these tools which appear on the coat of arms of the Worshipful Company of Curriers. The currying knife was also used to split the leather into different widths. Of course, the thickness required was dictated by the purpose for which the leather was intended. The suppler split leather was used for the uppers of shoes and boots. The heavier leather from the 'butt' or backbone of the hide was used for soles.

The finished product was frequently taken by other members of the family, living in the same village, for crafting into shoes, gloves, belts or use on saddles. This craft was practised in villages throughout Britain in both the leather centres such as Northamptonshire and also in smaller cottage leather treatment works. When an ancestor is recorded as a currier it is more than probable that other family members were also involved in the leather trade. There is evidence in London of curriers and the majority appear to have resided in the Farringdon Road and Fleet Street area. However, there is also evidence in other areas dating back to the medieval period with street names such as Currier's Lane off Fleet Street and Bristol Street and a Currier's Arms Inn Yard off Goswell Street (now Goswell Road).

Finished leather uses

Different types of leather were used for different end products. Most tanneries would have specialised, to some extent, in the type of leather treated as different processes would have been used. The most common were:

Cow hide: This was a tough, long wearing leather, used primarily for shoe making (both soles and uppers), machine belts and harnesses.

Calf skin: This was a fine grain leather withstanding scuffs and wear, used for book binding, gloves, handbags and suitcases.

Goat/kid skin: This was a sturdy, soft and pliable leather used for quality 'fashion accessories' and suede goods.

Sheep skin: This was a rather course grain leather used for parchment, textile mill rollers, piano parts and wash leathers (chamois).

Pig skin: This was usually taken from ordinary domestic pigs and of an unusual texture, used for wallets, sports shoes and razor straps.

There were also specialist leathers derived from Alligators, Kangaroos and Ostrich - then of course today we have the synthetics!

The Worshipful Company of Curriers

17. The Worshipful Company of Curriers.

The Worshipful Company of Curriers is number 29 in the order of precedence for City of London Livery Companies. The original trade is no longer practised in the City and the majority of the leather worked in the United Kingdom today is dressed and prepared overseas. However, modern-day currying continues to a limited extent in a number of centres of expertise around the country, including Walsall in the West Midlands.

The Curriers' Company has a long and sometimes complicated history, dating from 1272 when the 'Mistery of Curriers' first became a trade association. In the 14th century, the curriers became a guild and religious fraternity closely associated with the Carmelite Friars. They obtained their ordinances by an act of Common Council in 1415. By 1580 the Guild of Curriers had become a Livery Company of the City of London. Subsequently a grant of arms was made in 1583. It was not until 1605 that King James I granted the curriers their first Charter of Incorporation and a further charter was granted by James II in 1686.

Since then the Company has built six halls in the City, the last one being constructed in 1876. During the economic downturn of the 1920s the Company was forced to sell its sixth hall and move in with a partner, the Worshipful Company of Cordwainers, with whom it still enjoys a close relationship. The curriers no longer have a hall as the one it shared with the cordwainers was destroyed in the Blitz. It now holds its court meetings in the Tallow Chandlers Hall.

Records of the Worshipful Company of Curriers

The records of the Company are held at the Guildhall Library. The earliest record held is the 1473 Act but the majority of records were not compiled until after 1553. The registers of freedom admissions and apprentice bindings only date from 1658.

Constitutional records, including ordinances, charters and royal licences 1473-1729. Court records, 1628-1934 (including court minutes 1628-1658, 1689-1934 - abstracts only 1689-1724).

Membership records, including apprenticeship bindings, freedom admissions and freemen declarations 1554-7, 1658-1894, 1934-2000.

Financial records, 1553-94, 1627-1795, 1830-1938.

Trade records, 1700-1860.

Clerk's records, 1780-1929.

Charities and estates records 1558-1929, including the records of both Jacksons Charity 1827-1879 and Dawes Charity 1730-1902.

18. Curriers processing leather in the Tudor period.

Our ancestors as tanners and curriers

Leather was a major export and both the tanner and currier could be quite a wealthy member of any community. In the local trade directories there was a noticeable inter-relationship between tanner, currier and the leather goods producers such as cordwainers, saddlers, etc. Tanning and currying both involved hard manual labour, requiring strength, skill and specialist tools. Work would usually commence at about 5.30am and the average tannery processed 750 hides or skins a week. Like most rural trades, there was often a family tradition of son following in father's footsteps, many serving the mandatory seven year apprenticeship. Many of these apprenticeship records survive today, mostly for curriers, showing the names of both master and servant. These crafts were practiced in every part of the country. A look in any census will show that this is essentially a family business and other family members may also have been involved in the associated branches of the leather trade. In the 1841 census there were 6,601 tanners in England and Wales.

In Bishop's Stortford during the 15th century there was one area around Water Lane which contained 13 tanneries. The local records such as churchwarden's accounts and manorial court rolls frequently record 'tanners and skinners'. Even today a public house called the 'Tanners Arms' still exists in London Road. Doubtless there would have been a pub relating to curriers at some time in the town. The stench from the tanneries, mixed with smells from the various maltings within the town, would have been pretty pungent and the town was not a very environmentally friendly place in which to reside.

19. The processes involved in making leather.

The leather industry was also very much associated with Walsall in the West Midlands. The earliest records of a tannery exist from the late 18th century. The basis of the Walsall trade was in the supply of equestrian leather goods. Wherever a locality supported a leather industry, it was inevitable that nearby would be the tanneries and curriers. The first tannery in Walsall is mentioned in 1780. Its importance as a centre of the leather industry grew out of the skills of local trades people and the many natural resources such as animal hides, iron ore and limestone available in the locality. By 1925 there were eight tanneries and 39 curriers workshops in the town supporting almost 150 saddlers, harness makers, and bridle cutters factories or workshops. Many tanneries employed a small workforce, perhaps no more than eight or ten, and of these some would be skilled, others would have been tannery labourers. Like many industries, the leather trade in Walsall suffered from foreign competition and declined in the 1930s only to see a revival in recent times. There are now about 65 saddlers in the town but alas no tanneries.

Bermondsey Leather Market

Bermondsey Leather Market is perhaps mis-described as essentially it was a market selling hides. An early guide to Bermondsey c.1845 describes the market as follows:

'The neighbourhood in which it stands is devoted entirely to thinners and tanners, and the air reeks with evil smells. The population is peculiar, and it is a sight at twelve o'clock to see the men pouring out from all the works. Their clothes are marked with many stains; their trousers are dis-coloured by tan; some have apron and gaiters of raw hide; and about them all seems to hang a scent of blood. The market itself stands in the centre of a quiet block of buildings on the left hand side of Weston-street, the entry being through a gateway. Through this a hundred yards down, a square is reached. Most of it is roofed, but there is an open space lathe centre. Under the roofing are huge piles of fresh hides and sheep-skins. There is no noise or bustle, and but few people about. There are no retail purchasers, the sales being almost entirely made to the great tanners in the neighbourhood. The warehouses round are all full of tanned hides; the yards behind the high walls are all tanneries, with their tens of thousands of hides soaking in the pits. Any visitor going down to look at the Bermondsey hide-market should, if possible, procure beforehand an order to visit one of the great tanning establishments. Unless this be done the visit to the market itself will hardly repay the trouble of the journey, or make up for the unpleasantness of the compound of horrible smells which pervade the whole neighbourhood.'

20. The Leather Market (Exchange) Bermondsey - (modern photograph).

The market existed to enable the sale of the raw material and many of our ancestors would have been the sellers or merchants.

So - how was leather sold? The most economical way to buy leather was to purchase it directly from the tannery. Leather was usually priced by the square foot and sold as a complete hide measured on government approved devices at the tannery. Leather came from tanneries in various shapes and sizes depending on its intended use and the animal which it came from. Because of this, the exact size and shape of the finished leather is dictated by the size and shape of the actual animal hide that the tannery received prior to processing. For ease of handling during tanning, large animal hides were usually cut into smaller sections (sides, shoulders, bellies, etc.) at the tannery. Skins of smaller animals such as calf, goat, pig and reptiles were tanned and sold in their original shape. Although leather is sometimes cut into various shapes for the convenience of the customer, the price is always higher because of the additional costs for labour and waste resulting from trimming.

Both leather sellers and the merchant buyers had to understand what the different types of leather were used for, how different leathers were tanned and how large hides and skins were cut and sold. To make leather a uniform thickness, first the hides were run through a splitting machine. Since animal hides were not of uniform thickness, and since they were wet when they were put through the splitting machine, the thickness of the leather will not remain the same throughout the hide; there was always a slight variation.

Charles Booth and the leather trade

Charles Booth was a successful businessman, running interests in the leather industry and also a steam shipping line. His principle business was the importation to the USA of English leather for which they obviously needed ships as well.

21. Charles Booth of leather Industry fame (well known for the Booth Survey of London).

22. Booth Shipping Line ensign.

In 1862, Charles joined his eldest brother Alfred in a business dealing principally in skins and leather. Using money inherited from their father, the brothers set up offices in both Liverpool and New York. He ultimately but very quickly became the leading partner because of his energy and enthusiasm although the name of the firm was Alfred Booth and Company.

Charles Booth instigated a unique system and order in the handling of the firm's affairs and took it upon himself to master the details of the trade. He visited tanneries, inspected cargoes of skins, and gathered volumes of information summarised into facts and figures. People often questioned why he wanted so much information and detail from them but his inquiring mind and system management enabled the business to prosper.

His other claim to fame was that he was the self-motivated instigator of the social survey of London which he conducted between 1886 and 1903. He was one of the Victorians profoundly concerned by contemporary social problems. He devised, organised, and funded one of the most comprehensive and scientific social surveys of London life that had then been undertaken. Booth also added his voice to the campaign for state old age pensions to alleviate destitution in old age.

Sir Edward Thomas Holden

Edward Thomas Holden was perhaps the most prominent figures of the Victorian leather industry. At the age of 13 years he began work at the family tannery in Walsall which was established in 1819. On the death of his father, Edward began managing the tannery. He was then 19 years old. His company gained a reputation for the production of pigskins used in the local saddle, harness and upholstery trades. For most of its existence the tannery occupied a small and constrained site. Despite its location it was very successful, employing over 100 men and boys at its height in the 1880s. The leathers it produced were exported all over the world. In 1892 Holden also acquired a pigskin tannery located close to Glasgow.

Holden served as Mayor of Walsall and became Chairman of the School Board, resulting in him founding the town's Science and Art Institute. He was elected MP for Walsall in 1891 and was subsequently knighted in 1907. He died in 1926.

After his death the business remained family run well into the 20th century. Gucci were amongst the company's major customers. Holden's great grandson Thomas Holden relocated the business to Jedburgh in 1970, a move which was not economically viable. The firm ceased trading in the mid-1970s.

The Worshipful Company of Leathersellers

23. The Worshipful Company of Leathersellers.

The Company's origins date back to the trade guilds of the middle ages which existed to support and protect those engaged in particular crafts and trades.

Its origins probably began amongst the makers of fine white leather, known then as whittawyers and the pouch makers who traded in the City in the early 13th century. John and Roger Pointel were the earliest known leather sellers in 1297, although the earliest official use of the term 'leather sellers' relates to a group of London craftsmen in 1372 who complained to the Corporation of London about a group of dyers who had been dyeing sheep leather in order to pass it off as expensive roe leather.

In 1398, when Dick Whittington was the Mayor of London, the leather sellers applied for 'articles for the regulation of their craft and the prevention and punishment of dishonest practices in their trade'. This resulted in 'ordinances' (bye-laws) one of which related to the fact that all leather goods and hides sold in the City of London were to be inspected by the company.

By 1444 the leather sellers were organised and applied to Henry VI for a Royal Charter which established the governance of the Company by four Wardens, confirmed and extended the Company's right to inspect leather, and granted the right to meet, to wear a livery and to own land. Shortly after the grant, trustees acting for the Company purchased five properties on the south side of London Wall and from 1476 an upper room of one of the properties became the first Hall. The other properties were let out and part of the revenue distributed amongst imprisoned debtors in accordance with the will of Robert Ferbras, an early benefactor whose funding helped financially with the purchase of the new Hall.

During the Tudor period the Company amalgamated with the whittawyers, glovers, pursers and pouch makers thus eliminating rivals. Many members had also been generous with monetary and property bequests. In 1543 the Company purchased St Helen's Priory in Bishopsgate and converted it into a new hall. Benedictine nuns had been established at St Helen's in the 13th century and, being wealthy, owned most of the parish of St Helen's. The priory was surrendered on dissolution to Henry VIII in 1538.

24. The original Leathersellers Hall, London.

The Leathersellers Company purchased the site in 1543 using the money donated by John Haslewood a wealthy leather seller and in return leased part back to him and built a group of almshouses on the estate. The Company suffered as a result of levies imposed by the Crown and the City Corporation and it was subsequently forced to sell much of its plate.

The Leathersellers' Company received a second charter in 1604 because the original grant was out of date and the Company felt vulnerable because of the Statute of Leather which had opened the trade to non-freemen. The new charter confirmed all the then existing rights as well as establishing a new constitution which is still the basis of the Company's operation today.

Abraham Colfe, vicar of Lewisham had a connection with the Company through its then clerk, William Manby. Colfe and the Leathersellers' Company became trustees of Colfe's charitable trust, which included the management from 1652 of Lewisham Boys' Grammar School (later Colfe's School - which still exists today). It has been administered by the Company's since 1658 following Abraham Colfe's death. Many records of the Grammar School including early admission registers are held by the London Metropolitan Archives.

25. Colfe's School, Lewisham.

During the reign of Charles I the Company virtually lost control of its trade as many craftsmen moved into London's suburbs, with the full knowledge that the Company did not have the resources to search there. The plague and great fire were of further detriment. Court meetings were suspended during the plague and although the Hall was not damaged in the Great Fire, losses of Company property elsewhere in the City occurred. In 1684 Charles II revoked all existing Livery Company charters and issued restrictive new ones in their place.

The 18th century saw the Leathersellers' Company encounter difficulties much the same as encountered by many of the City Livery Companies during that time. The St Helen's estate was a constant drain on resources, and membership levels became very low. Although the Company had obtained an Act of Common Council requiring all leather sellers in the City to be members, it met with resistance and enforcement, already difficult to achieve, was abandoned. In the latter part of the century taxation further crippled the Company. In order to maintain its liquidity the St Helen's estate was redeveloped and John Nash was commissioned to draw up plans for a new square. However The Company abandoned those plans and in 1802 work began on a cul-de-sac of houses known as St Helen's Place which from 1807 produced increased rents. This improved the Company's finances and began to restore its wealth, helped also by the redevelopment of many of the Company's rural estates.

In an effort to manage costs the Company operated from a former merchants' house on the estate which became the third Hall. It was destroyed by fire in 1819, but all the records and possessions were saved. A fourth Hall which was built on the same site was opened in 1822. However, because of the increase in wealth and the re-establishment of social functions that Hall was deemed too small so a fifth larger and more lavish Hall opened in 1879. Almshouses had been built in Lewisham in accordance with the bequest from Abraham Colfe as well as on the St Helens estate. Additional ones were built in Barnet between 1837 and 1869.

In the 1880s, the Company was involved with Prendergast Girls School in Lewisham, founded under the terms of the will of the Rev. Joseph Prendergast. The Leathersellers' Company purchased the site for the school, which officially opened in 1890.

At the start of the 20th century the Company began rebuilding St Helen's Place. Work was affected by the outbreak of the First World War. During the war the Hall was used as a hospital, and the Company also funded an ambulance and field kitchen for the Red Cross. In the inter-war years, work resumed on St Helen's Place, and the Leathersellers' Hall was extensively remodelled. However bombing in the Second World War damaged or destroyed St Helen's Place, the Hall and many other properties owned by the Company throughout the London area including Colfe's School.

26. Almshouses owned by the Leathersellers' Company in Barnet, Hertfordshire.

42

Worshipful Company of Leathersellers' Archives

The Worshipful Company of Leathersellers' archives have survived despite the destruction by fire of the Company's Hall in 1819 and bomb damage to a later Hall during the blitz. Many volumes however are slightly damaged as a result. Unlike many Livery Company archives the Leathersellers' archive is still retained by the company. It remains a unique resource with records dating back to around 1250, covering most aspects of the Company activities. It is a working archive and modern documents are still being added covering its 750 year history. The company is 15th in the order of Livery Company precedence.

Most of its records are a valuable resource to family historians and comprise:

Registers of Members: comprising those records of most value:
Livery Lists dating from 1706,
Freedom Registers dating from 1629,
Apprenticeship Registers dating from 1630.

Court and Committee Minutes dating from 1608 to the present day.
Wardens' accounts dating from 1471 although they are not continuous

Title Deeds relating to property holdings dating from 1250 to the present day and covering the Company's estates throughout the City of London, and in Sydenham, Lewisham and Barnet. There are also some records in Lewisham archives.

Records also exist for almshouses and schools with which the Company is associated.

The Leathersellers' Company archives have limited facilities for public consultation. Access is by appointment with the archivist. They provide a research service for genealogical enquiries.

The leather trade outside London

Whilst the leather tanning, currying and selling businesses prospered in the main cities particularly London, the tanning and currier processes were very much provincial and rural 'cottage' industries. Throughout the country regional centres became established.

Leather was a vital Victorian commodity. Tanners were highly skilled workers, but they were forced to live on the fringes of society because of the noxious smell that went with the job. Raw hides were dipped in a sickly-sweet smelling lime solution for a week before the tanner scraped off the rotting flesh and hair. They were then soaked in 'bate', which was a warm, steaming gravy made from water and dog faeces, which removed the lime, softened the hides and stank the yard out something terrible! Over the next year, the hides would be soaked in various tanning solutions before the meticulous rinsing and drying out process began. The work was dull, strenuous and very, very smelly. Little wonder that tanners usually married other tanners!

As previously mentioned the town of Walsall in the West Midlands was perhaps second to Bermondsey in the industry and was typical of other areas around the country where the leather trade existed. Its importance as a centre of the leather industry grew out of the skills of local trades people and the many natural resources such as animal hides, iron ore and limestone available in the locality.

Despite its prosperity the county's leather industry was a mass of tiny and usually primitive backyard workshops, as well as a few factories often employing between two or three hundred people.

The report of the Sweated Trades Commission of 1889 detailed allegations of 'sweating' in Walsall itself and showed highly skilled tanners worked long hours for poor wages in bad conditions.

At the time (1889) typical earnings for a male was about 28 shillings for a 55 hour week. Women would earn about half that amount if they were lucky. Unlike the male employees, who were paid by the hour, most women were paid by the completed item so if there was no work they did not get paid. Within many of the so called 'modern' factories deductions were often made from wages for heating, lighting and 'shop room' in which the employees worked.

In rural areas the most important industries were those associated with agriculture. They used raw materials from the farms, supplied essential consumer goods and provided secondary employment for agricultural workers. The most important was the woollen textile industry followed closely by the leather trade as they were valuable to both the domestic economy and the export trade.

The clearest indication of the prominent role of the industry was the existence of legislation controlling the manufacture and sale of leather and leather goods particularly the Leather Act of 1563 and the Statute of Artificers. The leather industry was important as it provided the farmer with the goods he needed such as boots and shoes, saddles, horse collars and harness and other uses for general farm work and husbandry.

In many localities the manufacture of leather and leather goods was often combined with farming, although farming was often the secondary occupation. Many tanners and curriers ran their own independent cottage industry. The hides and skins used by tanners and leather-dressers abundantly came from farmers and butchers in the local communities. The sale of hides and skins also presented farmers with a useful source of income and in many local economies it is thought that the hide and skin market was often more important than the sale of meat despite the fact that the value of a beef carcass was often a lot higher and as such did not always make logical sense. Certainly with sheep the skins were much less important than the wool and meat. Clearly the supply of hides and skins fluctuated as meat consumption varied not necessarily because of an increased demand for hides. The result was that prices of hides and skins also fluctuated and often surplus supplies were just buried untreated.

In most villages there was usually only one leather dresser or worker of leather, a trade often carried on generation after generation which supplied the market towns where hides and finished good would be sold on market day alongside livestock etc.

Although leather and leather goods were made throughout the country, leather manufacturing was more prominent as an urban occupation since supplies and hides were available in the towns as a by-product of meat processing and consumption. The towns were also regional markets for finished leather goods.

In many parts of the country the leather industry was much more important to the local economy than it was to London. Some areas developed as specialised producing regions conducting a national trade in tanned leather or leather products. In other districts the leather crafts formed one of the most important occupational groups, even though their importance may have been confined to their own locality.

In eastern England the leather industry was important in several districts, although probably on a less extensive scale than in the west of the country. One region in which the leather industry existed was the pastoral area of Suffolk where the industry existed alongside dairying. Large quantities of tanned hides and calf skins were transported around the coast from Ipswich and Woodbridge, to London, where the leather was used in shoemaking, because it was stronger and more durable than many other leathers. There were differences between the Suffolk leather industry and that of western England. Suffolk specialised in tanning rather than leather-dressing and there were no urban centres where the leather crafts were practised. Although Ipswich was an important regional market for hides and leather the tanning was undertaken in the surrounding Suffolk villages.

Norwich was also an important centre for leather with a high number of leather workers becoming Freemen of the City. Well over half the leather craftsmen were shoemakers, and it is apparent there was no shortage of skins and hides as most of the leather produced in the city was used locally for footwear production. Peculiar to this area of East Anglia were the black cattle. The pastoral area to the south-west of Norwich produced calves whose skins and hides were used by the city's leather workers.

In parts of Lincolnshire the marketing of bullock calves leather was essential to the local economy. This was particularly so in the Lincolnshire clay lands, the marshlands and fens. The early centre of the industry was Stamford. In the Hall Book between 1657 and 1721, eighty of the 637 freemen followed occupations within the leather industry. Elsewhere in the county leather workers were to be found in many smaller towns and villages and numerous inventories of tanners, shoemakers, leather-dressers and other leather workers have survived alongside wills and other probate records. Most of the Lincolnshire produced leather was used locally as there was no evidence that distant markets were supplied.

The leather industry played an important part in the economy of the Midlands whose agricultural industry was centred on sheep and cattle-grazing fattened on locally grown grain, particularly corn, which gave a special feel to their skins and hides. As a result Leicester became a well-known centre for the tanning industry. By the latter part of the 16th century, and for a considerable time thereafter, tanners and leather craftsmen were the largest industrial group in the town, although their relative importance declined fairly rapidly during the early 19th century. Much of Leicester's leather was used locally, but its leather was also sold to more distant markets.

The other area of the Midlands which came to prominence for much the same reasons as Leicester was Northampton. Like Leicester, Northampton was situated in a sheep and cattle raising area and was an important centre of leather. It still remains so today. It developed notably as a shoemaking town. According to the subsidy of 1524 shoemaking was the leading industrial occupation of the town. By the late 17th century the town had become renowned for its footwear. A motto for the town states:

'Northampton may be said to stand chiefly on other men's legs; where (if not the best) the most and cheapest boots and stockings are bought in England.'

The development of Northamptonshire's footwear industry was not altogether economic, but also for military and religious reasons. The town had a long history of puritanism and it occupied a strategic position at the 'crossroads of England'. Hence, at the time of the Civil War (and for a long time afterwards) it became a vital garrison town for the parliamentary cause. It was inhabited by shoemakers adequately supplied with local leather so it was obvious that the town's shoemakers supply boots and shoes for the army. The town continued to receive orders to supply the army in Ireland with boots and shoes.

Tanning and leather-dressing flourished in Northampton as the town was inhabited by some fairly wealthy tanners and leather-dressers. Hides and skins came from the local farming community and oak bark was found locally mainly in nearby Salsey Forest. The many tanners and leather-dressers in the town constituted a threat to public health, so much so that the local authorities waged war on leather manufacturers who polluted water supplies and left carcasses in public places. Markets for Northampton leather were found at places as far afield as Stourbridge Fair near Cambridge, and of course in London.

In the north Midlands, tanning was a prominent industry in Nottingham. In the early 1800s there were 57 tanneries mostly along the river front. As in Leicester, Northampton and many other Midland towns associated with the leather trade, the number of butchers in Nottingham was high in relation to the population and there were no difficulties in obtaining hides. In the nearby town of Newark tanning was also an important occupation.

In the agricultural areas of western England the occupations associated with leather crafts were numerous. Following the imposition of excise duty on leather in 1697, many of the towns and villages petitioned Parliament. Around sixty of the 154 petitions received came from an area centred round the Cotswolds but extending northwards almost to the Mersey.

In the north of this region Chester was an important manufacturing and trading centre. Between the mid-16th and the mid-17th centuries the number of freedom admissions to the City amongst the leather trades was unprecedented although they later declined. The merchants of Chester exported large quantities of dressed calf skins from the port under licence. The dressing of skins and hides by curriers and the manufacture of gloves were common occupations not only in Chester but throughout Cheshire, Shropshire, Herefordshire and Worcestershire where many families were involved. Between 1790 and 1820 half of all glovers were based in Worcester.

Leather-dressers and the glovers of western England supplied a national market. London merchants frequently bought wholesale leather at Chester and Bristol and finished gloves at Hereford, Ross-on-Wye, and Brecon. Notwithstanding this a high proportion of the leather and goods was sold locally in market centres at Bristol, Chester, Gloucester and Oxford. Some 30,000 glovers were employed by 150 manufacturers.

The region had an abundant local supply of skins and hides but also supplemented the supply by importing skins, especially sheep from Ireland. The quality of the water supply also attracted the industry. It is said that in the Oxford district the water was such that:

> 'all skins of a more delicate kind ... are so well seasoned with it for the making of white leather, that more whiter, softer nor better is hardly found.'

The social structure of the region favoured the development of a local industry. The area was full of communities of small farmers pursuing a pastoral economy and as such a non-farming occupation was necessary to supplement the small incomes.

Tanners were able to locally source and buy oak bark from iron workers in the Forest of Dean, and it is likely that the existence of iron manufacturing nearby encouraged the growth of the tanning industry. Chepstow, because of its closeness to the forest rose to prominence both as a tanning area and for the export of oak bark. Thousands of tons of bark were sent to Bristol and to Ireland but the amount exported decreased when it ceased to be a Customs Port in 1882. To some extent the bark season was limited particularly in the Royal Forest of Dean and the season was only from April to June. In 1780 Chepstow had twenty two bark merchants but by 1880 the number had reduced to two. In the period of the Napoleonic Wars bark only realised £7 per ton whereas the average realised price in the later 1800s was in the region of £9 - £14 per ton.

There was also some connection between leather tanning and iron working in Shropshire particularly around the Rivers Severn and Teme. This seems to account for the prominence of Walsall as a centre district, where the manufacture of saddles and harnesses created a joint demand for leather and metal goods such as bits, buckles, and stirrup irons. Tanning was once a leading occupation in Birmingham, although it was gradually overshadowed by the advent of metal crafts.

Parts of Yorkshire, particularly the West Riding, were leather-manufacturing districts of note up until the start of the 18th century. Although it is known that the industry started by using and processing local hides, tanners became very dependent on supplies imported from London. Large quantities of raw hides were shipped to Hull, and then transported along the Humber and then overland to tanners and curriers who worked in the 'cottage' industry of the inner parts of the West Riding.

This area suffered decline in trade in 1626 when a Parliamentary proclamation prohibited the coastal trade in hides and leather due to an outbreak of plague. The West Riding tanners then explained that, in the preceding year, they had shipped nearly 5,000 hides from London, which exceeded the number which they brought in former years. According to this explanation:

'The reason thereof was the great visitacon which was in London the next year before which hindered us from buying hides there and so made a great scarcity thereof, and deerness of leather amongst us ... and so enforced us to buy more the last year for storing and replenishing of our tan pits and better serving of our neighbours with Leather.'

Eventually the Yorkshire tanners were permitted to carry 4,000 hides annually from London.

Elsewhere in Yorkshire the leather crafts were more obviously linked again with local agriculture. Both Beverley and York were typical of Yorkshire towns where the leather industry provided significant employment. Tanning of leather was for many years the principal trade of Beverley. Originally a cloth working town this industry had declined. So being set in a predominantly rural area it began processing hides and skins to support the agricultural industry. Hence the leather trade evolved.

A similar situation existed at York. Roughly 20% of the new admissions to the freedom of the city in the second half 18th century were leather workers. Hides were purchased from the local butchers, who in turn obtained animals not only from the mixed farming areas surrounding York but also from the rich pastoral region of the Galtres forest.

Although not as prevalent as in other areas of the country the south of England, particularly around the Kent and Sussex Weald was also a leather manufacturing area. It was a well-populated wood-pasture region, where local grazing provided hides and skins, and supplies were supplemented by occasional shipments from London into the Medway port of Rochester. In addition, there was plenty of oak bark available from the local iron masters. On occasions tanners became worried that the iron masters might fell oaks too rapidly and so threaten future supplies of bark. Sussex bark was especially suitable for tanning since it had a higher tannin content than usual. Rather than being centralised on any one area or town leather manufacture seems to have been widely scattered throughout the east Sussex area. Leather from this area was exported from Rye and other east Sussex ports. In the late 16th and early 17th centuries the Privy Council was frequently occupied with the problem of leather being smuggled from Rye by tanners.

The area of north-east Kent produced leather for the London market and raw hides were brought from London for tanning. There was a fairly regular trade of raw hides between London and Faversham, and tanned hides being sent the other way. Unfortunately, there is no evidence to show what happened to the hides once they reached Faversham albeit Canterbury had a huge tannery from 18th century founded in 1790 (see case history). Conceivably they were taken inland for tanning in the villages around Faversham but the Faversham region was devoted to corn and fruit growing. This area also had access to supplies of oak bark from the Blean Forest. There is little doubt that hides were being sent to this region because of a shortage of bark in the metropolitan area. Possibly London tanners were putting work out to the tanners of north-east Kent on a commission basis.

In Kendal in the north-west, six of the twelve early trade guilds were directly associated with leather working. The town was an important regional market for hides and leather. In Durham four of the town's twelve guilds in the early 17th century represented leather workers. In this area local tanners also worked with horse hides. In Hexham a leather market was established, in 1662.

Case History - the tannery in Stour Street, Canterbury

'When the St Mildred's Tannery site finally closed in 2002, it marked the end of over 200 years of tanning and leather work in Canterbury, associated with six generations of the Williamson family. Stephen Williamson (1770-1813) was born in Canterbury, and baptised at St Paul's church on 6 May 1770. His parents John Williamson and Susannah Row had been married at St Mildred's church (2 September 1760). Stephen founded the firm in the 1790s in premises at 18/19 Sun Street, but around 1810 opened a shop opposite at 5 Sun Street (now part of Debenhams). The outbreak of the Napoleonic wars proved good for business - 5,000 troops stationed in the area needed boots, harnesses and other leather items. Stephen died on 18 March 1813 and his body lies in St Alphege church. His son John James (1792-1881), grandson Stephen (b.1823) and great grandsons Stephen (b.1856) and Henry (b.1867) and later generations all carried on the trade. The family moved from Sun Street to Best Lane in the 1850s, and Stephen (b.1823) purchased Tower House in Westgate Gardens in 1886.

Despite complaints about the stink of the tannery processes so close to the city centre, the business grew and expanded across the Stour with a small bridge. By 1851 it was employing 7 men and a boy. This rose to 9 men and 3 boys by 1891. In the early 20th century the business became a major supplier to Connollys, a London firm with a specialist currying works in Wimbledon and contracts to supply fine leather for the new motor car trade. The relationship with Connollys thrived, and despite serious fires on the Stour Street site in 1931, Canterbury leather found its way into Rolls Royces, Bentleys, Daimlers, Ferrari and Jaguars, not to mention the House of Lords. Williamsons was acquired by Connollys in 1963.'

Canterbury Historical and Archaeological Society website (accessed 25 Sept 2014). **www.canterbury-archaeology.org.uk/#/tannery/45577S9185**

A tanning family

The 1841 census for Rickmansworth in Hertfordshire (HO107/438/21) shows the Wild family living at Mill End. Thomas Wild was a tanner. Although the census entry does not say so, his son Charles was an apprentice to him in that trade. His tannery was located nearby and at the time, Thomas Wild employed three other men. Charles, when he ended his apprenticeship, ran his own tannery in Kingston, Surrey with his elder brother and was c.1855 employing ten men. This tannery grew in size ultimately employing around twenty men and specialising in providing quality cowhide leather to the shoe industry. The Wild tannery supplied several factories established in Northamptonshire and in Ireland. Charles' sons did not follow in their father's footsteps when he died in 1878. The tannery was sold, presumably by his wife Jane, c.1880. Perhaps his sons benefited from the large sum of money left to them in Charles' will.

27. The family of Thomas Wild, tanner.

Further afield

The English took the oak-bark tanning process to America. Experience Miller, a tanner by trade, emigrated from Bristol. He arrived in Plymouth, Massachusetts in 1623 where he set up the first American Tannery, having learnt his trade in England. By 1650, fifty one other tanners had emigrated.

Trade and craft guilds

Outside London there were many trade and craft guilds many of which originated in medieval times. They played a very important role in a number of English towns, providing a basis for the maintenance of high standards in all crafts and allowing people better protection against excessive taxation. Tanners and curriers very often had their own craft guilds which in later years inevitably amalgamated with guilds of other leather and allied trades such as cordwainers, saddlers, glovers etc.

Guilds were so named from the Anglo-Saxon 'gilden' meaning to pay, and relates to the membership payments which all guild members contributed. As the feudal system of medieval Britain allowed lords to tax people and their trades, taxes became burdensome as trades increased. Guilds acted rather like modern unions in providing a degree of protection from over-taxation, as well as protecting consumers by providing a high standard of quality.

There were two aspects to guilds. They were either Merchant Guilds or Craft Guilds. A Merchant Guild was a trade association for either the tanners or curriers (or both), able to negotiate with local manorial lords in order to keep fair levels of trade levies. These guilds became the 'commerce government' in medieval towns and later developed into the role of civic administration or chambers of commerce. Many provincial towns can trace their foundation to charters established by local Merchant Guilds.

While the Merchant Guilds controlled overall regulations on all individual traders and craftsmen, those working in specific crafts and trades such as tanners, curriers and leather sellers began to set up Craft Guilds for the benefit of their own specific trades. For example all the leather workers in a town came together in Craft Guilds for each specialism, providing mutual aid and protection for all members. It was not possible for anyone to become engaged in any craft or trade without being a guild member. Membership of a guild was considered an honour as its members were recognised as being a skilled worker who had respect in the town.

The power exerted by the guilds was strong enough to ensure that anyone not maintaining the prescribed high standards would be excluded from following their trade. The provincial tanning and currier industry was often carried on generation by generation but parents could also pay for their children to follow a guild apprenticeship often from the age of 12 years. Apprentices would live and work with their masters, developing the skills of the trade within the guild's protective environment.

On completion of an apprenticeship the young person became a journeyman, able to ply his trade and ultimately set up his own business or inherit the family business as a master craftsman.

Some Craft Guilds and their successors were still admitting Freemen well into the late 1800s but the system began to fall into oblivion with the advent of industrial scale tanneries.

During their existence each guild was required to carry out its share of civic and public duties including the defence of the town. Most Guilds also engaged in welfare responsibilities for members and their families including such things as sickness and funeral expenses.

The following is a listing of known Tanner and Currier Craft Guilds throughout the United Kingdom where the records survive and which are normally deposited in County Archives. You will need to check the archive catalogues to see exactly which records survive and for what time period as this varies from town to town. In other areas it may well have been the case that tanners or curriers belonged to a kindred guild or were part of a general merchant guild.

Provincial tanners and curriers guilds (with dates of origin)

Alnwick	1611
Andover	1176
Barnstable	1303
Bath	1189
Berwick Upon Tweed	1249
Bristol	1188
Carlisle	1562
Chester	1711
Birmingham	1590
Coventry	1268
Devises	1614
Dorchester	1485
Durham	1411
Exeter	c.1600
Gateshead	1557
Gloucester	1200 (includes the Forest of Dean)
Hereford	1215
Ipswich	1410
Kingston upon Hull	1299
Leeds	c.1350
Leicester	1107
Morpeth	18th century
Newcastle Upon Tyne	1532

Northampton	1564
Richmond, Yorks	1587
Shrewsbury	1478
Winchester	1580
York	1130
Denbigh	1610
Chepstow	1410 (includes leather merchants)
Dublin	1292
Limerick	1292
Waterford	1205
Aberdeen	1520

Company, association and individual records

Held by the City of London Joint Archive Service (unless otherwise stated).

Tanners, curriers and leather merchants

Allsop Brothers Ltd, leather merchants, Northampton

Minute books and ledgers 1900-1957 - Northamptonshire County Record Office.

Bevingtons and Sons Limited, leather manufacturers

1792-1973 Bevingtons and Sons Limited were leather tanners, curriers and merchants based at Neckinger Mills, Bermondsey. Neckinger Mills produced light leathers primarily for shoes and fancy goods. The company moved to Leicester in 1980.

Minutes 1859-1931; property records 1792-1967; stock and finance 1862-1946 and staff attendance books and photograph album, 1860-1877.

Barrow, Hepburn & Gale, tanners & curriers, London

Company records and staff rolls, private archive held by Company.

Bullock Family, Stanwell

1366-1879 The Bullock family were leather dressers of some substance in London. Henry Bullock was admitted a freeman of the City of London in 1711. In 1715 the family acquired leather mills at Poyle in Stanwell. The earliest deed identifying the Mills is dated 1612.

The collection includes family settlements and wills of the Bullocks, and their connections to the Bland and Maw families.

Records include title deeds to Poyle Mills and related properties in Stanwell, Bullock family accounts and business papers.

Charles Case & Sons, tanners, Westbury, Wiltshire

Company records, wages books and pay lists of employees 1909-1960s, Factory register. Held by Wiltshire Archives.

DeClermont and Donner

1894-1995 DeClermont and Donner incorporates The South India Export Company, They carried on the business of tanners, curriers and leather dressers, and as manufacturers, importers and exporters of and dealers in leather, chamois, leather-cloth, hides, skins, shagreen, artificial leather, oilcloths, linoleum, leather coats, leggings, linings, gloves, purses, boxes, trunks, suitcases, portmanteaux, fancy goods, bags, saddlery, boots and shoes, hose, washers, belting. It had interests in Aden, Ethiopia and South India.

Business records 1894-1995 including minutes, accounts, papers relating to shares, and correspondence.

Dyster, Nalder and Company

1802-1950 Dyster, Nalder and Company were hide, skin and horn brokers and leather factors based at Leadenhall Market from 1770-1880 and from 1880 at Crosby Square, Pepys Street (Seething Lane) and later at London Wall.

Records include catalogues of sales of skins, hides, furs, horns, hair and tallow; and an out-letter book.

John Flemming & Co. Tanners, Warrington, Lancashire.

Register of members 1896-1910, Company records including Wages and Staff papers 1876-1960. Held at Warrington Library.

Herst Leather Corporation Limited

1900-1963 The Herst Leather Corporation Ltd was founded by Norbert Herst. a leather merchant based at 13 Market Street, SE1. Later of 51 Weston Street, Southwark, SE1 and 3 and 4 Leather Market, SE1. Herst also owned Leading Leathers Ltd and Avondale Tannery.

Records include administrative papers, correspondence to and from suppliers and clients, and details of products and processes at the Avondale Tannery; financial papers including records of sales and purchases, credit reports of companies they dealt with, publications and ephemera including leather samples, directories on the leather trade and surveys of the shoe industry.

J. Denman and Co, leather sellers, Tooting

c.1939-1941 Denman and Co were leather sellers of Furzedown Market, Tooting.

Records include receipts for goods appropriate to a shoe repairer, including shoelaces and socks. Suppliers (indexed) include some local and London businesses.

Leadenhall Market

1676-1978 Leadenhall Market is situated between Fenchurch Street, Gracechurch Street and Leadenhall Street and was originally the land of the Manor of Leadenhall, the Lord then being Sir Hugh Neville who permitted a small market to be held on the grounds in 1309. The market became known for poultry and cheesemongers. In 1408 Dick Whittington acquired the Manor of Leadenhall and in 1411 the freehold was given to the City of London. Initially the market continued to be used for the sale of fish, meat, poultry and corn.

In 1488 it was assigned the sole right to sell leather. However, the market expanded and in 1871 the City of London sought parliamentary powers to abandon the hide markets and to erect a market for poultry alone. These powers were granted in 1879. Records include administrative papers, letters, petitions, superintendent's reports and clerk's books, 1686-1978; collectors' books, 1779-1825, tenancy agreements, 1881-1913, and various accounts and dues, 1826-1889.

James Thomas and Thomas Powell

1848-1890 Records collected by James Thomas and Thomas Powell, leather and hide factors, comprising leather brokers' trade circulars, tables of prices and sales reports.

United Tanners Federation

1916-1919 Meetings were held at 176 Tower Bridge Road.

United Tanners Federation sub-committee minutes relating to trade after the First World War.

George Staynes and Sons Ltd., leather merchants, Leicester

1855-1959 George Staynes' was first established c.1855, trading as curriers and brush makers at 79 High Street and 101 Belgrave Gate, Leicester but by 1861 the company was described as leather merchants and curriers and also as 'manufacturers of leather machinery straps and uppers for boots and shoes, India rubber hose, sheet tubing, machine belting and India rubber washers etc. and agents to the Singer Manufacturing Company's sewing machine. One of the last mentions of the company in a trade directory is in Kelly's for Leicester, 1966.

Records held at Leicester and Rutland Archives include accounts, tanning progress books, bankruptcy, catalogues, letter books, photographs.

F. Hearn Ltd, leather merchants, Exeter

Company records including wages books 1895-1897, catalogues of products etc. held by Devon County Record Office

Henry Quick and Co

1852 - 1964 In 1850 the company began in Exeter as Joslin & Quick, shoe mercers. In 1857 became Henry Quick and later in 1889 became Henry Quick & Co, drapers, leather merchants, boot upper and boot tree last makers.

Devon Record Office hold various business papers including wages books.

Throughout the country county record offices and local archives are custodians of the business records of both individuals and companies involved in the leather processing industry. It will therefore be incumbent upon the researcher to determine where records are held and useful to undertake research if you know your ancestor owned or worked for a particular company. The following are just some examples of the scope of records deposited.

W J Kidd Ltd, leather merchants, Belfast

Company business records, staff wages book 1907-1909. Held by the Public Record Office of Northern Ireland (PRONI).

Wm. Sutton, Ltd., tanners & curriers, Scotby, near Carlisle

The records held at Cumbria Archives of the firm begin in 1837 and survive until 1912. Throughout this period the company was a family concern led by Elihu Sutton (died 1853) his son William Sutton (died 1879) and grandson, Alfred Sutton. The tannery was the major employer in Scotby and the Suttons played an important role in village life. The Sutton family were prominent local property owners and also provided a community reading room, gas works, and sickness benefit fund for employees and families.

Associated Industrial Tanners Ltd, Gomersal

The records are held at West Yorkshire Archives. The Association was formed by the following independent tanneries: Miles Rhodes, tanners, Shipley; John Harrison and Sons Ltd, tanners, Gomersal; Northowram Tannery Ltd, tanners and curriers; Benson Beltings Ltd, Gomersal; Benson Leathers, industrial leather manufacturers, Gomersal; and Benson Vee Leather Company, Gomersal; The business records include ledgers 1885-1988, day books 1946-1991, cash books 1979-1988, wages books 1911-1986.

William Paul Ltd, tanners and curriers, Kirkstall

The records are also held by West Yorkshire Archives. A unique and interesting document is the address book of employees 1863-1942, and other business records include sales ledgers 1898-1919, cash book 1919-1922 and piece work rate books 1961-1966.

S E Norris & Co Ltd. curriers, London

Company business records, price lists, photographs etc. Held by the Museum of Leathercraft, Northampton.

William Walker & Sons Ltd. Bolton. tanners and leather curriers

The comprehensive business records are held at Bolton Archives and Local Studies and cover the whole period that the company traded. The business was founded in Bolton in 1823 by William Walker, who originated from Co. Durham. The original tannery was in King Street but operations were transferred to Ridgway Gates in 1828.

Tanning also began at Rose Hill in 1850. The Railway Tannery, also at Rose Hill, opened in 1895. The firm also owned Bark Street Tannery, which it took over in 1864. The former Jackson's mill in Great Lever began the manufacture of 'Dri-Ped' leather in 1919. Two major subsidiary companies also formed part of the Walker Empire namely Dri-Ped Ltd and Bolton Leathers Ltd.

William Paul Ltd, tanners, Leeds

Company business records, employees address book 1861-1942. Held by West Yorkshire Archives.

Joseph Beaumont, currier, Beverley, Yorkshire

The records of this individual are held at East Riding Yorkshire Record Office comprising of account books, ledgers, waste books etc. from 1772-1825.

Turney Bros Ltd, leather dressers, Nottingham

Company records 1861-1979 including wages book, staff lists and employment records. Private archive held by the company.

W J Turney & Co. Ltd, Leather Dressers, Stourbridge, Worcestershire

Company records including wages books 1894-1903, accident book, young employees register. Held by Hereford and Worcester Archives.

George Dutton And Sons Ltd, Tanners Of Northwich, Cheshire

The records are held at Cheshire Archives for the period 1851-1965 including shares, accounts, operations, stock and waste, personnel, premises and papers relating to the Federation of Light Leather Trades of the United Kingdom which the Dutton's were instrumental in establishing.

Webb & Son, tanners, Stowmarket, Suffolk

Company records 1848-1971 including wages books. Held by Suffolk County Record Office, Ipswich.

Leather glossary

Aniline Leather: Leather that has been dyed by immersion, using aniline dyes, and has not received any surface coating. The process is not used today and the term usually describes leather without a surface coating.

Antique Grain: An irregular surface pattern of markings or creases, which are given a contrasting colour to produce a two-tone effect. The creases are produced by embossing, boarding or other similar means and usually relate to shoes or leather bound books.

Back: The main portion of a hide, obtained by cutting off the two bellies.

Badger: A maker of bags

Barker: A tanner, derived from the use of oak bark in the tanning process.

Belly: Part of the hide covering the underside and the upper part of the legs of the animal.

Belly Grain: The tanned outer layer split from a belly.

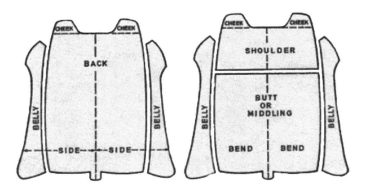

28. Each part of a hide and skin were known by different terms.

Blue Split: A process of chrome tanning where a hide or skin which has been split into two or more layers.

Bracegirdle: A belt maker, from 'breeches girdle'.

Brushed Leather: A velvet-like grained surface achieved by a process of controlled surface abrasion.

Buffed Leather: Leather from which the top surface of the grain has been removed by an abrasive or blade.

Burrell: A name for a harness maker, from the French 'boure' and 'bourellier'.

Butler: A maker or seller of leather bottles.

Buffing: Removal of the flesh side of the leather by abrasion to produce a suede effect.

Chamois Leather: Leather made from sheep or lamb skin, from which the grain has been removed. Generally the flesh split of a sheepskin or lambskin.

Chaucer: A maker of shoes or leggings, from the Old French 'chausse'.

Chrome Tanned: Leather tanned solely with chromium salts or with chromium salts with small amounts of other tanning agent used to expedite the chrome tanning process.

Combination Tanned: Leather tanned using two or more tanning agents, either chrome and vegetable, vegetable followed by chrome, or formaldehyde and oil.

Finish: The final process or processes in the manufacture of dressed leather.

Gant: A maker or seller of gloves, from the Old French 'gant'.

Grain: The unique pattern characterised by the pores of a particular animal and visible on the outer surface of a hide or skin after the hair has been removed.

Morocco: Vegetable tanned goat skin leather with characteristic grain pattern developed naturally and used especially in the fancy goods trade.

Nappa: Soft full grain gloving or clothing leather made from unsplit sheepskin or lambskin and usually tanned with alum and chromium salts and dyed which gives rise to the term used in the glove trade of napper.

Parchment: Non tanned material with a smooth surface suitable for writing, bookbinding and other purposes made from the skin of sheep or goats, by drying out the material without tanning. Made from the flesh split of a sheepskin.

Patent Leather: Leather, one surface of which is covered with a waterproof film which has a lustrous mirror-like surface. This coating was formerly built up by the application of various linseed oil based daubs, varnishes and lacquers, Today these substances include synthetic resins.

Rough Tanned Leather: Leather which after tanning has not been further processed but has been dried out.

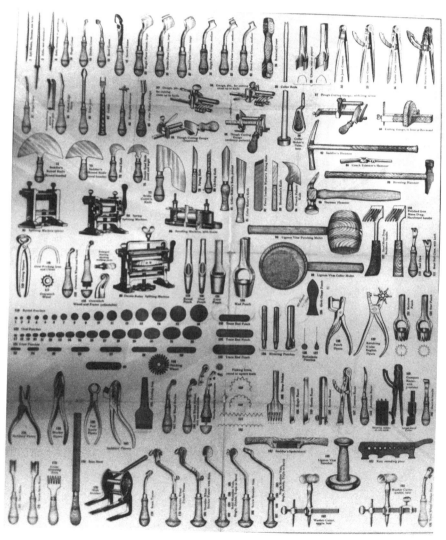

29. *Different jobs within the leather industry required many different tools.*

Harrold Leather Works

Harrold in Bedfordshire has long been associated with the leather industry. The author's great uncle, before moving to Rushden for employment in the boot and shoe industry worked for Pettits (specifically Charles Pettit as a leather dresser). The earliest record relating to the origins of this company held by Bedfordshire Record Office is a 1782 will for Stephen Morris, a fellmonger, who then devised his house to his wife Mary. She died without proving her husband's will which was subsequently proved by her executrix, Elizabeth Crawley, in 1786. Stephen Morris' estate was valued below £20. In 1795 a cottage and fellmonger's shop, yard and gardens in Harrold in occupation of Samuel Parsons at a rent of £4.15s.0d. formed part of the estate of James Milward and subsequently formed part of the Pettit factory.

Bedfordshire and Luton Archives and Records Service also holds a number of 19th and early 20th century directories and these include the following references to leather working in Harrold:

- 1839-1850: Samuel Parsons, fellmonger, perhaps the same man as mentioned in 1895, or a relative;
- 1847-1870: Thomas Parsons, described as a fellmonger, also, in 1853, a carrier;
- 1853-1870: Edward Rate, described as a fellmonger, in 1854 also a shopkeeper;
- 1877-1894: Charles Pettit, leather-dresser, in 1894 he was resident at Harrold House, he became a local JP;
- 1910-1920: Pettit & Company;
- 1924: Harrold Leather Company Limited, run by John Charles Tusting;
- 1928: Harrold Leather Manufacturing Company.

John Charles Tusting married Charles James Pettit's daughter and so succeeded to his business. A snippet from the *Bedfordshire Mercury* of 15th September 1888 shows how reliant on the owner the business, and its workers, was:

'Mr. C. Pettit, who was thrown from his trap a short time since, has been obliged to close his leather yard and go away for a change, thus throwing many out of work'.

The biggest leather works in the early 20th century, was to the rear of the southern part of the High Street. In 1927 the property in Harrold was valued under the Rating and Valuation Act of 1925 to set the rates. The valuer who surveyed Harrold Leather Manufacturing Company's premises stated that the site covered an area of about 1.5 acres and he noted the following groups of buildings - all shown in the plan on the next page:

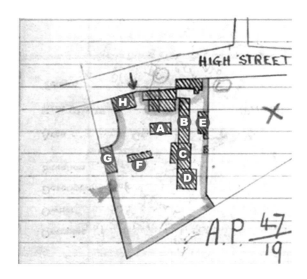

30. Leather Factory layout in valuer's notebook..

A: brick and tile and brick and slate offices and warehouse, wooden floor, 9 inch walls, one storey (56 feet by 22 feet by 13½ feet).

B: brick, stone and tile two storeys, 15 inch walls, part first floor with wooden shutters; finishing room and dye store (64½ feet by 15½ feet); heated drying room (67 feet by 18 feet by 22½ feet).

C: brick, stone and tile two storeys, 18 inch walls, heavy machines, 'good' machine room (51 feet by 19 feet), heated drying room (51 feet by 19 feet), brick annexe (36 feet by 16½ feet by 11½ feet).

D: new addition ('very good') brick and asbestos tile, two storeys, 14 inch walls, concrete floor; 'good' machine room 38 feet by 38½ feet; drying room (38 feet by 38½ feet); chimney shaft, square, 44 feet high.

E: new warehouse, brick and slate, one storey, 9 inch walls, concrete floor; 'good', 50 feet by 23½ feet; wood and corrugated iron store.

F: stone and slate old two bay open shed and two stores.

G: stone and tile barn used as garage and warehouse, concrete floor 24 feet by 60 feet outside.

H: brick and slate old stable with loft over used as store.

Also noted was the fact that the machinery consisted of a 24hp steam engine with a 13 feet by 2 inch main shaft and in relation to amenities, condition etc., that it had electric light and that the building was substantial and renovated with plenty of room but a shortness of water was a disadvantage as was no proper drainage.

CHAPTER TWO
The Shoemaking Industry

B oot and shoemakers are often referred to as 'cobblers' but the word cobbler is technically applied to a shoe repairmen rather than maker. Those who actually make footwear are better known as 'cordwainers.' This term has its origin in the word 'cordovan' which was reddish-brown goatskin leather produced in Spain. Hence, one who worked with cordovan was a cordwainer. However cordwainers also diversified to make other leather goods particularly bags and bottles. Shoemakers who made custom, made-to-order shoes were known as 'bespoke' makers.

Although shoes were being made and worn in prehistoric times, very little evidence has survived from before the Roman period. The early shoes were of primitive design resembling a moccasin and were essentially a leather bag shaped roughly like a foot. In these early settlements throughout Britain the shoemaker generally worked alone.

The Romans introduced more sophisticated shoes, and improved tanning methods to make better quality leather. Shoemakers at this time tended to congregate close to the centre of the town or village. Romans, used to wearing open footwear (sandals), cut the shoe uppers into straps and nets, and used rivets and hobnails. Evidence of shoemaking in the form of hammers, awls, lasts etc. have been discovered in many Roman towns in Britain including London and Bath as well as at some Roman military forts around Hadrian's Wall.

There has not been a basic change in the design of shoes since the middle ages. The chief developments have been on the technology processes such as welting and also in the tanning industry. A large amount of skill was devoted to the design by the makers of the 19th century particularly after the factories became established. This has been attributed in the main to the competition which existed between the different makers who competed for patronage based upon excellence of both design and quality in manufacture.

31. Typical shoe workshop of the late 1700s.

The designers of machine made shoes have gone to considerable lengths to preserve the looks and feel of the shoes that were once made by the hand sewers. Organisations like Bata and Clarks employed their own trained design teams. By 1860 rubber was being employed for the waterproof shoe. Rubber was frequently used for soles as it was more water resistant than leather, so much so that Bata had its own rubber factory to produce the component parts.

In London c.1850 there were over 28,500 boot and shoe makers but today that figure is probably no more than about 50. Elsewhere in the country similar patterns of occupation decline have also existed even in the predominant shoe making areas.

The shoemaking trade generally went through three phases of growth and decline. Outworking was prevalent in the late 18th and throughout the 19th century followed by a mechanised factory/manufacturing system which began in the 1850s and existed for about a century in varying degrees until the 1950s. After 1950 small specialist shoe companies making mainly high quality footwear have been in existence employing relatively small numbers of people. Why? Because of cheap imports.

The village shoemaker and cobbler

Throughout the British Isles most villages had their own shoemaker who inevitably repaired footwear as well as made shoes and boots for the local community. In many of the larger villages and smaller towns there were both shoemakers and cobblers working side by side. Until shoe manufacture became 'big business' in the key towns it was the craftsmen in the village who produced all of the boots and shoes for inhabitants and also repaired footwear if the agricultural labourer did not repair his own boots.

Most of our early ancestors who worked this trade would have been rural based and working as individuals or as a family with the trade following generations. It is unlikely that specific records of their business will have survived (if indeed they were ever kept) so it is necessary to use research skills to piece together information about their livelihood.

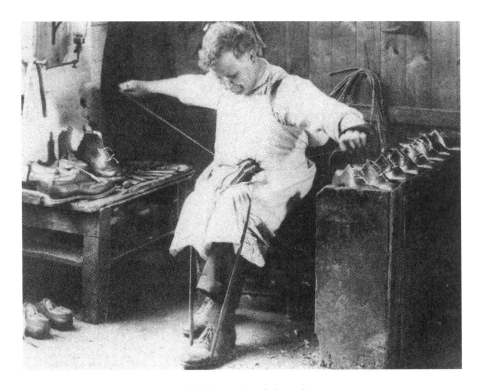

32. Eli Robinson hand-shoemaker.

The shoemaker could also double up as a currier. Boots were made to measure; and the shoemaker carried out repairs. He also provided the laces once using hempen fibres twisted with cobbler's wax (boiling hot pitch with a softening neat's foot oil) and a pig's bristle at each end to thread with. He was an important part of the village, cutting leather economically for shoe parts, making all boots and shoes including farm workers' boots which were simple and nailed for more grip. Shoes and boots were constructed with skill and made waterproof.

John Fountain and Son - shoemaker/cobbler/cordwainer

In 1773 William Tompkins, a cordwainer of Eaton Bray died leaving 'my tools used in business of a shoemaker' to his two sons Daniel and Thomas. They followed their father in his business. We know that Daniel was mentioned as a shoemaker in 1782, and when Thomas made his will in 1816 he was a cordwainer.

The Tompkins family were not the only family in the village to be connected with shoemaking. The Turpin family were also shoemakers and cordwainers in the same village working alongside the Tompkins family.

33. A typical village shoemaker/cobbler at work c.1935.

Shoemaking could not provide solely for a living so the shoemakers all had second occupations. With many of them this was farming with a small amount of land and perhaps a few animals. Examples from wills suggest that Richard Cooke left his cottage with buildings, barns, orchard, outhouses and gardens at Moor End to his wife in 1705. John Puddifoot in 1706 left his cottage and various closes and parcels of pasture ground adjoining. These were probably where his cow and pigs were kept. Some cordwainers seem to have had quite large holdings in the common fields which were divided into strips until the enclosure in 1860. In 1748 John Carter held strips in Orleing Field, West Field, Horsamill Field, Edlesborough Hill Field and Warehill.

An inventory in 1780 of one affluent cordwainer John Fountain, the author's 4th great grandfather, stated 'in whose house was to be found 'my large oval table, one chest with drawers' besides beds and bedding and at least one pewter dish. He held the office of overseer of the poor in 1757. His son, John Fountain combined the job of cordwainer with being the innkeeper at the Chequers. Most of his property was left to his son John in 1816, but certain items were for his widow, Mary. She was to have all her wearing apparel, 'my best bedstead', the furniture, sheets, household and table linen, 'the clock with the case standing in my parlour' and £315 worth of other household goods; 'but she may not choose my clock with the base standing upstairs nor my chest standing in my bedchamber' as these were for his son.

Most of the shoes made by the Eaton Bray village cordwainers were for everyday use by the villagers. The overseers accounts show that they made and mended shoes for the poor, which were frequently paid for by the parish. John Fountain senior sent in a bill for only four shillings in 1787 when eight pence was charged for mending a pair of shoes, whereas a pair of new 'high shoes' cost five shillings.

In many cases even village shoemakers or cobblers could not encourage all to use them and many of the poorer classes became enterprising do it yourself shoe repairers. The son of John Fountain's brother left this account in one of his diaries:

'My father, had to make ends meet on a limited wage so he saved money by repairing our family's boots, as that was what we all wore, apart from on Sundays and special occasions. It was cheaper for him to do it rather than to use my uncle who was the local shoe mender. Father did the repairs in his shed outside in the back yard of our house.

He was always ready to repair my boots once he knew that they needed it, but I was not always happy to tell him they needed repair. I well remember him asking to look at my feet, and there was a hole in the sole of my foot. There was a lot of 'tut-tutting' and questioning about the state of my boots suggesting I knew of the hole but seemed reluctant to tell him. I did, but one did not readily complain in my childhood.

My father mended our boots with leather which Uncle John let him have. First he soaked the leather in water to soften it. Then he took off the worn leather, put on the new and cut it neatly to shape.

My father had his own hobbing foot. This was a length of wood about 6 inches wide and about a yard high with a hole in the top to hold a piece of metal in the shape of foot.'

Bespoke shoemaking

Many of our ancestors would, as hand shoe makers have been involved in the bespoke shoemaking business. There was however, a difference in the organisation of bespoke establishments. The quantity and variety of work had a direct effect on the organisation required, but some general rules applied by all.

A firm involved in exclusively high-class business would evolve a system different from one involved in general work. There were many establishments in the West End of London and in the larger provincial towns and cities where bespoke orders were their exclusive work catering for a high-class trade, with some having their own sales representatives to take orders and measurements. Visits to the Continent and even to America by representatives of English firms were not uncommon. A general bespoke shoemaker was where only bespoke orders and the repairs of such work were undertaken and this often included the specialised making of surgical footwear. It was in this general business that the proprietor usually came into direct contact with his customers and took the measurements and other particulars himself. Then either he or a reliable worker executed or supervised the execution of the orders.

There were also a number of businesses in which actual shoemaking was not usually undertaken, but occasionally orders for bespoke shoes were received. The order was then sent to a manufacturer with necessary particulars which were very specific and detailed any variations required from stock patterns.

Name _Francis J. C. Esq_

Address _7 Bushy Park Road, Teddington, Middlesex_

Recommended by _Jos. H. Lawrence_ | Reference _Barclays Bank_

Date	Details of Order	Price
1. 3. 29	_Light glacé Derby boot, no cap, leather lining through. ay white to top., full ½ size, toch 1⅜" rubberettes_	RS/E
3. 4. 30	_Pair boots as last, but slightly larger by two point of right_	CS/E
6. 4. 30	_Pair glacé Oxon, straight caps, brogue vamp, linings. Same size as last pair of boots, but lighter sole. ⅝ edge_	RA/-

34. Individual record kept by bespoke shoemaker of customer orders.

Full particulars were sent by the retailer in regard to material to be used for the outside of the shoe or if the lining was to be of leather or drill; if there was to be a toecap and the style of shoe required. Of prime importance were the details of the foot, the length of foot; size of shoe required; measurements at the joint, instep, heel, ankle, and leg and if the order was for a boot, the height of the leg. A sketch or diagrammatic outline of the foot was also provided with indications of where any abnormal fitting was required.

With the advent of factory production some boot and shoe manufacturers organised a special department for making bespoke footwear; while some manufacturers catered exclusively for the bespoke trade in factory conditions. These firms, particularly with the passing of the established shoe maker craftsmen, proved to be a valuable resource to establishments offering bespoke orders but who were unable to find skilled labour locally.

Business premises

The premises in which the bespoke business was undertaken varied considerably in regard to accommodation. Some had tastefully appointed reception rooms, within high-class establishments and some were ordinary shops where orders and measurements were taken 'across the counter'. However to attract clientele a smart exterior and attractive window display was of real value. The windows generally contained samples of work, as customer satisfaction automatically brought further orders.

Whatever the class of business it was essential that facilities for a customer to be dealt with privately were available whether it was a cubicle or separate consulting room. Your bespoke footwear ancestor would in any case have wanted a pleasing environment and comfortable seating for a client. A counter or desk with a fitting stool was also essential. Most would have samples and illustrations of footwear and charts of feet when advising a customer as to style, etc. They would also have displays of sundries such as polishes, laces, spurs and foot appliances and often a selection of upper leathers, including perhaps reptile skins, so the customers could see the materials from which their footwear would be made from. Hand-made crocodile skin shoes were highly fashionable in the Edwardian period and makers referred to themselves as 'croc shoe makers'.

MEASUREMENTS

F.73

Date		Size	Joint	Instep	Heel	Ankle	Leg at 7	Leg at	Leg at	
2·3·29	R	6	9¼	9⅝	13¾	9	10	—	—	—
	L	6½	9½	9½	13¾	9	10⅛	—	—	—

35. Record of a customer's foot measurements kept by bespoke shoemaker.

Unless the premises were large, a single workroom would be used for most processes of shoemaking particularly to cut the patterns, the uppers and to fit the lasts (wooden or metal moulds made to the shape of a foot) and frequently to cut out the bottom stuff (tougher leather used for the soles of footwear) for the maker. This room was generally well lit, using both natural and artificial lighting. A fitted bench with a sectional cutting board was designed in such a way that there was ample room for the skins to be moved around when cutting the uppers. Shelving for the skins was also needed. A second bench was provided for fitting up the lasts and a separate room was considered necessary for dealing with the bottom stuff as a stronger bench was needed, but of course not all premises were able to accommodate such facilities.

It was from the main workroom that the work was given to the maker and to which the completed shoe was returned so that it could be prepared (finished) for delivery to the customer.

In general, workrooms allowed ample room for each worker to undertake his sewing and stitching work. Where a large number of hand-sewn makers (stitch-men) were working in one department, benches which provided workspaces for four workers were usual. These were usually secured to the floor and had divisions on the surface so that each man's tools and kit could be kept separate from those of his workmates.

In the absence of running water (frequently in the more rural workshops) a wooden tub was provided for clean water so that workers could wet his 'set of stuff.' A Bunsen burner was also provided for the heating of irons used in finishing. Sometimes a concave-convex roller was also provided but the older craftsman preferred to hammer the leathers which gave a superior finish.

Storage of lasts

In any bespoke business the lasts were their greatest asset. Once made, or fitted up from the individual measurements they formed part of the business archive and were usually preserved and catalogued. A bespoke shoemaker devised his own method of storage which varied with the type and volume of business. Some businesses had a last storage room where each pair of lasts was given a number and hung on a numbered peg, on a rack, or in numbered or named boxes. An alphabetical register was kept, showing the name of the customer and the respective last reference number.

36. Shoe makers kept labelled lasts for individuals on shelves.

When boxes were used patterns for the uppers were kept together with each pair of lasts. In addition to the storage and recording of lasts, records were also kept, which showed details of all the orders for pairs of shoes. This procedure prevented or minimised the possibility of complaints that a subsequent pair was not as comfortable as a previous pair.

Trade rates and conditions

Where a bespoke shoemaker employed workers rates of wages and conditions of labour were issued and enforced in the early years of the 20th century by the Ministry of Labour through an organisation known as the Boot and Shoe Repairing Trade Board. These regulations only came into operation when a person was employed as a wage earner by a business.

As an example from the early 1930s the regulations indicated different classifications of labour with the minimum time rates which had to be paid to workers engaged in particular sections of the trade. The rates for adult male workers ranged between 57s. and 72s. for a standard 48 hour week. For adult female workers, they ranged from 41s. to 72s. for the standard 48 hour week.

There were also special rates for workers under 21 years of age, learners and apprentices. For workers, who were neither learners nor apprentices, the rates ranged, according to age, from 15s. to 45s. for all male workers, and from 6s. to 36s. per week for female workers. These rates only applied if workers were engaged on operations falling within the scope of the Trade Board.

Apprentices

There were different rates for apprentices and learners, to which specific conditions were attached. In the case of apprentices, a model form of indenture was frequently used which, after allowing for a short probationary period, was completed and sent to the Trade Board Offices for certification. The apprenticeship then continued at the appropriate rate of remuneration for the class. The classes or branches of the trade were as follows:

(a) Bespoke (hand sewn making) including clicking and closing.
(b) All other branches of the trade.

The principal conditions applicable to apprentices were:

(a) That the apprentice was employed under a certified and executed indenture.
(b) That a clause in the indenture provided for effective instruction throughout the period of apprenticeship in the particular branch of the trade specified.
(c) That if required by the Trade Board, the Employer would submit for examination a sample of work done by the apprentice.
(d) That the apprentice was the holder of a certificate issued by the Trade Board.
(e) That the number of apprentices was not more than one to every two journeymen in the particular branch of the trade.

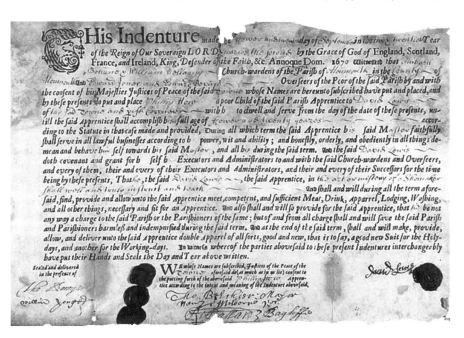

37. Example of entry from the IRI registers at TNA relating to tax paid for apprentices from 1710.

38. Example of a young boy apprenticed under the Old Poor Law in the 'mysteries of shoemaking'.

Learners

The difference between learners and apprentices was that the latter were engaged for a definite term of years as per the indenture, but learners were employed as time workers and were subject to a proportionate reduction if not employed for the full 48 hours in any week.

There were also some other conditions applicable only to learners:

(a) That they were instructed in a progressive manner in the particular class or branch of the trade for which he was certified by the Trade Board.
(b) That he was paid the appropriate rate for his age and the class of work in which he was being taught.
(c) That the proportion rule of not more than one learner to any two journeymen was observed.
(d) That he was the holder of a certificate issued by the Trade Board.

Exemptions

Exemption from any of the rates and conditions in the schedule could be obtained for any time worker suffering from a physical disability that affected his earning capacity. To obtain this, it was necessary to apply to the Secretary of the Trade Board, stating fully the grounds on which the exemption was sought.

Piece work rates

General minimum piece rates were also regulated by the Trade Board and contained various tables of rates for workers employed on piece rates, both for ground work and extras. There were also tables of rates for practically all operations of repairing work undertaken by cobblers.

Ground work

Different rates existed for different sections of work, and for the completed work. For making bespoke footwear, including surgical work, rates were determined for all classes and types of work, from the smallest children's shoe to the many varieties of ladies' and gents' work. They were so arranged that it was clear to see the exact rate for any specific operation. There was also a rate for the completed work.

Extras and overtime

There was also a comprehensive list of extras applicable to both hand sewn and surgical work. These were items considered to be additions to the normal boot or shoe making process and as an extra the rate has to be paid to the worker.

Rates ranging from time and a quarter to double time according to the amount of overtime worked, were payable if the worker was employed for more than nine hours each day. Overtime rates operated after 48 hours had been worked in the ordinary working week.

There was an exception where a five-day week was customary. In this case, overtime rates did not operate until nine and a half hours on four days, and ten hours on the fifth day, had been worked. In all cases work on Sundays and bank holidays was subject to double time rates.

An employer was bound under the orders issued by the Trade Board to pay the minimum rates applicable. He also had to provide all grindery (other than personal tools) necessary to perform the work. If he employed outworkers, there were other obligations he had to fulfil. The Trade Board was a statutory body and its orders were enforceable by law. A worker had to be paid at least the minimum rates for any time in which he was employed in any section of the trade as laid down in the Trade Boards (Boot and Shoe Repairing) Order of 1919, namely the repairing of boots, shoes, slippers, and all kinds of leather footwear, including the making of bespoke hand sewn, riveted, or pegged leather footwear, but excluding the manufacture of leather footwear on a large scale, the repairing of saddles and other leather goods not associated with the footwear trade.

An employer was subject to penalties on conviction if he failed to pay minimum wages as issued from time to time by the Trade Board. It was also necessary for him to keep wage and piece-work records for all work falling within the scope of the Trade Board. It was also an offence not to furnish an Inspector, appointed under the Trade Board Acts, with the information necessary for him to exercise his powers.

Book-keeping and costing

One of the prime responsibilities as required by the Trade Board of any bespoke business was the keeping of proper financial records and it is likely that these will have survived in any business archive. Such records will provide an in-depth picture of the business and what aspects of the trade they were involved with. Whether the business was large or small, the financial side was of prime importance.

For the average bespoke shoe maker, the requirements of the board were adhered to if the following records were kept:

(a) A day book, recording particulars of all goods dispatched or delivered to customers for credit.
(b) An index ledger for entering particulars of goods sold on credit,
(c) An index ledger, for recording all purchases of goods.
(d) A cash register, recording all cash transactions, including the payment of credit accounts.
(e) An analysis book, in which all financial transactions are summarised.
(f) A receipt book.
(g) Bank account into which all money received was paid.

It was necessary for the bespoke shoe maker to be astute in business methodology as he needed to make a profit and not undersell his services. He needed to have some system of costing that enabled him to form some idea of the gross cost of the goods he was making, and to give a quotation to a customer. It enabled him to cost the production of the boots or shoes being made.

Materials - In working out the materials cost, account was taken of cutting the leather for either uppers or bottoms, and the amount of waste which could not be avoided. Other on-costs needed to be accounted for including the leather for the outsides of uppers, materials used for linings, leather for bottoming, all of the eyelets, hooks, laces and polishes used for finishing, the grindery, hemp, flax, rivets, wax, paste and fillings.

Labour - All costs associated with the work of making the shoes was included.

The following is an example of the cost of a pair of bespoke shoes around 1930:

Outsides of uppers 3ft 4′ at 2s.4d. per ft. - 7s.7d.
Linings 3ft at 1s. per ft.- 3s.0d.
Soles and top pieces 1 lb. 3oz at 3s. per lb - 3s.6d.
Insoles, stiffeners and welts 12oz. at 1s.10d. per lb - 1s.4½d.
Linings, puffs, shank pieces, filling, etc., say. - 1s.0d.
Grindery, eyelets, hooks, laces, polish, say - 1s.0.½d.
Total cost of materials - 17s.6d.
Labour at Trade Board rate - 13s.3d.
Closing uppers - 2s.6d.
Cutting uppers and bottom stuff say, two hours at 1s.6d. per hour - 3s.0d.
Total labour costs - 18s.9d.

There were other on-costs involved which needed to be apportioned including utilities, insurance, boxes, clerical work, percentage profit etc. which may amount to an additional 40-50% of the costs.

St Crispin

The patron saint of shoemaking, Crispin was, according to English lore, born in Canterbury where he converted to Christianity. Some however will tell you that he originated from Rome. By the 15th century he was widely venerated and is frequently depicted standing and cutting the leather with another (who is believed to be St Hugh) sitting down sewing, which really typifies the shoe making process.

Within the shoemaking trade there are many legends and traditions which really begin with St. Crispin. Since medieval times, 25 October has been celebrated as St. Crispin's Day and still is the Shoemaker's Holiday in some of the manufacturing areas of Britain. In the past, boot and shoemakers traditionally closed their shops on this day, in

39. St Crispin the patron saint of shoemakers.

celebration and commemoration of St. Crispin. There are two stories about St Crispin and St Hugh one originating in France and one in England.

St. Crispin was supposedly born into a wealthy Roman family in the third century AD and fairly early on converted to Christianity. Since this was not an approved lifestyle for a noble Roman, legend says that he was disinherited and forced to rely upon his own resources, St. Crispin, who at the time was not yet a saint, became a shoemaker. Although teaching the gospel was his life's work, he made shoes in his spare time until he was executed in Soissons, France in 288 AD for his beliefs.

In Britain more is known about St. Hugh, the English counterpart of St. Crispin. Born Hugh, son of Arviragus - king of Powisland (modern day Wales), St. Hugh married a Christian princess, Winifred of Flintshire. She quickly converted him to Christianity and was disinherited. Having been thrown into poverty, Hugh became a shoemaker who preached the gospel by day and plied his craft by night. Both he and Winifred were put to death, ostensibly for rabble-rousing, about 300 AD. Legend has it that his fellow shoemakers kept a constant vigil and consoled him during the time of his internment. After his death, by hanging, his friends pulled his body from the gibbet and dried his bones which were then used to make tools for making shoes. A shoemaker's tool kit was commonly called St. Hugh's Bones. Since the death of St. Hugh shoemakers have historically been regarded as having an innate philosophical bent.

Turnshoes and beyond

The Anglo-Saxons introduced the 'turnshoe' to Britain, the process having originated in the Middle East. The turnshoe, as the name suggests was a process where the sole and the upper parts of the shoe were sewn together 'inside out', and then turned the right way round to wear. Shoemakers began to form guilds in towns from around the 12th century. Such guilds were known to exist in cities like Oxford from 1131 and London from about 1160. Many other provincial towns had communities of shoemakers such as Northampton where the guild was not formed until 1401 and Stafford, where the guild was formed in 1476. Although officially associated with Northampton in the 15th century, shoemaking in the county was established in 1202 by Peter the Cordwainer.

40. Some of the earliest forms of shoes were known as turnshoes.

By the 16th century a new type of shoe, called the welted shoe, was beginning to be developed. The process was more complex and the upper was attached to the insole and welt and then by a second row of stitches through the welt to attach the sole. This resulted in a much more flexible and comfortable shoe. This process still exists today.

As heels became popular during the 17th century, the design and process of shoemaking became more difficult and 'straights' were introduced. These were shoes which could be worn on either foot as the lasts were not shaped for either left or right. Nothing changed again until the early 19th century. By the time of the English Civil War many orders for army boots and shoes were given to shoemakers. Shoemakers in both Northamptonshire and London were at the forefront of manufacture. Northampton's shoemakers supplied the Parliamentary armies with 600 pairs of boots and 4000 pairs of shoes. It is said that they never received payment for these items despite meeting the terms of their contracts. Manufacturers in other locations also contributed particularly Oxford in the 17th century and York, Bristol, Norwich, Stafford and Stone in the 18th century. It is known that Norwich's shoe trade developed as a result of an influx of refugees from the continent. The slipper industry was centred on the Rossendale Valley in Lancashire, the reason being that it was a natural follow-on from its traditional felt making trade. Later still, around the 1830s, Leicester also emerged as a shoemaking centre as did Street in Somerset, home of Clark's Shoes and Kendal in Cumbria, home of K Shoes even later.

It is generally accepted within the shoe industry that Northamptonshire was the main producer of men's shoes whilst Leicestershire produced women's and children's shoes. Of course many other centres of shoemaking also existed such as Norwich and Staffordshire. The economic influences, the workforce and geographic location factors varied little.

In many areas prior to the 18th century towns had only enough shoemakers to supply the inhabitants but in major shoe manufacturing towns the wholesale manufacturers grew. From about 1793 there was a demand for standardised boots for the army. The impetus given to the trade first by the American War of Independence 1775-1783 and then by the Napoleonic wars 1795-1815 seems to have marked the transition from purely bespoke work to the making of shoes for stock.

The most prominent manufacturers of military footwear at this time were all based in Northamptonshire namely Thomas Gotch at Kettering, William Lee at Daventry and John Carey in Wellingborough. To give an idea of the extent of the trade; in 1813 Thomas Gotch produced 45,000 pairs of seaman's shoes, 10,000 pairs of boots for the Marines, 2,000 pairs of shoes for the Navy boys and 30,000 pairs of boots for the Army.

The bulk of the nation's demand for shoes was still, however, satisfied by the many bespoke shoemakers and clog makers. Work forces were swelled by the migration of displaced rural workers and also by many in the textile and stocking trades who saw greater security in the footwear industry. Even in 1831 Leicester was not really a shoemaking town, although a high proportion of the town's labour force was engaged in making shoes.

Other factors contributed to the expansion of the industry including the construction of the Grand Junction Canal connection to Northampton in 1815, the improvement of the road system thanks to the Tarmacadam system and above all the development of the railways. The Midland railway ran through both Northamptonshire and Leicestershire. The London to Birmingham railway close to Northampton ran through Roade, Blisworth and Weedon so much so that the local carriers saw an opportunity to expand and the shoe trade was rich pickings for them.

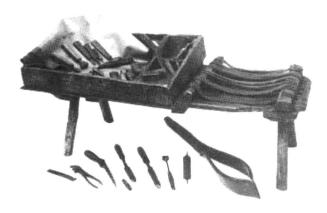

41. Hand Shoemakers 'Work station'.

At Weedon the establishment of a large Ordnance Depot during the Crimean War meant that military footwear could be stored 'on the doorstep' for later distribution which only served to help the trade in the Northampton area.

The making of shoes in the East Midlands, centred on Northampton and Leicester, was performed entirely by the traditional hand-sewing method. Many of the so-called manufacturers did not use machines or even had power in their factories and as such the factories were little more than central shops, operating a 'putting-out' system to outworkers who used the facilities rather than operate from their home. There developed in effect a two tier system: master craftsmen who employed a journeyman or two, or who worked alone perhaps with an apprentice, or the manufacturers who would employ anything between 20 and 300 workers.

Shoe craftsmen usually owned their own tools and produced around one pair of shoes or boots each day. Some village cobblers earned a living by 'Translatting', buying small lots of second hand boots or shoes and patching or repairing them to sell on at a profit. Virtually all villages had a local 'cobbler' until well into the late 1800s.

By the mid-1850s rolling-machines used for hardening leather and cutting-machines became popular, both of which were initially being driven by steam. By the late 1850s the leather-sewing machine, imported from America, was in common use amongst the outworkers involved in the closing trade. By 1853 the system of riveting the sole to the upper by machine proved to be an important advance towards factory production. This process, though known and used early in the 19th century fell out of favour with many manufacturers after the Napoleonic wars but was quickly re-established amongst the boot makers who supplied the army in the Crimean War resulting in an increased and cheaper rate of production.

Even more important to mass footwear production was the Blake sole-sewing machine, invented in 1858. This machine sewed the inner sole which was already attached to the upper, to the outer sole. Interestingly enough the company who made the Blake did not sell the machines, but leased them to the manufacturers. It is thought that the first manufacturer in the UK to use it was Stead & Simpson who were based in Leicester. The footwear industry was also stimulated in the 1850s and 60s by the development of elastic webs as a method of fastening boots, rather than laces and thus the elastic-sided boot became popular even with the military at the time.

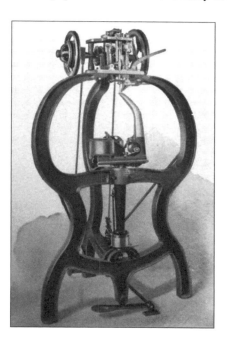

42. The Blake Sewer - the tool that revolutionised the shoe industry.

43. Rushden (a centre of the shoe making trade) - page from the 1871 census RG10/1498/57/33.

These technological advances were not particularly liked by shoemakers in the traditional centres of the industry, resulting in strikes at Northampton and Stafford.

Between 1851 and 1861 the number of people employed in shoemaking in Great Britain fell slightly from 274,000 to 250,000. A significantly large number of women were employed, chiefly in outworking and in the large factories and this trend continued through to at least the late 1960s due mainly to the use of the sewing machine.

Census returns need to be interpreted because in both the 1841 and 1851 returns it is clear that most of the population was served by local cobblers who spent a good deal of their time mending and patching up shoes and boots as well as occasionally making a pair for the individual customer. In 1851 5% of the population were involved in the footwear industry. In Northamptonshire this was represented by 17,204 workers most of whom were outworkers as opposed to artisan shoemakers. In contrast by 1951, a century later, 28% of the population was represented by 35,034 workers. By 2000 only 4,759 shoe workers lived in the county.

The main emphasis within the industry was on the 'Wholesale Manufacturers' who co-ordinated large groups of outworkers producing shoes for the wholesale warehouses located predominantly in London.

Why London? Because it was the centre of a major domestic market and also the home of the Army and Navy Boards who placed large orders for military footwear.

There were three basic phases of the industry:

1. Outworking in the 18th and early 19th centuries
2. Mechanised factory based systems with their heyday between 1870 and 1920
3. Period of small specialised high quality shoes from the 1950s onwards.

One also has to be aware of the cheaper imports which were flooding into the country from the late 1880s.

Throughout the second half of the 19th century the organisation of the industry was such that those with only small amounts of capital could easily set up as manufacturers. The expanding economy was able to absorb most of those who wished to pursue such a venture, but some firms came and went fairly quickly particularly during times of depression. As a result the industry grew from small family firms, which went on to become household public or private companies after the First World War. However no real family fortunes were made in the 19th century industry, but most families who were manufacturers were considered, by Victorian standards to be comfortably off.

Until the late 1880s machinery in shoe factories was generally powered by steam which was replaced around a decade later by gas engines. Few machines were automatic and newly invented ones for the various sub-processes were experimented with. In the early years of mass production only the heaviest and most permanent machines, such as those for cutting or stiff sewing were power driven. The remainder were manual machines driven by handles or treadles.

In most factories, clicking which was the most skilled operation was almost entirely carried out by men, as was the cutting of linings although this was very often done by apprentices or by juniors who were still training. Clicking demanded skill and knowledge of the differences in thickness, shade, markings, and quality of leather. Women and girls were also employed in large numbers, both within factories and in the 'putting out' processes of closing of uppers using sewing machines. In the 1860s such machine work was being done more in the homes of the workers and within small workshops rather than in factories. However, most leading manufacturers employed many women in their factories. Although the factories were town based some of the women and girls travelled from neighbouring villages to learn 'hands on' how to use the machines and when proficient they were able to do their work at home. This type of work, as well as the making and finishing, which was given out to the country districts, was often referred to as 'basket work' particularly in Northamptonshire, Leicestershire and Staffordshire. Trade union agitation against it became strong in the late 1880s and early 1890s, (discussed later) but the outworking system was seen as very advantageous to the manufacturers from an economic viewpoint as it enabled them to obtain the necessary labour more cheaply.

The machines used by the women in their homes or workshops in both the town and villages were usually hired from the employer. In the mid-1860s the rents were anything from 1s.0d. to 2s.6d. a week, depending upon the cost of the original machine and its value to the employee. 'The cost of a machine' was around £11 or £12, and each had a working life of about three years maximum. Occasionally women bought their machines at a discounted price at the end of the period and this meant that they could work independently.

Irrespective of whether the uppers were closed in factories or in homes, they were collected together at the factory warehouse, inspected, costed and given out again to a shoemaker together with an appropriate number of soles and a certain amount of rivets and thread. Until the 1890s the bulk of the actual 'making' was done outside the factory in small workshops. Where soles were attached to the uppers using a process known as wax-thread sewing, a specialist class of men known as 'sewers to the trade' evolved. The Blake machines as previously indicated were hired out upon a royalty basis, based on the number of shoes made. This royalty system was established for three reasons:

1. because of the fear that if too many machines were installed, outlets for improved versions would be limited.
2. as an incentive to men with little, if any, capital.
3. in the belief that a steady, if not smaller revenue, was better for the shoemaker than a one off or periodic larger amount.

There is no doubt that this policy of leasing machinery did make entry into the industry easier.

The other more established method of 'making' was that of riveting, which was a cheaper process, producing an inferior shoe. The workshop system usually had four or five men hiring a small room and these would often employ two or three lads whose job it was to scrape off bottoms and rasp the heads off the rivet. Periodically an assistant employment commissioner would visit the maker's workshops to check on standards of working conditions. Facilities were frequently found to be overcrowded and this proved unacceptable. In one commissioners report after he had visited four workshops in Ebenezer Terrace in Rushden it was stated 'One room was tolerably ventilated and not very dirty, but the other three were in all respects detestable; the ceiling and walls black with gas soot; the faces of the workpeople, men and boys alike, colourless and grimy: the children literally in rags of the dirtiest description, the heat of the atmosphere almost unbearable. The homes of the men who let out benches to different journeymen were miserable hovels and their workrooms dreadful places'.

When several riveters worked together, the work room was fitted with long narrow counters, divided up into bench compartments each large enough to accommodate a man and boy standing side by side. Each bench was fitted with two iron rods on which a pair of movable lasts were placed, one for the left and one for the right foot. When the shoemaker had fitted the material over one of the lasts and lightly tacked the sole to the upper, he passed it to his boy, who drove the nails into the holes which had been made by a hand or foot driven light pricking machine. A man working by himself would normally last up and rivet around a dozen pairs of shoes in a ten hour day and around 18 to 20 pairs if he had a boy to nail for him. However to put this in context a Blake sewer operated by a treadle would turn out 200 pairs in a ten hour day and 300 pairs if it was steam driven.

On completion of the 'making' process, the boots or shoes were then finished usually back at the factory where the conditions in which the process was carried out were normally unhealthy. The finishers sat very close together on each side of a low table, on which several broad gas flames always burning to heat their burnishing and where other irons were installed. The unions described finishers as amongst the 'most degraded of the working population'.

As shoe factories became more common so specialist workmen with distinctive occupational names began to appear in the many records. This had its downside amongst the young men and women entering the trade because as more and more operations were machine based the need for the apprentice diminished. Apprenticeship began to decline from the first expansion of the industry, as there was no longer a need to learn all the stages of shoe making. However after the initial thrust of shoe factories from 1860 onwards some forms of quasi-apprenticeship reappeared. Machinists could be 'apprenticed' at 14 or 15 years for either two or three years, receiving wages of between 5s.-9s. per week. Some would pay a small premium to an adult for the use of a machine. Some apprentices were bound to foremen but in general they either learnt from the machinist or worked without payment in a factory for a few months. Boot making work was the domain of boys but there was rarely any formal apprenticeship, except in the bespoke trade. In later years the need for training was taken care of by the 'boot and shoe technical colleges'. The one exception was perhaps in existence in the wholesale factories where boys served a form of apprenticeship to learn clicking earning between 10s.-20s. per week. Shoemaker journeymen in the sewn trade sometimes took learners under agreement for two or three years but to become a riveter little teaching was required. Finishers sometimes also took boys under agreement for a short period. The riveters' boys in workshops earned between 2s.6d. and 5s. per week, but in the factories sums of 8s. or 9s. were fairly common. Apprenticeship was almost unknown in the shoe trade by 1892 and neither the employers nor the trade unions ever attempted to revive it.

As the footwear manufacturing industry grew so did its distribution system. In the 1930s there were around 13,500 distributing units serving only around 1,050 manufacturers. This network developed from the crude marketing methods of the 1850s when the manufacturers were their own distributors. As the industry expanded, specialised footwear factors appeared. To illustrate how the distribution system evolved consider George Oliver who was apprenticed to a shoemaker in Barrow upon Soar. In 1860 he opened a retail shop in Willenhall (Staffs.) later opening another outlet in nearby Neath (Staffs.). He continued to open other shops and in 1869 he set up a factory in Wolverhampton to self-supply those shops. After only a short time he decided to concentrate on distribution. The factory was closed after which he set up a warehouse in Leicester. By 1890 he had over 100 outlets and advertised himself as 'the largest boot retailer in the world'. Whether he actually was is difficult to prove or disprove.

44. Typical closing room in a large shoe factory.

Before the turn of the 20th century there was little variety in the style and colour of shoes. Most of the larger manufacturers competed in the same market place which had a tendency to eliminate the less efficient producers. In order to overcome such limitations many opened their own retail shops. At the same time some of the distributors competed by making their own shoes. One good example of this is William Timpson. The increase in retailers promoted both variety in style and fashion. This was not without its drawbacks and advantages. The extensive advertising undertaken by the multiple retailer of a wider choice of shoes affected the independent retailers, who were forced to order styles of shoes different from those offered for sale by the multiple retailers. Conversely as the multiple retailers gained an increasing proportion of the distribution market, they were able to obtain a wider choice of shoes.

Such moves were particularly noticeable in the market and manufacture of both women's and children's shoes as the number of manufacturers and employees in this speciality began to rise. In Northampton for example those employed in 1881 numbered 10,500. Just ten years later the number had risen to around 13,000.

By the mid-18th century shoes shoes could be bought from warehouses as well as from the shoemaker direct. Like most warehouses they began to stock a fairly wide range of shoes and from this time on footwear was deemed fashionable. In urban areas most shoes were assembled by outworkers working in a small shed or outbuilding attached to their homes. The manufacturers employed a large number of such workers and stored completed boots and shoes in warehouses.

The thousands of boots and shoes made to supply the army during the Napoleonic Wars not only saw a growth in the shoe trade, but also encouraged the development of methods to enable mass production. In 1810 for example a sole-riveting machine was introduced. This was perhaps the first machine to aid mass production but its life was short. However at the start of the Crimean War in 1853 Thomas Crick of Leicester patented a better and quicker method of riveting.

A pegging machine was invented in America in 1833, which used wooden pegs to attach the sole, rather than iron rivets. Singer also invented the leather sewing machine and the first to be used in England were introduced in 1855 in a shoe factory belonging to Edwin Bostock in Stafford and was soon introduced in factories in Northamptonshire and London. It was often, however, the cause of unrest amongst workers. It was from about 1857 after the introduction of such machinery that shoe factories grew in number providing much needed employment for many including women. These early machines were only used for closing the uppers, which was traditionally women's work. Other processes were still carried out in the shoemaker's home. Over the next twenty years further inventions enabled all shoemaking processes to take place in a factory but outworking still survived well into the twentieth century. Pegging and riveting machines were adopted in Britain during the 1860s. Finishing was the last process to be mechanised making the mass production process complete by about 1895.

The industry, as change took place, suffered from labour troubles throughout the 19th century particularly as exports to Australia, Canada and the Colonies declined. At this time the USA began to flood the British market with their products and in order to try and counteract this, the shoe factory owners sought to extend working hours in their factories. Various (and some infamous) strikes occurred as workers tried to resist extended working hours and depressed salaries. Perhaps the most well-known of these was in May 1905 with the army boot makers from Raunds, Northamptonshire marching to London in protest.

After the First World War, a slow decline began but the traditions established by the manufacturers helped the industry through the downturns of the late 1920s and early 1930s. In the aftermath of the Second World War the number of manufacturers and the volume of shoes made continued to decline. However, Northamptonshire, which at the time was the centre of the shoemaking trades, supplied most of the boots to the British armed forces during the two World Wars.

An innovation in manufacture particularly for women's shoes was the use of adhesives to attach the sole to the upper. This new method was pioneered in Britain from 1949 by Clarks of Street in Somerset. The first direct moulding machine was introduced in 1950 and has since become the common way of producing shoes, moulding the sole on to the upper.

By the mid-1960s leather soled footwear accounted for less than 10% of boots and shoes worn. British shoe manufacturers had for some time found it more difficult to compete with cheaper produced foreign imports from both Italy and the Far East.

The centre of the shoe trade - Northamptonshire

The association between Northampton and shoemaking dates back to the 15th century, when the 1452 Assizes regulated prices and weights for various trades included cordwainers:

> 'The Assize of a Cordwainer is that he make no manner of shoes nor boots but of good neats leather and that it be thoroughly tanned.'

Northampton boasted a large weekly cattle market where the local leather merchants purchased cattle for the tanning industry virtually securing the access to the raw materials necessary to shoemaking. Northampton's geographic location also allowed a wide distribution network by road, canal/river and ultimately by railway, to be established (the LNER and LMS railways ran through the town). As a result shoemaking developed into the town's major industry. In 1642, a group of 13 shoemakers, led by Thomas Pendleton, obtained a contact for boots and shoes to be used to equip the British army before going to Ireland.

The 1841 Census lists 1,821 shoemakers in the town. Around this time there are clues of a transformation taking place in the town's shoe industry. Some of those shoemakers were beginning to describe themselves as manufacturers, as opposed to shoemakers. These manufacturers would go on to employ a large number of shoe-hands, as well as supplying materials and collecting the finished product from outdoor shoe workers, and then selling them on to buyers.

The Northamptonshire shoe workers were affected early on in the Industrial Revolution as mechanisation and the factory system became accepted practise.

Northampton's shoemakers initially feared the onset of machinery because they perceived mechanisation as a threat to their craftsmanship and livelihood. The nature of the town's shoemaking industry meant that the transition from an individual artisan's workshop to employer's factory would not be without trial and tribulation.

In 1851, Northamptonshire was the leading provincial centre of footwear manufacturing in the country. Boot and shoemaking was the third largest source of manufacturing employment in Great Britain. The 1851 Census reported, 274,451 in boot and shoemaking, with 94,175 'shoemakers' wives' in addition designated as such because they had an active role in making footwear, often working at home as closers or machinists, alongside their husbands and sons. 17,204 were in Northamptonshire, representing 8% of the national total. By contrast in 1951 there were 35,034 footwear workers in the county, approximately 28% of the total. In 2001 the industry provided direct employment for 16,987 people in England and Wales, 4,759 of them in Northamptonshire still 28% of the total.

H E Bates, the Rushden born author, describes the small footwear factories of the early 1890s in both his novel *The Feast of July* and his autobiography, *The Vanished World*.

'The plan of these old factories, all built just before the turn of the century, was very much the same: three storeys of brick, windows of thick opaque glass, heavy wooden front door, widish wooden staircase, and a little matchwood office on the first floor where clerks dealt with wages, kept books and made use of the wall fixed telephone.'

From *The Vanished World*

'In the shabby little towns the factories were lit with mantleless gas-flares, the flames fan wise, darkish yellow and blue-pricked if turned too high. But sometimes there were still oil lamps nailed to white-washed walls, with crinkled reflectors often of tin in the shape of shells. ... The pattern and odour of them was the same; always the steep wooden stairs and the walls soaked with grease, always the dark imprisoned odour of leather, the sing and stink of gas flames, the hollow rattle of iron treadles on sewing machines.'

From *The Feast of July*

These factories formed part of the street vista: a run of brick pavement lined terraced houses, then a small shoe factory, more houses, then another shoe factory. This pattern existed in virtually every town street. Many of the houses had small brick workshops at the rear, with rear alleyways providing access denoted on the street by an extra door between the houses or a pathway at each end of a row of six or seven houses. This local industrial scene had been effectively bricked-and-mortared into the domestic architecture. So too had the public houses, the small working men's clubs and the nonconformist chapels.

45. Shoe factories formed part of a residential street vista.

Shoe factories in Northamptonshire

The following is a selective chart showing the growth and decline in shoe factories in the county of Northamptonshire. A similar pattern emerges in other key shoe manufacturing areas around the country including Leicestershire, Norfolk and Staffordshire.

Location	1911	1921	1956
Northampton	50	54	48
Rushden	28	42	37
Wellingborough	18	21	26
Kettering	34	35	29

The main shoemaking centres in Northamptonshire were Desborough, Kettering, Raunds, Rushden, Wellingborough, Earls Barton and Long Buckby but other towns and villages along the Nene Valley were also contributors to the trade.

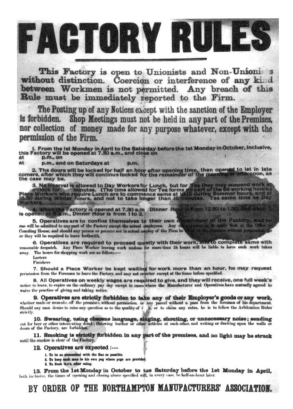

FACTORY RULES

This Factory is open to Unionists and Non-Unionists without distinction. Coercion or interference of any kind between Workmen is not permitted. Any breach of this Rule must be immediately reported to the Firm.

The Posting up of any Notices except with the sanction of the Employer is forbidden. Shop Meetings must not be held in any part of the Premises, nor collection of money made for any purpose whatever, except with the permission of the Firm.

1. From the 1st Monday in April to the Saturday before the 1st Monday in October, inclusive, this Factory will be opened at 7.30 a.m., and close on _____ at ___ p.m., on _____ at ___ p.m., and on Saturdays at ___ p.m.

2. The doors will be locked for half an hour after opening time, then opened to let in late comers, after which they will continue locked for the remainder of the morning or afternoon, as the case may be.

3. No Interval is allowed to Day Workers for Lunch, but for Tea they may suspend work ___ o'clock for ___ minutes. (The time allowed for Tea forms no part of the 54 working hours.) Piece Workers who require Lunch are to commence same at 10.15 during Summer hours, and at 10.30 during Winter hours, and not to take longer than 15 minutes. Tea same time as Day Workers.

4. When the Factory is opened at 7.30 a.m. Dinner Hour is from 12.30 to 1.30, and when it is opened at 8 a.m., Dinner Hour is from 1 to 2.

5. Operatives are to confine themselves to their own department of the Factory, and no one will be admitted to any part of the Factory except the actual employees. Any ___ are to apply first at the Office Counting House, and should any person or persons not in actual employ of the Firm be found in the Factory or they will be required to leave forthwith.

6. Operatives are required to proceed quietly with their work, and to complete same with reasonable despatch. Any Piece Worker leaving work undone for more than 24 hours will be liable to have such work taken away. The hours for shopping work are as follows :—
   Lasters
   Finishers

7. Should a Piece Worker be kept waiting for work more than an hour, he may request permission from the Foreman to leave the Factory, and may not re-enter except at the times before specified.

8. All Operatives on weekly wages are required to give, and they will receive, one full week's notice to leave, to expire on the ordinary pay day except in cases where the Manufacturer and Operatives have mutually agreed to waive the practice of giving and taking notice.

9. Operatives are strictly forbidden to take any of their Employer's goods or any work, whether made or unmade, off the premises without permission, or any parcel without a pass from the foreman of his department. Should any man desire to raise any question as to the quality of ___ or to claim any extra, he is to follow the Arbitration Rules strictly.

10. Swearing, using obscene language, singing, shouting, or unnecessary noise ; sending out for beer or other intoxicating drink ; throwing leather or other articles at each other, and writing or drawing upon the walls or doors of the Factory, are forbidden.

11. Smoking is strictly forbidden in any part of the premises, and no light may be struck until the smoker is clear of the Factory.

12. Operatives are expected :—
   1. To be as economical with the fine as possible.
   2. To keep each man to his own peg where pegs are provided.
   3. To finish work before leaving.

13. From the 1st Monday in October to the Saturday before the 1st Monday in April, both inclusive, the times of opening and closing above specified will, in every case, be half-an-hour later.

BY ORDER OF THE NORTHAMPTON MANUFACTURERS' ASSOCIATION.

46. All shoe factories had rules made in conjunction with the unions.

Clog making

From the start of the 20th century clogs as a choice of footwear for the British worker has been in decline, and they are today usually worn as a fashion item or for clog dancing.

Before the turn of the 20th century clogs were an extremely common type of footwear worn by virtually everyone from farm labourers to ministers or teachers and as such clog making in Britain was booming. Clogs were also long lasting and easier to repair than other types of footwear. Farmers and farm workers, male and female, wore clog-boots because wooden soles kept their feet out of the mud, road workers wore clog-boots as insulation from the heat generated by newly laid tarmacadam and in winter particularly, school children would compact snow on the bottoms of the clogs and then use their footwear as makeshift skates. Even during the Second World War you could buy as many pairs of clogs you required because rubber-soled footwear was on ration.

The clog maker was a specialist craftsman, concerned only with making wooden soled clogs. In addition to the many itinerant cloggers almost every village and rural community had its clog maker, who made unique footwear for each individual.

The clogger measured the customers feet accurately for the 'men's', 'women's', 'middles' and 'children's' styles and transferred those measurements to a paper or card pattern. In many clog makers workshops, patterns representing the feet of generations of local inhabitants could be found. After highly-skilled work with the stock knife, a similar knife with a convex blade some three inches wide was used to shape the top surface. This was known as the hollowing knife and it was followed by the morticing knife or gripper, whose narrow V-shaped blade cuts a channel all around the edge of the sole for fitting the leather uppers. Finally the sole is finished with rasps and short-bladed knives until it is perfectly smooth

47. Tools used by clog makers for cutting clogs.

To make them durable a 'cacker', similar to a small metal horse shoe, was nailed on both the toe and heel to stop the wood wearing out. Most people repaired their clogs at home, replacing cackers or even fitting new leather uppers. With fashionable shoes becoming more affordable to the masses the wooden clog shoe went into decline. This change in demand has seen the village clog maker almost vanish particularly in Scotland and the North of England where clogs were frequently worn.

48. A clog maker cutting a clog sole.

The Welsh clog makers reckoned that a sycamore tree cut from the hedgerow produced far superior soles to any other type of wood. The trees were felled and immediately converted into sole blocks; first with beetle and wedge, then with an axe and finally with the large stock knife. The process adopted by seasoned cloggers meant a few deft strokes with a guillotine-like stock knife reduced the blocks of wood to nearly the correct shape.

For most village clog makers and shoemakers their workshop contained some basic equipment including manual sewing machines, hammers of all sizes, riveting machines, various machines fixed to benches for cutting soles and uppers, shelves of coloured dyes and racks of wooden lasts for stretching the leather uppers of shoes into the right shapes and sizes. The lasts were made to an individual's foot pattern and no two were the same.

The clog making process was slightly complex. The process revolves around a pattern and the pattern making process is much the same for both clogs and shoes. Pattern making is a very precise art because if it is wrong then the footwear is of no use to the wearer.

For clogs it is necessary to first get the pattern of the wearer's foot and draw around it on the back or flesh side of the hide making sure the hide is smooth, without flaws and not ruffled at the back. Pattern making is something which had to be worked out to a fraction of an inch as the smallest variation will affect the finished article. (It is said that your feet feel everything.)

49. Shaping the clog.

Once the pattern is correct the next step is to produce the upper which involves pieces cut to form an upper and lining for each foot. This is done using a curved very sharp knife with a rounded wooden handle that allowed the clogger to cut curves and corners easily. The pieces were then glued together, incorporating a stiffener at the toe of each foot. This was important for industrial clogs where heavy objects dropped on a foot would cause injury. The next process was to use a skiving machine which removes the top layer of leather off around the edge of a piece. The skiver is adjustable so only the right amount is taken to the depth to which it is set. The object of the skive is to make the top edges so they can be folded over without creating too much of a gather. Once skived the edge is paint glued and when tacky a small incision is made and the edge is folded over, pressing it flat using a pressing wheel which squeezes the leather together to ensure it sticks. The uppers were then ready.

They were tacked in place, hammered into shape and left in the last for a few hours to be moulded into the correct shape. Unlike a boot, the clog is removed from the last before assembling. The clog upper is nailed with short flat-headed nails. A narrow strip of leather is cut and placed over the junction of uppers and sole. Great care had to be taken to ensure that the nails used in assembly pointed downwards and were in no danger of damaging the wearer's feet. Replaceable grooved irons were nailed to the sole and heel; a bright copper or brass tip was tacked to the front and the clogs were ready for wear. With constant use and the replacement of irons at regular intervals a pair of clogs may have lasted without resoling for at least twelve years.

50. The finished clogs.

The wooden base which was frequently made of beech and the upper were then combined. The upper was held in place with nails around the edge until the bend by the ball of the foot was reached. Today nails have generally been replaced by staples. The leather was then softened and the last was inserted pushing it home right to the tip of the toe of the wooden base. Some clog makers steamed the leather to make it more pliable but in any case a converted kettle with a piece of pipe attached to the spout was used. The leather was then pulled over the toe with grips, specially shaped to hold leather without marking or tearing it. Once the clog was completed it was left overnight. The lasts were taken out the following morning. The clog was then finished with dubbin, varnish etc. to make it ready to wear.

The process of making a boot or shoe

There is a traditional adage that a shoemaker worked on his own turning out a few pairs a week but shoe manufacture in large factories required a division of labour and this evolved over a fairly short period of time. Our ancestors who worked in factories frequently came to it from other walks of life and served short apprenticeships or even trained on the job becoming skilled at their particular trade very quickly.

H E Bates the writer who was born in Rushden (prominent in the Northamptonshire footwear manufacture) wrote in his book 'Vanished World' of his grandfather George William Lucas:

'... he could after the fashion and tradition of centuries create a boot or shoe from the sole upwards, stabbing and stitching with his own hands. The world in which he plied his craft knew of no machines except perhaps a treadle machine for stitching uppers. Consequently I am still to see him to perfection in the mind's eye; shoemakers last between his knees tossing handfuls of tacks and sprigs into his mouth, to my extreme consternation his awls, threads and leather, files, hammers all about him.'

This was a description of a hand shoe maker just before the First World War. How things changed.

A shoemaker had a standard tool kit and many took pride in the tools that they used, some being handed down from generation to generation.

Curved knife, straight knife, narrow skiving knife, rounded head hammer, feather knife, channel knife, edge cutter, awl, shoemaker's rasp, lasting pincers, bone folder, edge iron, heel iron, finishing wax, and hemp thread.

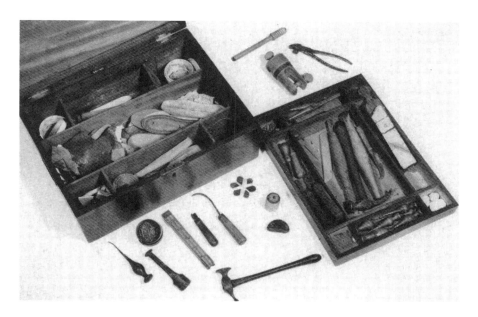

51. A shoemaker's treasured possession - his toolbox.

To understand the process of shoemaking it is necessary to know the different parts of a shoe.

A shoe consists of sole, insole, outsole, midsole, heel and an upper or vamp. These are included in all types off shoes but depending upon the style and use of the shoe other parts are also included such as a lining, tongue, quarter, welt and backstay.

Sole: The exterior bottom part of a shoe.

Insole: The interior bottom of a shoe, which sits directly beneath the foot. They can be removed and replaced. In some styles of shoe, extra insoles are often added for comfort, foot hygiene or orthopaedic reasons.

Outsole: is the part of the shoe that is in direct contact with the ground usually made of leather or synthetic rubber. We usually refer to these as heels or soles.

Midsole: The layer between the outsole and the insole for shock absorption is the midsole. Some special shoes have materials incorporated beneath the heel for shock absorption. Materials used for midsoles depend on the shoe manufacturers.

Heel: The rear part at the bottom of a shoe supporting the heels of the feet. Heels of a shoe are usually made from the same material as the sole. Fashion often dictates whether a heel is high or flat.

Upper or Vamp: The upper part of a shoe helps in holding the shoe onto the foot. This part is often embellished or given different styles to make shoes attractive.

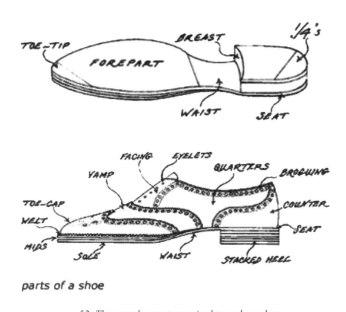

parts of a shoe

52. The complex parts required to make a shoe.

Boots and shoes are amongst the most complicated items of clothing we wear. A great deal of skill is needed to make a shoe using a large range of tools. Whilst there are only four basic operations to shoe making either by hand or machine i.e. Clicking, Closing, Lasting and Finishing there are over twenty different processes used to make a shoe whether by hand or using machinery. Until shoemaking became mechanised during the 19th century, a shoe would be hand made by one person. Some shoemakers would employ or work with a journeyman (a trained, but junior shoemaker) and an apprentice, and the work would be divided between the three. In later times outworkers would be employed for certain processes (see later). The process of shoe and boot making together with the terms used are explained below. It was not unusual for persons to be identified by the process they performed. The census returns particularly relate to occupations such as riveters, clickers, finishers rather than shoe makers so it is important to be aware of both the terminology and the process your ancestors performed.

The designer

The designer worked to the dimensions of the last which was made of wood or plastic to what evolved into standard shoe sizes and produced a sketch or painting of the shoe. This was done on either a canvas fabric or a plastic cover for the top of the last. He also made a mock-up of the shoe itself.

Pattern making or cutting

The process of pattern making was not that much different to clog making. The first stage was to make the last (the model of the foot around which a shoe is formed) and the pattern for the different pieces which make up the shoe. Lasts were normally made of wood but sometimes iron was used. Today, they are more often made of a hard plastic. Patterns have always been made of card or paper. They were then 'graded' to make a complete series for all the different shoe sizes required. The paper patterns were then made into permanent sheet metal or cardboard versions.

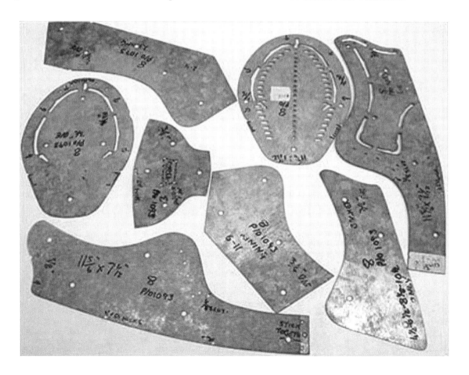

53. Patterns were used to shape each part of the shoe

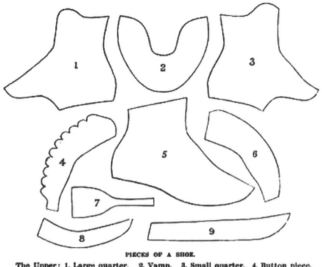

PIECES OF A SHOE.

The Upper: 1, Large quarter. 2, Vamp. 3, Small quarter. 4, Button piece. 5, Drill lining. 6, Glove button-piece lining. 7, Heel lining stay. 8, Button stay. 9, Top stay.

54. Every different design started on the drawing board.

British shoe size

The length of a foot is defined as the distance between two parallel lines that are in contact with the most prominent toe and part of the heel. Foot length has to be measured whilst standing barefoot with the weight of the body equally distributed to both feet. In most cases the sizes of the left and right feet are slightly different and to establish this both feet are measured. Each size of shoe is suitable for a small interval of foot lengths. To fit comfortably the shoe must typically be 15-20 mm longer than the foot, but this varies between different styles and fashion of shoes.

One important aspect for shoe size relates to the length of the 'last'. This measure is the easiest one for the shoe maker or manufacturer to use, because it relates only to the tool used to produce the shoe. It makes no promise about manufacturing tolerances or for what size of foot the shoe is actually suitable. It leaves all responsibility and risk of choosing the correct size with the wearer. A last can be measured in several different ways resulting in different measurements.

Sizing systems also differ in what units of measurement they use. This also results in different increments between shoe sizes because usually, only 'full' or 'half' sizes are made. In the United Kingdom the Barleycorn system of shoe size is still used.

The barleycorn equals to ⅓ inch. Half size shoes which are commonly made use of increments of ⅙ inch. This ancient measure is the basis for current UK and U.S.A. shoe sizes. The largest shoe size is taken as thirteen inches (a size 13).

Sometimes size systems also include the width of a foot where the measured width is assigned a letter (or combination of letters), that is taken from a table which is indexed to length and width or just assigned on an ad-hoc basis. In the UK the most common are:

D, E, F, G. The common UK; 'medium' is usually F, but this often varies by manufacturer for example Edward Green and Crockett & Jones, among others, use E instead. Alternatively some manufacturers use N (*narrow*), M (*medium*) or R (*regular*), W (*wide*).

Clicking

55. Clicking was the most skilled operation in shoemaking.

Clicking is the process of cutting out the different pieces of leather which make up the shoe upper. The shoemaker uses a clicking knife or a clicking press to cut out the different pieces from the leather, using the patterns as a guide. All the different pieces for the shoe upper are cut out from leather hides. The placing of the patterns needs great skill so that the clicker wastes as little leather as possible. With a large hide the clicker worked to a recognised system for cutting but if he was working on smaller skins then he needed to use his skill and judgement in the pattern layout using a couple of simple rules, Straight lines to straight lines and curves to similar curves.

The most important tools for a clicker were and still are a good quality clicking knife and many clickers had their own, as well as a flat level board which was frequently oiled and buffed.

The cap of a boot or shoe and the front are cut from the best part of the skin. The remaining parts of the shoe can be cut from poorer quality skin. The tongue needs to be of cut from light pliable leather because of its function.

If your ancestor was a clicker he needed to have an understanding of the lines of tightness and stretch of a hide in order to cut the material correctly so that the resultant item of footwear was not misshapen.

In some shoe factories the clicking press was used which meant that less skilled clickers could be employed. The machine, if set correctly meant that the outline is cut true to shape, the edges were square and it saved time. Of course the presses cost money and power to run them.

When the shoe parts have been cut the clicker colour coded them to show the size of the shoe to be made. He would normally use a metal stamp or water based paint on parts of the leather which would not be visible on the finished shoe. Most shoemakers adopted a universal colour scheme and half sizes were marked twice with the same colour.

Closing

Closing is one of the main processes in the making of a shoe. The caps, fronts and other parts come from the clicking department marked with different colours denoting the size and also stamped with the size, fitting, shape and sample number for identification purposes while the shoe was in the shoe room. Traditionally, closing operatives were women.

An awl was used to pierce the leather to prepare for the thread. The thread was taken through the stitch holes using a hog's bristle attached to the end of the linen thread. After stitching, a closer's hammer is used to flatten the seams and smooth out wrinkles. This process was known as seaming.

The experienced closer would produce a perfect seam holding the same resistance as the original material. Seams join the various sections together and have to be strong enough to withstand the other manufacturing processes of lasting and abrasive friction as well as standing up to final wear. Various systems of seaming were used depending upon the type and ultimate purpose of boot or shoe.

Seams were normally stitched with silk, cotton or linen each having their own characteristics. Silk is elastic, strong and uniform and its fine texture makes it suitable for high class fashion footwear. Cotton is strong, produces a smooth and firm seam and capable of withstanding damp and heavy wear. Linen is harsh and is mainly used on footwear made from heavy leathers because of its strength and resistance to friction.

56. The Closing Room was where the shoe was 'made'.

The women who worked in the closing room sat at either a sewing machine or a semi-automatic flat bed, cylinder arm or post-closing machine. Most of these machines were manufactured in America by the Singer Sewing Machine Company and were in common use from around the mid-1850s. The closers were skilled at their job and stitch formation was as important as the clicking process. The stitch tension was vital as each stitch had to bed down to the upper and be in keeping with the style of the shoe. The high standard required 'sixty-four to the inch'. Northamptonshire, as the center of shoemaking in England, is the origin of the legendary '64 stitches to the inch' - a reference to the detailed and painstaking quality that went into the shoes.

57. The closing operations were undertaken with a sewing machine.

Lasting

Lasting was undertaken either by hand or machine. Once it left the closing room the upper had no interior shape so it was the work of the laster to mould the upper to the wooden or metal last to give the shoe its shape and set it to retain the shape when the last was removed. Moulding or 'drafting' is a process to mould the upper to the shape of the last. Lasting pliers are used to pull the leather uppers tightly over the last.

There were two methods of lasting that were used in both hand and machine produced shoes. The hoisted method was used for hand lasting and the seats up method for machine lasting. Both systems required the use of pincers.

Before an upper can be moulded to the last an insole, side lining, toe puff and a stiffener had to be produced. The insole held the upper to its shape and the stiffener enabled it to keep its shape. The side lining as the name suggests supported the side of the upper and the toe puff enabled the toe end of the shoe upper to retain its shape.

Part of the Lasting process involved skiving and this was a noted occupation. A 'skiver' undertook a process of tapering the leather so that where the joint between upper and sole occurred the thickness was the same. This was a very skilled job which is today undertaken by machine but used to be done by hand using a skiving knife.

Soles and heels (the bottom stuff)

My grandfather was a rough-stuff department foreman for a local shoe factory in Rushden. The rough stuff department is where the soles were worked on which involves a number of important processes.

58. Leather was sorted in the rough stuff department for the different process in shoe making.

106

The first process is called tempering. Preparation can not occur until the material is tempered. Different materials require different tempering depending on their quality. This is done by submerging cut parts under water so the soles are soaked long enough to loosen the fibres and render the parts pliable enough to work.

59. The sole press was used for the cutting of soles.

The next process was done by machine known as a grader and leveller. It basically makes all the parts level grading the material to a tolerance of 192ths of an inch. The machine is a series of rollers and knives. The sole passes through the front set of rollers where feelers feel for the thinnest section of the cut part. As it passes through the machine the knives cut off the surplus material thus making the sole level.

The process then continues with rounding, again by machine which is basically a process to trim the sole. The next process is the channelling, perhaps the most important part of the job. Bad channelling makes for bad stitching. For stitching the channel should not be more than ⅛ inch from the edge of the sole although some machine stitched shoes allow up to a ¼ inch from the edge. Finally the sole is moulded and this determines the shape of the whole shoe. If moulded correctly the shoe keeps its shape.

The sole is then attached to the shoe by means of different methods including Blake sewn (chain stitch), riveting (metal rivets which ares stronger than the stitching), screwed or welted. Each of these processes gives rise to a shoe hand describing himself with a speciality. It is not unusual for a person to have an occupation as a shoe riveter, Blake sewer or welter.

One process which was common and gave rise to the occupation of 'pegger' is known as pegging. This process is not used very much today. Pegs were machine cut from a coil of strip wood and a hole was made through the sole and insole to receive them similar to dowelling in the carpentry trade. The points of the pegs which protrude through the insole are trimmed off so the insole is left smooth. This method was used mainly for wet wear boots and shoes particularly for those supplied to fishermen and the navy. They were also used during both world wars by people working in munitions factories where metal rivets or screws could have created sparks thus causing explosions.

Heels which were usually made away from the shoe factory to standard sizes still required building up and required two processes for attachment, slugging and compression. The 'slugger' was again a skilled job although is undertaken by machine in modern footwear production. The heels were then attached to the insole usually by nailing for which various processes and methods were used depending upon the style of shoe being made.

The maker (sometimes referred to as a separate operation)

The maker is a combination of several skills and is the person who actually joins together the upper, sole, insole and heel together with all other minor components and accessories. These were frequently known as a 'boot-man' or if making ladies' shoes a 'woman's - man'.

Finishing the shoe

Once the upper and the bottom stuff have been attached the shoe is sent for the finishing, polishing and shoe room processes. As many as twenty processes are undertaken to finish a shoe. Finishing is the final trimming and polishing of the completed shoe. Many different tools are used in this stage. Shaves are used to trim rough edges off the leather. Finishing and glazing irons are then heated over a spirit burner or gas flame and used to apply wax, dye inks and polishes giving a smooth, polished finish to the leather, especially to the welts and face edges of soles and heels.

If decoration is added to the shoe this is done by something called a fudge wheel (giving rise to the occupation of 'fudger') and used to imitate hand stitching around the upper edge of a welted sole. Seat wheels are used to add decorative marking around the edge of the seat of the heel.

The final stage involves a general inspection of the finished shoe, making minor repairs, removing stains, inserting socks and laces, general polishing to make sure the shoe is water-resistant and final wrapping and boxing. The shoe is now ready to be sold.

Outworkers

Before 1855, most shoemaking relied upon skilled hand processes which took place in people's homes or individual workshops, with outworkers playing an important role. Women and children would work together sewing the leather uppers, while men would carry out the tougher work of sewing the uppers onto thick soles.

The prosperity and survival of many shoe manufacturers relied upon a band of outworkers. Outwork is the making of part of a shoe outside the factory. Outworkers were involved in various processes including closing, lining, hand stitching and hand finishing. Pieces would be collected from the factories and would then be made up by the shoemaker in his or her home or perhaps a small shed or workshop. From the time of the introduction of sewing-machines in 1857, groups of workers, mainly women, set up small closing shops in their homes or in purpose-built closing rooms, the machinery often rented from the shoe manufacturers.

60. Outworkers collecting and returning shoes to the wholesaler factory.

An article relating to The Long Bugby outworkers appeared in a Northampton newspaper of the day:

'You see most of them worked at home in them days and they would have one of the bedrooms as a workroom and they had the bench in the middle and they would sit, place themselves round on little stools. They wouldn't be stools, what they'd be was chairs that'd broke and they'd sawn the legs down and made little stools of them you see. Well at night-time I used to go up my granny's... they lived with my grandma and I used to run errands for them... at night-time while they were working I used to sit and read the newspaper to them.

When people took the work back when they had finished it, which we called 'shopping' the work, when you 'shopped' your work... he booked it down... you got paid for what you did and he was a passer and he was known as 'foreman at the wicket' and that was his job.'

Shoemakers enjoyed a largely autonomous, independent position. They decided themselves what days and hours they worked, often deciding to work on Sunday in order to have more cash to spend in the pub on Sunday night. The habit of taking off Monday or 'Saint Monday' as it was known, (after St Crispin) is testimony to the freedom enjoyed.

As shoemakers effectively ran their own business, they had to keep business records and conform to measurements to ensure shoes fitted correctly. This high level of literacy combined with the fact that many had been granted freeman status meant that any perceived infringement on their autonomy and flexibility would be vigorously opposed.

In 1857, when the first machines for shoe production appeared in Northampton, the town's shoemakers feared that there would be massive unemployment and that those who managed to keep their job would be forced to work in a factory. The idea of having their working lives controlled by someone else and having set working hours was totally alien to their way of thinking.

Shoemakers' cottages and workshops

In many manufacturing towns shoe manufacturers either built or owned houses which were occupied by either their factory workers and/or outworkers. One such terrace exists in Rushden, known as Ebenezer Terrace, where most of the occupiers carried on the trade related directly to shoe making.

61. An outworker's workshop.

The terrace of houses built in 1861 by the Radburne family, consisted of a sitting room, a kitchen and two bedrooms. Beyond the back yard there was another row of buildings which housed a workshop, known locally as 'shop', where the occupants would undertake their work as shoe makers or as pattern makers, clickers or cut parts for other footwear makers.

Of course, as time progressed, trades of the occupiers diversified. The *Phillipson's Directory* of 1910 extracted by Rushden Research Group on their website www.rushdenheritage.co.uk shows that there was a tinsmith, who made dust extraction equipment for the shoe factories, and a baker.

By 1920 one of the cottages became a general grocery shop where the occupier used the front room of her cottage. The cottages have since been demolished but the original date stone has been incorporated into the boundary wall of the small car park which replaced them.

In the rear gardens stood a row of outbuildings incorporating the cobblers' workshops. Most were of single leaf brickwork with either pitched pan tile or slate roofs. Whilst most were single storey some were two storied contemporary with the construction of the terrace.

62. Shoemakers had workshops at the rear of their houses.

It was not unusual for the outbuildings to vary in layout and size. Maybe they were built for specific trades or even to occupier's specifications? Fronting Newton Road at the end of the terrace next to number 55 was a low single storey building with two large windows. The two storey workshops had the shoemakers' workshop at first floor level, usually with ample window light and at ground floor a washroom or storage facility. Other schemes had much smaller workshops which were all the same such as East Street in Long Buckby.

Typical workshop space measured about 8-10ft square. These workshops were basic and contained little more than a bench in front of the windows and perhaps a store cupboard adjacent. Heating was by means of an open fire (the coal was stored at ground floor level) and gas lighting was provided.

Often this accommodation was shared with other shoemakers, an apprentice or other family members particularly the womenfolk who were the outworkers. Many small family businesses also used such facilities so if your ancestor called himself a shoe manufacturer then it was inevitably on a small scale even though hand making of shoes was being replaced by machine produced shoes. Most occupiers of such accommodation managed to scrape together a living and were frequently outworkers for one or more of the larger shoe factories. However an important element for the workforce in the mid-19th century was the collectiveness of working in small groups or in small workshops. The factories mainly took care of the rough stuff and to some extent clicking and had the warehouses where the leather was stored. By the late 19th century the processes originally the domain of the outworkers had become largely factory based. In many areas finishing still remained very much an outworkers' operation.

Children as young as 6-8 years old were often involved in the closing process. Most outwork was undertaken at piece work rates although they still had to queue at the warehouse for their work at a specific time of day or they lost out to someone else. Even payments in kind existed.

63. Plan showing the layout of a typical two storey workshop attached to a cottage.

Living conditions amongst shoemakers varied. In the villages most had an allotment or good sized garden attached to their cottages. It was not unusual to see shoemakers working the land during harvest time. By contrast in the towns the houses were often squalid and overcrowded, partly furnished and usually had one room devoted to shoemaking restricting living space for the family.

Many outworkers originated in villages and rural communities and were sceptical of the factory system. H. E. Bates described a typical factory in *Vanishing World:*

'Three storeys of brick, windows and thick opaque glass, a heavy wooden front door, widish wooden staircase and a little matchwood office on the first floor.'

64. *Most shoe factories were three or four storey often incorporated within predominantly residential streets.*

During the evolvement of the factory system married women were allowed to take work out to their homes. Family members were still 'apprenticed' to learn the trade, male and female workers were generally kept separate. Each group or 'room' in the factory elected its own overseer and above all there was no sub-division of labour, so all was not bad.

The development of the factories did however transform the urban landscape. Many of the small 19th century manufacturers became household names, Manfield, Start-rite, True-form, Church, Grenson, Tecnic etc.

Bata at Thurrock - the shoe makers garden city

In 1933 a factory was opened at East Tilbury by the Bata Shoe Company. Bata was originally based in Czechoslovakia having been established by Tomas Bata, who was killed in 1932 in a plane crash.

The Bata Shoe Co was the largest shoemaking organisation in the world. Its largest works were established at East Tilbury in London where they employed over 5,000 people who lived and worked at Bata. As part of Tomas Bata's ideal it was recognised that there was a need for on-site housing. As the factory took shape providing a lot of employment for the local Essex people, a garden city was planned. The houses were designed by top architects of the time, the first street to be completed being Bata Avenue. The company also had its own farm, shops, cinema and sporting facilities which included tennis courts and a swimming pool. Play areas were supplied for the children of the workers and a school and college were built.

The first factory was a single storey building but expansion was necessary and three more buildings were constructed, one for the Leather Department, one for Rubber and one for Administration, design and merchandising, and service department.

The Bata estate was perhaps the first truly international one. Many of the first inhabitants were from Bata's establishment in Czechoslovakia together with people from around the British Isles and from Poland and Malta. As Bata grew others came from around the world. The Bata Community also had celebrities visiting. Professional athletes and sportsmen were involved with the development of sports shoes. West Ham United Football Club used the sports ground for training, Workers' Playtime on the BBC Light Programme was frequently broadcast from the cinema on site and may other radio and TV personalities visited.

65. *Residences for BATA employees.*

Over the next 70 years Bata played an important role in the East Thurrock economy. A multi-national community lived and worked on the Bata Estate and to recognise this, the Bata Reminiscence and Resource Centre was established to better understand some of the social history of the 20th century.

The Bata Record was a weekly publication costing 1d. per copy. It was purchased by the majority of employees and contained information and photographs of life within the Bata Community. It was proposed that they should do away with the 1d. charge because it raised so little revenue but the management decided that people would only read it if they had paid for it so it stayed at 1d. for the duration of its publication. The Record served as a communication medium between company and staff recording such information as births, deaths and marriages of staff and families, sporting reports and items of importance from the management regarding the running of the factory.

Bata employees who served in the armed forces during the Second World War were guaranteed their jobs when they returned after the War. During the period of service they were sent copies of the Bata Record and food/cigarette parcels by the company. Many of them wrote to the Bata Record about their exploits. Many of the wives took over their husband's jobs whilst they were away. Some employees never returned and they are recorded on the Roll of Honour.

The Bata Reminiscence and Resource Centre holds a large collection of these magazines in hard copy as well as a complete collection on CD. More recently a twice yearly newsletter has been published (available on-line in PDF format) which includes extracts form the Record and other items of topical interest for those descendants of former Bata employees.

ROLL OF HONOUR	ROLL OF HONOUR
ARCHER ALBERT	LINDSELL FRANCIS
ASHDOWN STANLEY	LYNCH JAMES
BARRETT ARTHUR	MANSFIELD SYDNEY
BELEC JEROME	MCLEARY THOMAS
BING EMILY	MEREDITH FREDERICK
BLOOR RICHARD	MERRIFIELD KENNETH
BRADD DENNIS	MILLS THOMAS
BRANDON HENRY	MUNDAY FRANK
BURCH GEORGE	NORMAN EDWARD
CHAPLIN GEORGE	PAGE HORACE
COLE JOHN	PHILLIPSON JOHN
COUVES WILLIAM	PRATT DONALD
CROOKS LEONARD	PRITCHARD RONALD
CROOKS STANLEY	RAYMENT MAURICE
DAWSON RONALD	REYNOLDS SYDNEY
DORRELL STANLEY	RICHARDS WILLIAM
FAIRCHILD HERBERT	ROMPEN LEONARD
FARAWAY ARTHUR	SANDWELL JOHN
FOLEY WILLIAM	SAPSFORD LESLIE
FROST JOHN	SAVAGE IVY MURIEL
FROST WILLIAM	SAWKINS HERBERT
GAME GEORGE	SEDA FRANK
GARDINER LESLIE	SHINWELL HARRY
GARRAD ERIC	SHORT HENRY
GILES LES	SMITH EDWARD
GOULDING ROBERT	SMITH FREDERICK
HARMONIAUX GORDON	SMITH LEONARD
HARVEY JOHN	SPIGHT HEDLEY
HAWKINS GEORGE	STAMMERS ERNEST
HAYES REGINALD	TANN HORACE
HOCKLEY LESLIE	THOMAS DAVID
HOLLINGTON HORACE	TUCK ALFRED
HUGHES JOSEPH	TUCKER KENNETH
HUGHES RONALD	TURNIDGE FREDERICK
JACKMAN PETER	WAKEFIELD ROBERT
JONES WILLIAM GEORGE	WEBB ALAN
KEMPSTER JOHN	WELLER JAMES
KING PETER	WILLIAMSON MAURICE
LEGG HENRY	WINDLEY FREDERICK
LETCH ARTHUR	WRIGHT ARTHUR
	WRIGHT JOHN

66. BATA employees who lost their lives in the Second World War.

The Bata Reminiscence and Resource Centre is staffed by volunteers and based at East Tilbury Library. The opening hours are restricted.

Bata Shoe controlled the supply of its own raw materials so its factories received the right quality material and that they would be available when needed. They acquired other specialist companies within the UK and opened additional factories at Cumnock and Maryport.

The factory at Cumnock produced two million pairs of uppers for the East Tilbury leather and rubber factories but also produced shoes in its own right.

67. The factory at the centre of the Bata community.

The Maryport factory, built in 1940, specialised in rubber footwear using and pioneering the vulcanising process. It was based on East Tilbury and was outside the traditional British shoemaking centres in an area of heavy unemployment at the time thus providing jobs and retraining for many.

Bata also acquired the Blackburn and Derbyshire Cotton Mill in Adlington, Lancashire to produce linings and outer parts of sports and casual shoes. After plant modernisation the mill diversified also making fabrics for furnishings, cars and mattresses.

J. Hardy Smith and Sons, a Leicester tanners was acquired in 1944 and processed all the leather to meet the needs of the Company.

Hampton and Brothers at Netherton, Dudley, Worcestershire became part of Bata in 1949 producing football and industrial boots.

Cordwainers

During the Middle Ages, the tradesmen of London and many other major provincial towns formed themselves into fraternities. The workers in manufacturing industries such as metal, cloth and leather formed 'trade guilds' to present a united front for their craft and to control their trade within their towns and cities.

68. The Cordwainer statue on the boundary of the Cordwainer Ward, City

Those who worked with the finest leather were called Cordwainers because initially their material came from Cordoba in Spain. From this they developed Cordwain which was a soft and durable goatskin leather which played an important role in the growing prosperity of London. Those who processed the leather ultimately formed their own guilds but the shoemakers remained part of the 'Cordwainer' guilds and this is why today shoemakers are known as cordwainers.

The Guild of Cordwainers has existed from 1272, making it one of the oldest Livery Companies in the City. It subsequently obtained its Royal Charter from Henry VI in 1439. The charter confirmed the operations of the Company and allowed it to own property. It was one of the first to own its own hall.

John Fisher bequeathed property in Fleet Street and adjoining Falcon Court in 1597. It has served the Company up to the present day.

The Great Fire of 1666 was disastrous as the Company lost both its Hall and other property. Most of its records to that time were also lost. Dr William Marsden, founder of the Royal Free and Marsden Hospitals was their Master in 1849-50, and Sir Henry Doulton, founder of the Royal Doulton pottery company was the Master in 1889-90.
The Industrial Revolution resulted in a swift decline to the guilds' control of their trades. In the late 1800s their role in education and their value as advisors to their trades became paramount to their survival ultimately founding the Leather Trades School.

Like most of the City Livery Companies the 20th century saw them having a distinctly charitable role which included the provision of almshouses, pension schemes and care of the poor and the infirm amongst its membership.

69. The Worshipful Company of Cordwainers.

No less than five halls existed near St. Paul's Churchyard, a site which had been associated with the Company since 1316. The last hall was built in 1909 but this was destroyed in the Blitz and since then the Cordwainers have shared facilities at the Law Society and later at the Clothworkers Hall. It no longer has its own hall.

The records of the company as they survive are lodged with the City of London Joint Archive Service and consist of microfilmed copies of the original records including:

- Freedom registers 1595-1961
- Apprenticeship binding books 1595-1965
- Court minutes 1622-1874 (there are some gaps)

York cordwainers

The earliest reference to the trade of cordwainer in York comes from the Freemen Rolls dating from 1272 which lists over 200 cordwainers with the first entry relating to a 'Thomas de Fulford, Cordwainer'.

The oldest surviving ordinances of the Company are contained in the York Memorandum Book dated around 1395. Later ordinances, dated 1417 and c.1430, also appear in the same book. At the time the cordwainers of York were variously described as a 'Craft', or 'Mysterie'. The first reference to an incorporated company appears towards the end of the 16th century. Throughout this period the cordwainers, alongside other city trade guilds, exercised great power in the City. The senior officers of the guild were known as searchers and like London were entitled to inspect all leather and shoes coming into York and reject any they found to be of inferior quality.

The Cordwainers' Company, like other associated trade guilds, had as its main objectives religious support, the maintaining of standards relative to its craft and trade, including the control of apprenticeships. All persons engaged in the trade were required to be members of the guild. Because of this the guilds exercised significant influence over the affairs of the community in general particularly as their power developed. The ordinances, the rules accepted by the trade, related to the way leather was prepared and sold, both raw and tanned. There were stringent regulations for the methods of tanning as well as the quality of the shoes.

The leather trades were the most important in York in the middle ages particularly in the late 13th century. This is clear from the number of freemen from the cordwainers which made up around a third of the freemen. During this time the Freedom list names 220 cordwainers, 150 tanners and 200 pelters and skinners.

In the 15th century the cordwainers constructed their hall in Hungate. There was also a Maison Dieu in Fishergate maintained by the cordwainers. It is also clear from historical documents that not only craft workshops but also their associated households tended to congregate in particular areas of the city. It is possible that within the Hungate area, as well as the Cordwainers' Hall, that both houses and workshops of cordwainers existed. Archaeological excavations undertaken in 1949 unearthed a number of shoes from the medieval period.

In 1808, without explanation the Company ceased to function, but not before the remaining 26 members had sold all the property the guild owned including its Hungate hall. It was revived in 1977 by around 50 local people connected with the footwear and leather trade. Its objectives are now mainly centred around charitable and civic life but its main purpose is in promoting knowledge of the British footwear industry.

Records

The records of the York Cordwainers Guild are held variously between York Minster Archives and York City Archives and include minutes, accounts and ordinances between 1580 and 1808 although there are significant gaps.

Oxford cordwainers

The cordwainers or corvisers guild in Oxford was recognised to be the oldest guild of its type in the country, originally established in 1131. A charter of Henry II dated 1260, acknowledged the existence of and recognised the customs and liberties of the Oxford cordwainers (corvisers) as granted by Henry I. At least nine, possibly ten, royal confirmations of the guild dating from 1390 were subsequently approved by assize. An annual rent payable to the Crown of 1oz. of gold, estimated at the time of the charter to be worth about fifteen shillings was subsequently increased by five shillings in 1260 and a further two shillings in 1319.

In 1319 the university complained that the renewal of the guild's charter threatened the university's privileges and agreements with the town, and an inquiry was ordered. Presumably the guild's cause prevailed, for in 1321 the king was censuring the town bailiffs for failing to enforce the charter of 1319. In 1321, however, when the university complained again, this time that high admission fees were keeping out many shoemakers and raising prices, the king ordered the guild to admit anyone seeking entry without charging the fee. In 1465, after various disputes relating to admission fees, the guild agreed that those qualified for membership as a result of apprenticeship or patrimony should pay forty shillings. Strangers wanting to become guild members who had lived in Oxford for a minimum of one year had to pay a minimum of fifty three shillings and provide a breakfast for senior town officers. In 1484 there was another dispute between town and guild, and in 1500 the university intervened against the guild on behalf of an individual shoemaker.

From the 16th century the guild meetings continued to take the form of courts until c.1530. The chief officers were a master and a steward (later known as warden) and essentially the 'legal' officer. The other officers included four key-keepers, two leather-searchers and, because of the guild's religious connections, two keepers of a light of Our Lady in the church of the Carmelite Friars which offices ceased to exist after the reformation. All were elected annually on the Monday nearest 18 October. However some evidence existed that the steward's office was at the nomination of the master. The leather-searchers role overlapped with that of the leather-searchers appointed by the town council.

As there were few shoemakers in Oxford for much of the 16th century there was little turnover among company officers. William Spenser was master eight times, steward twice and held each of the minor offices over a dozen times. The master and warden were jointly responsible for the company's finances. The master usually held an annual guild dinner and by the end of the 17th century received an allowance for it. No such dinner appears to have been held between 1613 and 1629. The warden's duties which were not peculiar to Oxford included summoning members to meetings. Membership consisted of three classes; masters, wardens, and commonalty. In a somewhat unique ruling it was decided that the commonalty should not attend meetings other than elections and that the masters and wardens could make orders for the whole company. It later became possible for members to purchase the place of master or warden rather than serve in the office.

The commonalty entered through apprenticeship, patrimony or purchase. In 1560 the guild's admission fees were set at £3.6s.8d. for apprentices of Oxford masters, £5 for sons of freemen and £10 for strangers. In 1575 the City Corporation successfully persuaded the company to admit strangers for a lesser fee. Most entrants irrespective of class paid £3.10s. with a dinner. In 1634 admission fees were reduced to 3s.4d. with £1 for a breakfast, and remained unchanged until the early 18th century. Under an ordinance of 1633 only freemen's sons and apprentices were admitted with very few strangers joining the company. In 1644, however, a journeyman could be admitted for £5, a silver bowl and dinner for the whole company.

Cobblers and workers in old leather were not admitted as full members but were licensed by the company. In 1633 entrance was restricted to apprentices of Oxford cobblers. There were however relatively few cobblers and numbers dwindled in the late 17th century, increasing significantly in the 18th century. Widows of members were also allowed to continue their husband's trades.

The company's main source of income was from admission fees, fines and quarterage (quarterly subscription payments). In addition each member was expected to contribute a sum at election meetings. The company owned plate, including a chalice, and a number of the silver spoons given by entrants.

From the middle ages the cordwainers' shops were grouped around Northgate Street, sealed by the purchase of Bocardo House and Shoemakers' Hall, which was for a time sub-let to the keeper of the prison until the lease was sold in 1633. At some point in time the company was prosperous enough to invest in land at Kennington in Berkshire, but shortly thereafter the land, the hall and the plate were sold and the proceeds divided amongst its members. The company held little capital thereafter.

Little changed until the mid-1800s but abuses of many of the regulations and of the statutory seven-year apprenticeship term was not uncommon. The company closely controlled the craft but in the 19th century declining membership meant that control weakened to the extent that its authority was removed as a result of the Municipal Corporations Act of 1835.

In 1807 the company established a loan fund and by 1819 the money was handed over to the City Corporation as trustee with the intention of them loaning money to cordwainers in sums not exceeding £50. Again the company was wound down and the fund together with other company assets was divided among members in 1845.

Records

The Bodlien Library in Oxford holds many of the records relating to the Oxford Cordwainers Guild dated between 1260 and 1846. These records include various manuscripts, minutes, accounts and ordinances. Few lists of actual members have survived.

Newcastle upon Tyne cordwainers

The ordinary and agreement establishing the guild is dated 17 December 1566, and mentions their meeting house in the Blackfriars monastery and states that every apprentice should serve ten years and that foreigners (those not a native of the city) could be admitted on payment of £5, one half of which would go to the guild and the other to the repair and upkeep of the Tyne Bridge.

According to *Descriptive and Historical Account of the Town and County of Newcastle upon Tyne* by Eneas Mackenzie, 1827, in 1617 the company received a grant from the common council stating that:

> '... divers persons, for years, under colour of exercising the trade of a cobbler, who should only mend old shoes that are brought to them to be mended, do buy great number of old shoes mended and made fit to be worn at London and elsewhere, and cause them to be brought to Newcastle upon Tyne, and in the cobblers' houses, and in the market within the said town, sell them to the best advantage, whereby the fraternity of Cordwainers of Newcastle aforesaid is much impoverished. The common council then proceeds to empower the stewards to fine the aforesaid 'cobblers,' for the preservation of their 'ancient customs, rights, and privileges.'

In the early 1700s several members of the guild practiced as 'sharers' which meant they joined together in purchasing their leather and dividing it afterwards. The records of the transactions appear in an old book, 'The Company's Sharers' Book'. In 1748, they allowed twelve persons by grant known as the 'Cobblers' Bond' to follow the trade of cobblers, at a quarterly cost of 6d.

Over a period of time, those who processed the leather formed their own guilds as tanners and curriers but the shoemakers continued in the original guild and kept the name Cordwainer.

Records

The records of the Incorporated Company of Cordwainers are held by the Tyne and Wear Archives and include apprenticeship bonds 1618-1798, Order books 1390-1945, admission entry books 1628-1755, names and addresses of company members 1601-1940, fines and attendance records 1663 - 1915 as well as various records relating to property, finances etc.

Cardiff cordwainers (and strangely) glovers

In the middle ages, Cardiff had various trade guilds. The guilds were associations regarded as the benefit clubs and trade unions of medieval times. Besides its primary object of protecting a particular trade, the guild took on a religious character with a chaplain and chapel. The guild meetings were devoted to religious exercises, business and conviviality.

King Edward II on 4 March 1323/4 granted rights and privileges 'to the burgesses of the arts or crafts of Cordwainers and Glovers of the town of Cardiff and to their successors for ever.' A new confirmation was given by Richard, Duke of Gloucester, on 25 March 1444 ratified by Queen Elizabeth in 1589.

The two most important of these associations were the Guilds of Holy Trinity and Saint Mary. Saint Mary's seems to have been the Cordwainers' Guild and Holy Trinity was the Guild of Glovers. The Cordwainers and Glovers were involved in some dispute with the law officers of King Edward VI relating to their property at Cardiff. The amalgamated associations of the Cordwainers and Glovers of Cardiff preserved their corporate existence down to the 19th century.

The charters of this guild (or these guilds) are known by a translation made in the 17th century and deposited along with the minute books and papers of the Masters and Brethren. In 1861 elements of the charter and some of the related minutes appeared in the Cardiff and Merthyr Guardian.

Within the registers or minute books of the Company of Cordwainers and Glovers, there is a list of Journeymen dating from around 1630 although regular updates do not begin till 1663. The minutes refer to business as grants of freedoms, imposition of fines and the costs of legal proceedings defending trade rights.

From 1801 to 1806 there was no election of either masters or wardens and the end of a guild which had existed for more than 500 years came when, in 1806, the last elected masters John Hussey and John Bird, shoemakers, sold the Shoemakers' Hall for the sum of £28.2s.6d.

The Glovers, like the Cordwainers, chose an annual master and each trade admitted members into their common corporation. This accounts for the appointment of two Masters and two Wardens; the senior was the head of the Cordwainers and the other of the Glovers. The Glovers were allowed their share in the use of the Shoemakers' Hall, for a yearly rent of five shillings; while the profits of the Hall and the quarterage money of the Journeymen Cordwainers were to belong to the senior craft. All the other profits of the united Guilds were to belong to both in common.

Other town and city cordwainers guilds

Throughout the country many other trade guilds were established, the most notable being:

Alnwick 1535
Berwick on Tweed 1249

Bristol 1603

Canterbury 1518

Carlisle 1560

Records for this Guild are fairly comprehensive:

    CARLISLE SHOEMAKERS GUILD

    1595-1934 Books and papers

    1732-1836 Admission certificates

    1799-2003 Lists of members

Chester 1573

Coventry 1340

Daventry 1383

Devises 1614 (this guild included the leather sellers)

Dorchester 1630

Durham 1565

Exeter 1387

Gloucester (date uncertain but certainly by the mid-1500s)

Helston 1201

Hereford 1215

Ipswich early 17th century

Kendal 1490

Hull 1624

Leeds (earliest record 1710 but believed to have existed much earlier)

Leicester 1720

Lincoln 1307

Maidstone 16th century

Morpeth 18th century

Northampton 1566

Norwich 1565

Preston 1628

Reading 16th century

Richmond Yorkshire pre 1836

Salisbury 1612 (Shoemakers, Last Makers and Curriers)

Shrewsbury 1387

Stafford 1729

Stratford upon Avon 16th century

Winchester 1580

Worcester 1504

There were also specific Cordwainers Guilds established in some Welsh, Scottish and Irish towns during the 1200-1600 period.

Records

The records associated with the various town and city guilds will be available in county record offices where they survive.

The title 'cordwainer' tended to die out of use in the late 18th / early 19th century.

National Union of Boot and Shoe Operatives

By the 19th century, a number of local trade unions or unions representing one particular trade had emerged throughout the industry such as the Edinburgh Operative Cordwainers, established in 1822, and the Amalgamated Society of Journeymen Cloggers, established in 1830.

The most prominent and perhaps the most influential of the early unions was the Amalgamated Cordwainers Association which was established in 1840 representing the skilled craftsmen responsible for making hand stitched shoes and who were not enamoured by the new mass production techniques that began to emerge after the 1850s.

The Association encountered difficulties in the recruitment of tradesmen who were riveters and finishers who worked in the manufacture of down market footwear. The union seemed to be involved in two distinct purposes; namely their recruitment (they even changed their name to the Amalgamated Association of Boot and Shoemakers in 1873) and in obstructing efforts to organise workers in the factories.

The union was not that successful and in December 1873 split. Representatives from the Associations' branches in Glasgow, Newcastle, Chester, Bristol, Norwich, Leicester and Northampton met in Stafford and formed another union under the guise of the National Union of Boot and Shoe Riveters and Finishers (NUBSRF).

This was the first new union with any degree of influence over the trade and their members called themselves 'The Sons of St Crispin' Within a short time from formation they had 4,000 members in 35 branches and by 1875 were able to offer members sick pay and also establish a funeral fund. In just over a decade membership had grown to just under 10,000 and continued rising until 1895, when progress was halted because William Inskip, General Secretary of the NUBSRF was at loggerheads with G. E. Green, General Secretary of the former Union of Clickers and Rough-stuff Cutters, which had merged with the NUBSRF in 1892. This culminated in Green taking the London clickers out of the union in 1898.

Another influencing factor was the 1897 strike for a minimum wage, coupled with a 54 hour week and constraint in the employment of child labour. This crippling and almost ineffective strike lasted for 34 weeks. Not surprisingly following this defeat union membership numbers fell significantly and it took about a decade for those numbers to recover. Within an industry that was heavily reliant on outworkers and casual labour, it was difficult for any union to prevent employers undercutting wage rates.

By 1898, when it affiliated to the General Federation of Trade Unions (forerunner to the TUC), the union had changed its name to the National Union of Boot and Shoe Operatives (NUBSO). The NUBSO experienced turbulent times through disputes and disagreements, both national and local. In 1916 the Amalgamated Association of Boot and Shoemakers which then had debts of around £500 approached NUBSO with a view to a merger. Despite the misgivings the NUBSO absorbed the older but smaller sibling Association.

70. Badges worn proudly by members of the Union.

71. Each branch of the NUBSO had its own banner.

The first half of the twentieth century was a good time for NUBSO. During the First World War membership nearly doubled and by 1920 stood at more than 100,000 (although this figure included men serving in the armed forces who remained members of the union). Throughout the 1920s and 1930s, membership remained fairly static which enabled the NUBSO to become better organised and employ more full time officers.

However during the second half of the century things worsened as the import of cheap footwear caused an untold downturn in the British shoe making industry. In 1971 NUBSO joined forces with the Amalgamated Society of Leather Workers, the National Union of Leather Workers and Allied Trades and the National Union of Glovers and Leather Workers to form the National Union of Footwear, Leather and Allied Trades. After a further series of mergers, that union is now part of 'Community' which looks after workers in the clothing and textile trades as well as the steel industries.

Boot and shoe trade unions and societies

Throughout history there have been many other Unions both large and small that our shoe making ancestors may well have belonged to.

Amalgamated Cordwainers Association - formed in 1840 as a loosely connected federation of cordwainers' societies and associations all joining forces. The association failed to respond to mass production methods and fell into decline in 1873 when most of the constituent organisations became part of the NUBSO.

Amalgamated Society of Boot and Shoe Makers - established in 1880 with around 1,300 members principally in the London area. There was also a kindred society formed in Ireland in 1892.

Amalgamated Society of Journeyman Cloggers and Allied Workers - a small society formed in 1830 amongst the clog making workers. This was short lived and faded into oblivion.

Bolton Cloggers Friendly and Free Gift Society - founded in 1819 and was the forerunner to the Bolton Journeyman Cloggers Society which then became part of the Amalgamated Society of Journeymen Cloggers in 1844 after suffering financial ruin.

Bury Cloggers Friendly Society - formed in 1865 with its own office and administration working out of the Arthur Hotel, Haymarket Street, Bury. This became part of the Amalgamated Society in 1872.

City of Dublin Union of Hand-Sewn Boot & Shoe Makers - was in existence between 1820 and 1830 although believed to have formed much earlier. It was one of several Irish shoe unions that attempted to rival the British NUBSO in Ireland.

City of Glasgow Operative Boot and Shoe Trade and Funeral Society - believed to have been established to help pay towards funeral costs of shoe workers' families rather than as a trade union. It was still operative as late as 1958 but its origins are unknown.

Cork Ladies' & Gentlemens' Boot Makers Union - founded in 1858 and existed in Cork up to 1919 when it became known as the Cork Boot and Shoe Makers Union.

Dublin Hand-sewn Bootmakers Society - claims to have descended from the ancient trade guild within the city and from 1890 was absorbed into the Amalgamated Association of Boot and Shoe Makers with its centre in London. In 1895 it broke away to become part of the London & Provincial Hand-sewn Boot and Shoe Makers. That association was short-lived and it returned to the Amalgamated Association in 1897.

National Union of Boot and Shoe Riveters and Finishers.

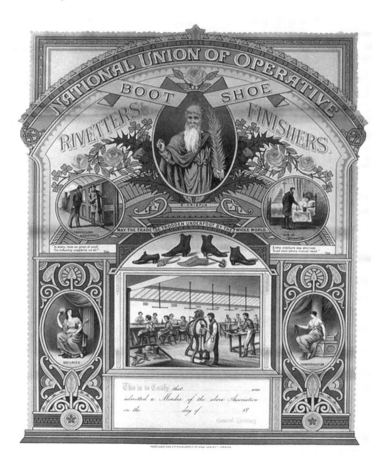

72. Banner of the Riveters' Union.

Dundee Hand-Sewn Boot and Shoe Makers.

Edinburgh Operative Cordwainers Trade Protection and Friendly Society - founded in 1822 and was still operational in the early part of the 20th century.

73. Trade Unions set the wages for their footwear operatives.

London Jewish Boot and Shoe Trade Union - origins are unknown but it is believed to have originated in Germany. The London branch started after the mass migration of German Jews in the 1870s. It was not registered as a trade union until 1921 and lasted as such for only two years.

Manchester & Salford Operative Clog Makers Society - founded in 1866 but from 1912 was known as the Manchester, Salford & District operative Clog Makers Society. Dissolved in the early 1920s. Members became part of the Journeyman Cloggers and Allied Workers Society.

National Union of Boot and Shoe Clickers, Pressmen and Machinists - founded in Hackney, London in 1899.

Newcastle on Tyne Slipper Makers Society - origin unknown but was dissolved in 1901.

Rossendale Union of Boot, Shoe and Slipper Operatives - established in 1870 and in the early years only skilled clickers and riveters were allowed membership. Membership peaked in 1947 with around 9,500 members (at the time the second largest union after the NUBSO).

Scottish National Amalgamated Union of Operative Boot and Shoe Workers - was formed in 1866 and was still operating until 1968.

Western District Ladies Hand-sewn Boot and Shoe Makers - founded in 1895. Held its meetings at the Prince Arthur Pub in Westbourne Park, London.

Other unions which have existed over time throughout the United Kingdom have inevitably been registered under the Friendly Societies' Acts. Some details can be found in the FS class at the National Archives. They include:

Aberdeen Hand-Sewn Boot & Shoe Makers Union
Amalgamated Association of Boot & Shoe Makers
Amalgamated Society of Boot and Shoe Makers
Amalgamated Society of Boot & Shoe Makers and Repairers
Amalgamated Society of Cordwainers
Amalgamated Society of Female Leather Workers, Stitchers and Machinists
Amalgamated Society of Journeyman Cloggers
Association of Pattern-Makers And Allied Craftsmen
Friendly Society of Operative Boot Makers
Glasgow Boot Makers' and Boot Repairers' Society
International Boot & Shoe Workers' Union
International Journeyman Boot Finishers' Society
Jewish Mutual Boot Finishers' and Lasters' Benefit & Trade Society
Ladies Shoemakers Society
Leicester Clickers Union of Boot & Shoe Trade
Leicester Shoe Foremen's Association
Leicester Union of Clickers and Pressers
Society of Shoe, Rivet and Wire Nail Makers
United Society of Boot & Shoe Makers
Walsall & District Amalgamated Leather Trades Union.

Many of these have now been amalgamated with the larger unions, in which case any surviving records are likely to be amongst the larger union records or deposited in local record offices. In some cases the unions and associations were short-lived and no records of their existence survive.

Unrest in the shoe trade

Not many unions have had a famous jazz musician record a song about unrest within their industry, but Acker Bilk recorded a song specifically for the NUBSO relating to the formation of the union in 1873. This song remained their 'Anthem' and was often heard at their rallies.

74. The anthem of the NUBSO.

Raunds Strike

Up to the end of the Boer War, Raunds boot makers had a large government contract for a supply of boots to the military. After 1902 there was a dramatic fall in the demand. In order to survive, factories became ultra-competitive in order to win contracts and in doing so, their worker's wages were reduced placing many on the 'bread line'. The Union decided that from March 1905 the manufacturers must pay the workers 15s. a week, or 5s. a week from funds in case of a strike.

A dozen factories refused to comply and by mid-March 1905, 500 workers were on strike. The worst payers seem to have been the Co-operative Societies and in particular, the St Crispin's Productive Society. After one week the situation became intolerable. The strikers peaceful protests became riotous, sometimes violent, and the strikers barracked those who had broken the strike. Strike breakers in the village who mainly worked at home had to run the gauntlet in order to collect their 'out' work each day. They were openly called blacklegs and stones were thrown at their house smashing windows and causing minor structural damage. The situation worsened so by the end of March, a police sergeant, ten constables and 200 men, women and children regularly accompanied the strike breakers to and from home particularly those who lived in nearby villages.

75. A photograph taken as the Raunds Marchers passed through Rushden.

On 7 April, 1905 at Thrapston Magistrates Court 17 pickets were charged with, persistently following the shoe workers with a view to compelling them to abstain from working as shoemakers for Lawrence & Co.

With the strike seemingly not having any effect, a good number of the strikers gradually drifted back to work and by April it looked like the Union had been defeated. In order to escalate the strike the union came up with an idea headed by a local convenor Mr James Gribble. To plight their cause hundreds of workers volunteered for a march to London but only 115 workers including a marching band, were selected from the town of Raunds and from Ringstead a nearby village.

The march left Raunds on 8 May 1905. When they arrived in London's Hyde Park two days later around 10,000 people had gathered to meet them. Some marchers managed to access the Strangers' Gallery in The House of Commons and disrupted a debate on Women's Suffrage. The striking workers were intent on seeing the then Minister for War, Mr Arnold Foster.

The men were ejected, but their plea was not without results. Before the close of business that day, a lawyer had been instructed to make an enquiry into the dispute in Raunds. On the following Sunday afternoon, Keir Hardie, Labour Party Chairman 1906-1908, spoke in their favour at a rally in Trafalgar Square. The march achieved its objective, bringing attention to the plight of Raunds boot and shoe workers. The local evening newspaper stated that the march had: 'created an historic precedent in the matter of laying grievances before the highest authorities' and, although it was not the first time such a march had taken place, it was the first by an organised body. As a result the Raunds workers were paid a standard rate that was enforced by the War Office. This in itself initiated an enquiry that resulted in a change in the conditions of all contracts for boot and shoe workers starting in 1906.

Rotherham Strike

In May 1857, owing to pressure of business, one of the master shoemakers in Rotherham hired men who were not connected with the union. As a result the shoe hands who were members of the union refused to work until the non-union men were discharged.

A meeting of the masters was held, at which it was resolved to support their brother tradesman in the course he had adopted and also to discharge every union hand in the town, unless the men went back to work. This did not happen and all the refractory workmen were discharged; the masters adopting a resolution never in future to employ any workmen connected with the Journeyman Boot and Shoemakers Union.

The Northampton Strike

In the 1850s shoe manufacturers wanted to introduce machinery and mass produce shoes which would speed up production. The first shoe factory was built in 1859 and belonged to Isaac Campbell. The factory owners distributed posters and leaflets announcing that they were to be using closing machines in the factories. These were used for sewing the shoe uppers. The shoe workers became worried that machines would be introduced for all areas of production and that they would be forced into a factory environment and as such be subject to poor conditions. The shoemakers voted overwhelmingly to go on strike.

In the following two years the striking shoemakers travelled to other towns to make boots and shoes and as such the Northampton Mutual Protection Society to which all the strikers belonged paid subsistence to wives and families left behind. At the time around 1,500 men left Northampton but many returned when they could not find work elsewhere. Within a couple of weeks most were back at their old jobs.

Nantwich Strikes

In 1872, in Nantwich, it was a William Cooper a currier who inadvertently found himself at the centre of a bitter wrangle between the shoe makers and their masters and who became an arbitrator and finally helped settle the strike. The strike occurred after a period of prosperity in the trade. The Nantwich shoemakers asked for 3d. per pair increase in rates, whereas the riveters and finishers demanded an overall 25% increase in pay.

The masters countered this action by refusing to employ any riveters or finishers and this resulted in a lock-out, though the dispute was confined to Nantwich. As a result, around 200 workers went to other towns to seek better rewards. The Cordwainers Union of London and Stafford entered the negotiations but the Nantwich masters said they could not match the rates being paid elsewhere because of increased local costs in raw materials.

Altogether about 500 men were laid-off, along with the women in five machine shops, because of 'the shortage of boot tops'. William Cooper, who knew the union leader suggested the two sides enter into negotiations, an idea that met with a favourable response. The negotiations were held at the Crown, Nantwich, with both parties in separate rooms and William Cooper acting as arbitrator. Eventually a compromise deal was made whereby the men agreed to accept half their original demands and the masters promised there would be no victimisation.

During the negotiations a large crowd, mainly those laid off, gathered outside the Crown, eager for an end to the dispute. Many local tradesmen, especially drapers, grocers and publicans, had also been badly affected by the strike, so the news it had ended was met with relief on everyone's part. However in 1873 they were all back where they started, another strike, more lock-outs and a three-day week.

A further strike erupted in May 1873 and it was reported in the 'Crewe Guardian' under a notice about men leaving Nantwich for Stafford, whilst their families were locked out by the masters. Those not otherwise involved were working a three day week.

The strike, like the earlier one, was over a wage demand but this time there was no compromise or arbitration. By mid-June the strike had become a 'matter of endurance' and the workers' demands were getting smaller.

Some physical and moral intimidation was aimed at suspected scabs resulting in one case ending in court. A dispute was heard between Thomas Sutton a shoemaker and William Wild, a shoe manufacturer. Thomas Sutton was a presser at William Wild's factory. Thomas Sutton had requested to be sent 29 pairs of tops and bottoms with lasts, presses and rivets so he could make them at his home. When William Wild asked for the competed work to be returned Thomas Sutton stated that he had not completed them for fear of reprisal by the other men, and returned the shoes in an unfinished state. William Wild said he would not press the case if the work was done, which Thomas Sutton was bound over to complete by the court on a £10 bond.

By July there were signs of a possible breakthrough. The masters offered removals of restrictions on union men and exactly half demands on everything. The men refused and the strike continued. The next week the men sought interviews with their masters and meetings were held almost daily. Terms were telegraphed to the Nantwich men working in Stafford. On 18 July a meeting was held that ended the strike, when delegates from the local union and national officials from Stafford and London agreed with the masters a formula of roughly 50% of the claim on most items. Work recommenced the following Monday. The trade remained fairly quiet from then on, with few if any disputes. The master's victory was somewhat pyrrhic as other centres encroached on the Nantwich markets but the masters seemed prepared to face these consequences rather than concede to union demands, even though the main demand was only for pay parity with nearby centres.

Boot and shoe manufacture and its effect on religious beliefs

There is said to be a definite link between the boot and shoe industry and the growth of nonconformity in many areas associated with shoe manufacture. This is true of the author's home town of Rushden in Northamptonshire. As areas became urbanised more churches were built to cater for the growth of population especially in the latter years of the 19th century. The churches played an important role in both the social lives of the many factory workers and also in support of the Temperance Movement which was advocated amongst many of the employers, for perhaps obvious reasons, particularly to help prevent shoe workers taking Mondays off to get drunk which was an old tradition in the county. In many areas, particularly the manufacturing towns, the nonconformist churches were the major religious denominations and as such our ancestors would almost certainly have been involved with them as opposed perhaps to the traditional Anglican churches.

Both Anglican and nonconformist religions tended to grow side by side. Northamptonshire's Victoria County History indicates that mid-17th century Northampton specialised in footwear, and refers to the *'Liber Custumarum'* which was the regulation governing tanning and bootmaking, and the *'Ars Allutariorium'* for the Cordwainers Craft. These documents available at Northamptonshire Archives were dated much earlier (mid-15th century). In its earlier history it is known that Northampton supplied boots and shoes to Cromwell's army. In order to meet this need, footwear manufacture large and small, spread to the areas along the River Nene, effectively the start of the outworker system where the ready cut leather was sent out to outworkers in the nearby villages for closing, a process which started in the late 1780s. Eighty years or so later Wellingborough became known as the centre for outdoor closing. At the time the industry was still very much home based with all family members participating.

The introduction of machinery and thus factory manufacture of footwear reached its impetus around the 1870s which was also the time that many nonconformist chapels were built and inaugurated.

As shoemaking became more specialised, factories became centralised in the larger towns and workers began to leave the home and work together in groups under a somewhat strict regime. However, this was not the end of homeworking for the women and children and in some of the villages families set up their own workshops to the rear of their houses. A prime example is the community of Long Bugby, Northamptonshire.

The industry was the largest single employer of labour in 'shoemaking towns' and almost half the men so employed worked in the factories, with the women still heavily involved in either domestic service or as outworker machinists. Eventually the machinists were also taken into the environs of the factory and this was heavily enforced by The National Union of Boot and Shoe Operatives who in 1894 demanded that all work except for closing and hand-sewn work should be done in the factory. Further improvements from union intervention meant the workmen were subject to regular hours. Up to this time it was possible and indeed frequently the case for shoemakers particularly in the villages to work late into the night and tend their garden or allotment in the middle of the day. 'Saint Monday' was also frequently observed.

The 1851 religious census measured church attendance and the distribution of denominational strength thus providing a picture of religious practice amongst various groups of population. The synopsis suggested that church attendance in urban centres was worse than that in rural areas and:

> '... it must be apparent that a sadly formidable portion of the English people are habitual neglecters of the public ordinances of religion.'

There were, of course, regional differences and there appears to have been a tendency for nonconformists to outnumber Anglicans in large manufacturing areas. In some areas there was evidence of dominance of one religion's congregation over the others and this varied between towns. This is highlighted in Rushden as there were 67% nonconformists (predominantly Baptists) to around 32% Anglican. Similar figures occur in other shoe manufacturing conurbations.

The growth of nonconformity in industrial areas and particularly villages was due to the emergence of a lower middle class rather than the expansion of the working class. As an example, in the author's home town of Rushden the Baptists were granted their first 'preaching licence' in 1672 although the first record of a chapel was not until 1722. The first recorded Baptist preacher John Woolston used his home for meetings initially. As the Baptist movement progressed and the congregations grew, the community split off into different groups albeit following the same basic beliefs.

A similar situation seems to have occurred within the Methodist movement where a Sunday school class was first recorded in 1781 but no chapel existed until 1828. The first Methodist church building was actually rented from a local shoe manufacturer. Again as congregations grew new chapels were constructed and Sunday schools enlarged. By 1889 the Primitive Methodists purchased a piece of land to build their chapel which was opened the following year. Signatories on the original conveyance included several shoe workers (as opposed to shoe manufacturers).

Perhaps the biggest success in nonconformity was from the Salvation Army who in early 1883 took Rushden by storm. In June, the *War Cry* reported that 'Rushden had 86 soldiers and had sold over 400 copies of the *War Cry* in its first week'. So large was the movement that Mrs. Bramwell Booth wife of the founder addressed over 400 attendees at the opening ceremony of the Salvation Army citadel in the town.

To balance this, the Anglican Church had also experienced growth as had the town and the shoe factories. A second parish church St Peter's was built serving the northern part of the town. Nevertheless the dissenting population was estimated to be about two-thirds of the total, in part due to the political stance of the Anglican Church at the time. This pattern was repeated in other shoe manufacturing areas throughout Northamptonshire and Leicestershire. The picture was slightly different in Staffordshire where the nonconformist movement was not as strong. In Norwich the strength of the Anglican Church with many parishes within the city walls, meant that fewer nonconformist denominations had a presence.

For many years the social life of the shoe worker was mainly centred around either the church, working men's clubs or the local athletic, football and cricket clubs. Experience and research suggests that shoe workers were either involved with the churches or not. Somehow the two communities seemed to live side by side.

In many shoemaking communities, as shoe factories replaced the individual shoemaker, from the middle of the 19th century there was a move from a religious to a secular society. However nonconformity was still strong and many shoe making communities exhibited a steadfast religious belief.

The nonconformist churches in many communities provided weekday and social activities to cater for the increased leisure hours enjoyed by the shoe worker.

Virtually every chapel had its own Sunday school. Classes usually met twice on Sundays, and the members were also encouraged to attend the chapel services. Sunday school attendance was often larger than secular educational schools, so much so that it was not unusual to find that they quickly outgrew their buildings thus requiring larger and additional premises. Some chapels re-organised meetings to cater for their large numbers. Many built additional facilities or even new chapels. To cater for more local needs these new buildings were often located away from the established chapels in different areas of the towns.

The Sunday schools had a dual role providing both religious education and developing the moral character of their participants. In the early 1880s the Baptist Movement began to offer library facilities holding only 'good literature' which included publications by the Sunday School Union and Cassells. Most of the libraries held runs of the 'Boys' Own' and 'Girls' Own' papers. They ultimately combined with the Teachers' Library, which was originally founded in 1858, to pave the way for the Carnegie Public Libraries which were established in most towns in the pre First World War years.

Sport also played an important role in the communities catering for all the family whether as players or spectators. Most chapels had a football and cricket team. Emphasis was also given to music and this interest gave rise to choral societies in both the Anglican and the nonconformist churches. The formation of brass bands, amongst factory workers as well as by church and town, provided concerts in park bandstands and also played for parish garden parties and teas. Some of the most famous are a result of factories establishing top class brass bands such as the GUS Brass Band and the John White Footwear Band.

The nonconformist churches ultimately became a way of life in many boot and shoe towns also influencing and drawing in shoemakers and their families from the surrounding villages. Many gave the opportunity for young people from different communities to meet and find marriage partners.

There was also a degree of integration and co-operation between the different chapels as they frequently invited each other to meetings and Sunday school activities so instead of being rivals they complemented each other both socially and religiously. This may well explain why many families changed allegiance from time to time. The nonconformist churches provided preachers at special services such as harvest festivals in the different denominations and as such the Free Church Councils played an important role in different religions working together. Because many of the shoe manufacturing bosses were nonconformists they were further able to cement relationships with their employees as they could work side by side to better the communities in which they lived. This was further enhanced during the First World War when the Anglican Church clergy and nonconformist ministers shared congregational preaching.

Working men's clubs and the temperance movement

Alongside the chapels with both their secular and religious aspects, the leisure hours of the shoe workers in most towns also led to the development of the Working Men's Clubs. The first Working Men's Club in a boot and shoe community in Northamptonshire was established in 1860s some ten years after the movement began. They settled into a regulatory club with the formation of the Working Men's Club and Institute Union in 1862 which was led by the Temperance Movement. Their aim was to help working men to establish clubs where they can meet for conversation, business and mental improvement, with the means of recreation and refreshment, free from intoxicating drinks. The first Secretary was the Rev. Henry Solly whose main aim was to raise funds for the establishment of clubs all over the country. To some extent he encountered a rough ride from his colleagues to the extent that in the 1870s and 1880s there was an unprecedented rise of self-governing clubs and the introduction of alcoholic beverages. Also, the social side of the cubs complemented politics and education. These self-governing clubs in the boot and shoe towns drew most members from that community, almost to the exclusion of others. Many areas had more than one club.

The clubs provided reading rooms where, besides books, newspapers and journals could be reviewed and bought by the members. Regular concerts were held and a string band and brass band section was set up. Sport was catered for by cycling sections and cricket clubs. Inter-club competitions in darts, whist, snooker and billiards and skittles took place. Other recreation included quoits, bagatelle, cribbage tournaments, shows and fishing. Sick members were given financial help and could avail themselves of the union's convalescent homes. Donations were also made to the Transvaal War Fund and to the Relief Fund in 1898 for 'those in distress in Wales arising out of the Coal Strike'.

The clubs exercised strict discipline over their members cautioning or suspending them for breach of rules such as bad language, gambling or causing disruption. Letters were sent to parents who kept their children late at the club and names of any suspended or expelled member were distributed to other clubs in the area to prevent admission.

It was necessary for the Working Men's Clubs to present a sober, industrious image of the working man, as it was for the churches, and to encourage a sense of belonging to a respectable family group. The temperance movement tended to break through denominational barriers and drew together all the churches. The movement originated in the 19th century but really made an impact in the early/mid 1840s particularly in the shoemaking communities around the country. The pledge of the temperance movement was:

> 'We voluntarily agree to abstain from all intoxicating liquors except for medicinal purposes and in a Religious Ordinance'.

Before the temperance movement there was literature published against drunkenness and excess; total abstinence from alcohol was very rarely advocated or practiced. 'Shoe Monday' was very popular and shoe makers liked their drink often to excess. The earliest temperance societies, inspired by a Presbyterian Church of Ireland minister who poured his stock of whiskey out of his window in 1829, concentrated on abstinence from spirits rather than wine and beer.

In 1838, chartism, the mass working class movement for universal suffrage to which most shoe workers belonged, included an organisation called 'temperance chartism'. Faced with the refusal of Parliament to give the right to vote to working people, the temperance chartists saw the campaign against alcohol as a way of proving that working class people were responsible enough to be granted the vote.

In 1847, the Band of Hope was founded in Yorkshire, with the stated aim of saving children from working class backgrounds from the perils of drink. In Northamptonshire amongst the shoe makers there were eight known Band of Hope groups set up. The members had to pledge to abstain 'from all liquors of an intoxicating quality, whether ale, porter, wine or ardent spirits except for medicinal purposes'.

The temperance movement received a boost due to government intervention at the beginning of the First World War. Public house hours were regulated by licence. Beer was watered down and was subject to a penny tax per pint. In 1916 some breweries were nationalised. At the same time, prohibition movements sprung up throughout the country, many associated with the shoe manufacturing towns. There were also secular temperance organisations.

As the shoe making towns expanded so did the 'migrant population' particularly amongst young men who lodged with families in the urban areas. This was a natural progression as many had worked in the trade in the villages. As such they were considered without roots. With a number of single young men there was inevitably a greater degree of drunkenness. Whether or not this was an accurate perception of society at the time, the nonconformist chapels and the temperance societies believed that there was a problem and that they had a responsibility to wage war against intemperance and to wean people from the belief that drink was essential to their very existence. The 1881 Annual Report of the Rushden Temperance Society stated that the New Temperance Hall building:

'... shows the public that there is a strong Temperance element in the town and that the promoters are anxious to show that they are doing something to stem the torrent of drunkenness in Rushden.'

The nonconformist chapels had their own reforming crusades ranging from Temperance Sundays and missions for their own congregations to more positive outside action by organisations like the Salvation Army.

The national trend within the Temperance Movement focused on both the political and secular aspects but also retained a considerable part of the early evangelistic appeal. The archives leave us in no doubt regarding the energy and zeal of the movement within the churches and of its concern for the sobriety of the shoe workers.

Throughout the archives in England and Scotland there are deposited records relating to individual societies as well as those of the national federations and the women's temperance organisations. The local and provincial newspapers carried reports of the activities of the temperance societies and many archives include scrapbooks of those cuttings.

Some also acted as benevolent organisations and many had 'Sick and Burial Clubs'. Those records reveal important genealogical information about the recipients and their families. It is unlikely that you will be able to fully research your shoe worker ancestor without recourse to such records.

Training to become a shoemaker

Leather Trade School

76. Many schools and industrial schools established shoemaking classes.

The Leather Trade School was founded in Bethnal Green in 1887 by the Leathersellers and Cordwainers' Company, City and Guilds Institute and the Boot and Shoe Manufacturers' Association. In 1914 it was incorporated and became the Cordwainers Technical College, with the aim of developing the work of the Leather Trade School. The College moved to Hackney in 1945, under the auspices of the Inner London Education Authority. Between 1956 and 1977 the college buildings were enlarged to give an additional larger technicians' section, lecture room and work room. The College provided specialist education and training courses in footwear, accessories, leather goods and saddlery. In 1991 the College was renamed the Cordwainers' College and ultimately became part of the London College of Fashion in 2000.

Records of Cordwainers' College exist from 1948 and include the Board of Management papers, such as inspection reports, reviews and handbook for Governors; prospectuses, prize giving programmes, photographs, press cuttings 35mm slides of shoes, digitised images of the historic shoes collection, comprising approximately 700 shoes from the 18th-19th centuries; Honourable Cordwainers' Company newsletters, 1989-1994.

College records relating mainly to correspondence, are amongst the City and Guild Institute papers held by the London Metropolitan Archives (MS21926).

Boot and Shoe Technical Colleges

Many of our ancestors who started work directly in the shoe factories would have trained 'on the job' and also by attending one of the Boot and Shoe Technical Colleges.

Rushden in Northamptonshire which was a centre of the boot and shoe industry had one such college. The Rushden and District Boot and Shoe Manufacturers' Association founded the Boot and Shoe School in 1928 in a former converted shoe factory which was opened by Lord Eustace Percy, President of the Board of Education. Classes in the principles of boot and shoe manufacture had been established in the county since 1892 primarily within the existing elementary schools rather than in a separate institution. The result of which meant that some elements of the training were, through necessity, curtailed. The establishment of a similar establishment at Wellingborough had not came about because of the outbreak of war but in 1920 the Northamptonshire Education Committee undertook to provide three small boot and shoe schools at Wellingborough and Kettering besides the one at Rushden.

77. Colleges were established for day release training courses.

In 1921 the Wellingborough centre commenced activities and in response to a generous offer of £1,300 from the Kettering and District Boot and Shoe Manufacturers' Association a second school was instituted at Kettering in 1924. An offer of £1,250 in 1927 by the Rushden and District Manufacturers meant that the Rushden School could go ahead.

By the time of its official opening the Rushden school had 150 students enrolled with the prospect of further enrolments from the surrounding villages. The school offered 'state of the art' facilities for the time with a lecture room, a pattern cutting and clicking room, a closing room and a room for bottom stock cutting and preparation and hand lasting and welting together with a machinery workshop equipped with machines provided by the British United Shoe Machinery Company Ltd and the Singer Sewing Machine Company Ltd.

The syllabus provided courses for all prospective entrants and existing employees within the boot and shoe industry, covering every aspect of manufacture, design and economics. The County Council who administered the school produced a series of instruction books and course material on all the processes used and instituted a series of examinations and awards to honours stage level for students who normally attended on a day release basis from their full time employment gaining both the practical experience as well as the training.

78. Colleges promoted their courses with the publication of prospectuses.

The school's log books, which are comprehensive, cover the period from 1928 to 1973 and are deposited at the Northamptonshire County Record Office which also holds photographs of many of the student groups and staff.

In Leicester the School of Art began to run classes in shoe design from the 1880s. Shoe design was undertaken from the early days of the industry but took various guises. In the early days it would have been called 'cobbling trades'. After the end of the Second World War when soldiers were de-mobbed, the school held classes, to teach ex-soldiers, how to make and repair shoes, enabling them to earn a living in civilian life.

Northampton, the centre of the shoe trade, did not open a technical college until 1924 after which it began to offer various courses in shoe making, design and repair. In 1994 the Leathersellers' College of London was integrated into the Northampton College under the auspices of the University of Northampton and is now the British School of Leather Technology having extended its remit to more than just the shoe industry. The college had its origins in 1909 when the Leathersellers' Technical College was first set up in Tower Bridge Road, London.

The Bata Organisation at Tilbury also had college facilities where young men were trained in the art of shoe making. These young men came from all over the country and were trained in either the leather or rubber side of the industry, or administration. At Bata the participation in sport was considered important and many of the young men went on to play for the company's first team in various sports.

There were usually no more than 30 students in the college. The company enrolled ten students per year for the three year course. The ten students who completed their course each year were available to work for Bata anywhere in the world. Some went to the Canadian factory with all expenses paid.

The students rose at 6.15am then breakfasted in the Bata Hotel. Work commenced at 7.30am. As the time neared 7.30am clocking in gates were closed. If you were late, entry was then via the Personnel Department where late arrival was recorded on your personnel record.

Students could specialise in leather shoe manufacture, rubber footwear manufacture or engineering and were given a training book listing all the manufacturing operations to be performed over the first two years. In the third year students specialised in one particular aspect. During each week students spent three days in the factory and two days at the Hackney Cordwainers' College where they learned technical and managerial aspects. The rubber students went to the Rubber College in London. Evening classes did not end until 9pm but that meant students were not required to be in the factory until 10am the following day.

There was the opportunity some weekends to work in the Bata shops. If you chose a London branch then you had your fare paid to London and could spend Saturday evening there.

From 1948 until its closure, British Bata ran a scholarship scheme whereby 18 year-old school leavers were recruited from all over Great Britain to be trained as eventual key employees in the Bata organisation either at home or abroad.

'All-found' accommodation in the purpose-built college building and a weekly allowance was given to every student, together with the sandwich courses at London colleges in order to obtain professional qualifications in either leather or rubber technology, or business studies and accountancy. The College 'boys' as they were known worked at the East Tilbury site when not attending their study courses and were guaranteed placements after graduating.

Shoemakers to the famous

Peal and Company made bespoke footwear between 1791 and 1965 for many famous people. Samuel Peal, the founder originated from Wirksworth, Derbyshire and set up the original business in Stepney. Peal had patented a water-proofing system for clothing and extended this to his boots and shoes which became renowned for their durability. The firm outgrew its Stepney premises and relocated, first to Tottenham Court Road, and after a couple of further moves, finally ended up in Wigmore Street in Soho.

Six generations of the Peal family ran the business until its demise. The second owner, Nathaniel Peal, displayed a selection of footwear at the Great Exhibition of 1851 and one hundred years later were again exhibited at the Festival of Britain Exhibition. The firm's speciality was riding boots and Peal's had stands at such events as the Burghley and Hickstead horse trials, as well as other horse shows around the country.

The reputation built up by the organisation was attributed to its highly trained commercial travellers and salesmen who in the latter part of the 19th century travelled throughout the world securing a large number of foreign orders.

In addition to taking foot measurements, the salesmen made outline drawings of every customer's feet. These were kept in a series of over 600 'Feet Books' which are deposited as part of the company archive in the London Metropolitan Archives. Orders were sent to the firm's factory in Acton Vale. Each pair of boots or shoes was individually made from the patterns, a process which took about six weeks.

When the original skilled shoemakers left or retired, the company had difficulty replacing them which unfortunately led to its eventual demise.

The archive collection consists of administrative records such as account books and ledgers as well as the Feet Books. Every Feet book contains around 150 orders and each was given a running number. The earliest surviving book no. 23 dates from the 1870s and the last book is no. 1002 for 1965.

The celebrity customers included:

Fred Astaire, dancer/actor	Humphrey Bogart
Lauren Bacall	Sir Charles Chaplin
Gary Cooper	Henry Fonda
James Garner	Cary Grant
Rex Harrison	Boris Karloff
Steve McQueen	Sir John Mills

Sir David Niven
Sam Wanamaker
Henry Ford
Richard W. Woolworth
Dean Martin
Dickie Valentine
John F Kennedy
HM King Edward VIII

Sir Laurence Olivier
Guy de Rothschild
Howard Heinz
Frank Shuttleworth, Old Warden
Yehudi Menuhin, musician
Rt Hon Sir Anthony Eden
Karl Marx
Lord Louis Mountbatten

Shoe machinery and support industry

Not only did the shoe factories employ large numbers of people but the support industries also had an impact upon the local community. Many people became involved in the production of shoe machinery but that is a different story. However a book about shoe making cannot go without mention thereof.

Technical innovations meant that new machinery to undertake operations in shoemaking were being continually introduced. This meant that local shoe-machinery firms were designing and improving on the various American produced machines which were introduced into the country after 1870. These new innovations accelerated production. In 1872 the Goodyear welt sewing machine was introduced into England although it had been invented some ten years earlier. These machines proved to be over 50 times faster than traditional stitching using an awl and thread. With this machine and also the chain stitcher it was claimed that footwear of similar quality to any hand sewn boot or shoe could be produced in a significantly shorter time. In 1899, an improved version took under half a minute to do what had formerly been done in an hour. More and more processes were beginning to be undertaken by machines, and this gave rise to the system of standard sizes and half-sizes.

In 1859 a new method of boot making was inaugurated by the introduction into this country of the Mackay or Blake sole-sewing machine. It did not make much headway until after the exhibition of 1861, at which it was shown at work, but soon after was taken up freely by the trade in Northampton and elsewhere. This was a chain-stitch machine, which in one operation sewed through the sole, middle-sole, upper and insole, the thread passing through heated wax on its way to the needle. For more than twenty years the machine-sewn boot was held in high repute. The greatest objection to the Blake sewer was the fact that inside the boot where the sole of the foot rested was a ring of waxed thread, an insuperable trouble to people with warm feet. Nevertheless, immense numbers of boots were made using this method, which was, apart from riveting, the cheapest system.

With the increased use of machinery, competition between manufacturers of footwear machinery was based upon the output capacity of each machine. This competition resulted in the formation in 1899 of the British United Shoe Machinery Co. Ltd. (BUSMC). The company began in Leicester and amalgamated Pearson & Bennion, which was a machinery manufacturer in the town with the British arms of American companies in alliance with the United Shoe Machinery Co. However the company was administered in the USA and all the decisions were made there. The BUSMC system was only to lease rather than sell their machines and even today, apart from sewing machines, only a small proportion of the machinery used in many shoe factories is owned by them. The cost of machinery leased from the BUSMC was exactly the same irrespective of the size of firm, as the lease payments were assessed at a fixed sum based upon the number of processes performed by that machine. There were of course still many independent producers of machinery that existed around the shoe centres and these also thrived.

79. Just a couple of the machines manufactured to speed up production of shoes.

80. The Leicester factory of BUSMC.

The BUSMC secured patents on some important machines and the system of tied leasing operated by the company forced independent machine firms either to close down or join the company almost creating a monopoly. In the early 20th century it was thought that less than a quarter of machines found in shoe factories were acquired from firms outside the B.U.S.M.C and by the start of the Second World War, 90% of the machines used came from BUSMC

Besides the provision of shoe machinery and companies establishing themselves within the shoemaking towns, the industry relied upon the provision of other components.

Besides the obvious industries associated with tanner and currier for the provision of raw leather it was necessary for shoe makers and factories to have easy access to wax polishes, adhesives, boxes, knives, buckles and linings, stiffeners, socks and various stains. Although your ancestor may not have been directly involved with the shoemaking trade they may well have played an important role in making sure the industry survived.

Cobblers

81. Village cobbler mending shoes.

Many of our ancestors would have been cobblers, or to be precise, shoe repairers. Cobblers have been working with shoes for centuries and in many rural areas cobbling was an integral part of the shoemakers' daily toil. Cobblers carried out such repairs as re-heeling and re-soling, stretching and re-shaping shoes, dying and re-lacing as well as polishing. In most towns, cobblers' shops were located in residential areas. Immediately opposite the author's home in Rushden was a small shop attached to a bungalow and occupied by a cobbler who had a Blake Sewer and a very cluttered workbench. Perhaps the best known cobbler in Rushden at the time was Shortland's who had a shop in Portland Road. Unfortunately he closed down in the 1960s but was one of the iconic cobblers of the day supplying not only shoe repairs but also repair materials to many of the men who worked in the shoe factories who undertook their own family shoe repairs.

82. Shortland in Rushden - local town cobbler and shoe repairer.

It took around four years, usually by apprenticeship to learn the trade (apprenticeships had fallen out of favour in shoe manufacture) and part of that training was to understand how a shoe was made. You will find that many cobblers perhaps worked as shoemakers before the advent of the factory system or elected to become cobblers if they were displaced. In the mid-20th century many factory workers when they retired became cobblers.

Shoemakers trivia

The 'Cobblers' Football Team

83. The logo of 'The Cobblers' Northampton Football Club.

Northampton Football Club is known as 'The Cobblers'. According to the 1841 census there were 1,871 Shoemakers in the town. The football team was not officially formed until 1897 after meetings were held at the Princess Royal Inn on the Wellingborough Road, Northampton between the town's schoolteachers and Mr A J Darnell a local solicitor. The main sport amongst many of the shoe workers was football and in particular, schoolboy football was strong in the county due in part to the enthusiasm of the local teachers. They were dissatisfied with the arrangement of arranged friendlies between schools so they felt that forming a town team would answer some of those challenges. Many of the shoe factories also had their own 'friendly' teams. A J Darnell also travelled to Leicester with the local rugby team (now Northampton Saints) where he was a spectator of an exhibition football match between Leicester City and Notts. County which made him enthusiastic about starting his own club. Darnell and the local schoolteachers came together through their shared aims and, on 6 March 1897, Northampton Town Football Club was formed.

James Bond

Northampton is the place to go for prestige shoes. The town's manufacturers supplied James Bond stars with shoes used for five films including Casino Royale. Shoes from one company, Church's, were also used in the Da Vinci Code movie.

Shoelaces

The small tube that binds the end of a shoelace to prevent fraying and to allow the lace to be passed through an eyelet is known as an aglet which has Latin origins. The modern shoelace was invented in England on 27 March 1790. Up to that time shoes were usually fastened with buckles.

Hobson's Choice - a play about a bootmaker

Henry Hobson runs a successful bootmaker's shop in 19th century Salford. A widower with a weakness for drink, he frequents the pub opposite his shop, the Moonrakers' Arms. He tries to rule the lives of his three somewhat wayward daughters, Maggie, Alice and Vicky who work in his shop unpaid. When he says 'no marriages' to avoid the matter of expensive settlements, Maggie rebels and sets her sights on marrying Will Mossop, Hobson's bootmaker. Maggie and Will start up in competition, after which Maggie turns her mind to helping her sisters marry their chosen partners.

The timing of the play corresponded with a feminine revolution enabling the strong sisters to forge their own world when at the time this was frowned upon. Behind the boots and clogs are individuals who must also be determined and strong in a society that gives them little credence. Although very humorous it portrays the life of the Salford folk and the social connections and customs that gave their life order, until they were challenged and eventually changed.

One day, Mrs Hepworth, a rich customer, demands to know who made her boots. It is of course Will Mossop. She insists that all her and her daughters' boots must from now on be made by Will, and tells him to inform her if ever he should leave. Maggie, an astute businesswoman, considered too 'fuddy duddy' to marry, proposes to Will who reluctantly agrees. She tells Hobson that she intends to marry Will, but he laughs at her and threatens to beat Will for courting her. As a result Will leaves the shop, and Maggie goes with him. They borrow £100 from Mrs Hepworth, set up a shop on their own and marry.

Later, Hobson falls into the warehouse belonging to the father of Fred Beenstock, Vicky's love. Remember in the plot that Hobson has refused marriage settlements which means that without any money they are unlikely to find decent husbands. With the help of lawyer Albert Prosser, Alice's love, they issue a writ claiming damages from Hobson for trespass, damage to corn sacks and spying on trade secrets. Hobson eventually agrees to pay, the money is settled on the girls and they can now get married.

Thanks to Will's skill as a bootmaker and Maggie's business acumen, their shop is very successful and, within a year, they have taken nearly all of Hobson's trade. Hobson is almost bankrupt and drinking himself to death. After an attack of delirium, he asks each of his daughters to look after him. They all refuse, but eventually Maggie agrees to do so provided that Will takes over his business, with Hobson remaining as a 'sleeping partner' only.

The play is thought to be based upon a true life character, a friend of Henry Brighouse's father, who owned such a shoe shop. Whether that is true or not - we may never know.

Well Heeled

The heel of a shoe itself is a symbol of nobility, the high heel being used for riding. This appears to date back to invading Mongol tribesmen wearing bright red wooden heels. Mongols were experienced horsemen and their battle victories left a mark on European society. In times past owning and caring for a horse required some wealth and being on horseback, riders appeared superior to the common man. Consequently, high heels became associated with nobility. Today, the saying 'well-heeled' is used to describe someone of wealth or aristocracy. In the Northampton Museum are examples of riding boots which have 2' stacked heels and are dated around 1630.

Wellingborough Bankrupt Shoe Makers, Manufacturers etc.

It was not unusual with the advent of shoe factories and mass production for shoemakers and small manufacturers to end up with financial difficulties and subsequent bankruptcy. Perry's is full of them as the example below shows.

Perry's Bankruptcy Weekly Gazette

Mid-1800s
Joseph Wright, shoemaker 1842
Samuel Randall, shoe manufacturer 1855
William Allen, boot & shoe maker 1859
John Watts jnr., shoe machinist 1864
David Kirby, boot top closer & clicker 1865
James Betson, shoe manufacturer 1867
William Faulkner, shoemaker 1867
Thomas Keller, shoemaker 1867
James Watkins, shoemaker 1867
Alfred Young, boot upper maker 1874
Thomas Hughes, boot closer 1869
Thomas Slinn, boot & shoe manufacturer 1874
Edward Dunmore, leather merchant & upper manufacturer 1876
Charles Clayson, machine upper closer 1877
John Andrew Gent, boot closer & shoe dealer
Alfred Beale, closer 1878
John Hacksley, boot & shoe manufacturer
Thomas Watts, boot & shoe manufacturer
John Cox, boot upper maker 1881
George Burrell, shoe manufacturer 1883

Both local and national newspapers carry reports of creditors' meetings, voluntary liquidation and bankruptcy proceedings and should be researched where it is known that your ancestor may have resorted to such financial measures.

Rushden Argus 1888

Charles Perkins, shoe manufacturer, Rushden - In this case, at the Northampton County Court on Wednesday an application was made for the debtor's discharge. The Official Receiver reported that in this matter the proceedings were initiated by an order of the Court on the 7 January 1888, and the public examination of the bankrupt was concluded on 8 May 1888. The bankrupt had omitted to keep proper books of accounts and had contracted debts which he had no reasonable expectation of paying. He had carried on business without knowing he was insolvent and he had used up certain goods obtained by him shortly before his bankruptcy in making clothes for himself and family. Mr. Jas Heygate (Wellingborough) represented the bankrupt. During the hearing of this application his Honour made some pointed remarks as to the prevailing lack of proper book-keeping by those who entered into business and said such neglect in a trade in which credit was given generally ended in bankruptcy. When all was said in that case, the fact, and it was an ugly one for the creditors, remained that commencing business with a small capital the debtor's liabilities had amounted to £2,168, with only about 3s.6d. in the pound to pay them. He would grant the debtor's immediate discharge on condition that he entered into an agreement with the Official Receiver to increase the dividend from 3s.6d. in the £ to 5s.0d but no proceedings against him should be taken without the leave of the Court.

Other bankruptcy reports in Rushden newspapers

Advance Boot Co. 1923
Ainge & Haseldine 1925
Perkins & Eden 1893
Nurrish & Flawn 1908
Darlow & West 1913
Colson & Co. 1889
Barratt & Barratt 1898
Brown & Co. 1898
George F Brown 1898

In many cases the official records of the bankruptcy have not been deposited with The National Archives (class B) even if they survive so the information contained in official notices is all the information that will be available. The *London Gazette* will also carry official notices of all bankruptcy cases and can be accessed on line at: **www.gazettes-online.com**

Records held by Northamptonshire County Record Office

Many deposited company records only contain administrative information such as directors' board minutes, order books, brochures, trading ledgers etc. as opposed to actual staff/employee records. Nevertheless if your ancestors worked for those companies then such records are likely to be of interest. Some company records currently remain uncatalogued.

Company and individual archives containing staff and wage records:

Allen & Caswell Kettering
Photographs c.1910-1960.

Avalon Footwear, Rothwell
Personnel records 1907-c.1985, wages book 1902-1910.

W. Barratt and Co. Ltd. Northampton
Photographs, c.1920.
William Henry Addington papers: Addington was managing director of Barratt's. Biography and obituary, notes on employees who served during WW2.

William Bruce, Duston
Account book 1891-1903, Duston parish records.

Desborough Shoe Co. Ltd.
Wages books 1912-1913, 1920-1921.

R Griggs and Co. Ltd. of Wollaston
Wages books and sheets 1955-1961, 1965-1973.

Chater and Underwood, Northampton
Wages Ledger 1884-1885.

G T Hawkins Ltd, Northampton
Wages register 1890-1894.

Haynes and Cann Ltd. Northampton - Formerly Youngents Ltd.
Staff records 1941-1946, wages register 1956-1962, and administration records.

John Mason Hodgkin, Northampton, boot lift manufacturer
Wages book 1896-1897.

Jaques and Clark Ltd. Rushden
Admission of 1866, wages books 1937-1941, 1948-1950.

Loake Brothers Ltd. of Kettering
Wages books 1925-1929, 1933-1935, 1943-1944, holiday fund accounts 1919-1936.

Manfield & Sons Ltd, Northampton
Staff magazine vol. 1, 1930, register of members 1920-1937, wages records 1952-1967, welfare trust fund minutes 1922-1924.

Mounts Factory Ltd. Northampton
Outworker's account book 1894.

Pollard & Son, Northampton
General ledgers, including wages 1904-1910, 1913-1920, production books including 'out' work 1884-1920, log books 1908-1942, employee and wages records 1889-1893, 1909-1944 including war bonus record 1915-1919.

Septimus Rivett Ltd. Wollaston
Wages book 1955-67, pay roll 1955-1962.

John Shortland Ltd, Irthlingborough
Wages records 1937, 1939-40, 1942, 1952-56, history 1962.

Tebbutt & Hall Bros Ltd. Raunds
Staff records 1969-1993.

Tecnic Boot Co. Ltd. Rushden
Register for employees under 16 1927-1938.

George Webb & Sons, Northampton
Mentone Services Bulletin issued by the Company for employees in armed services 1941-1945.

Wellingborough Boot & Shoe Manufacturing Co. Ltd. Wellingborough
Wages books 1925-1928, 1934-1941, 1944-47, 1950-1952, share records 1890-1960.

John White Footwear, Rushden
Wages records 1923-1966, Company history.

Whitney & Westley Ltd. Burton Latimer
Wages books 1897-1909, 1910-1920, 1929-1937, 1943-1952, office staff 1915-1922.

Some prominent company records held elsewhere:

C & J Clark Archives 1825-1990

The archives of the company fall under the responsibility of the Alfred Gillett Charitable Trust, whilst acting as a resource to those interested in history of the business, the staff who worked there, genealogical, local and social history research. C&J Clark was founded in 1825, but the archive has material that predates the 18th century. Business-related collections include a collection of adverts, films, accounting/financial records, minute books, original documents, printed sources and industry-specific objects such as collections of shoe machinery and footwear.

The Clark family papers collection includes photograph albums, diaries, inventories, letters and wills; as the Clarks were Quakers there is amongst the collection religious books, letters and papers relating to local Quakerism.

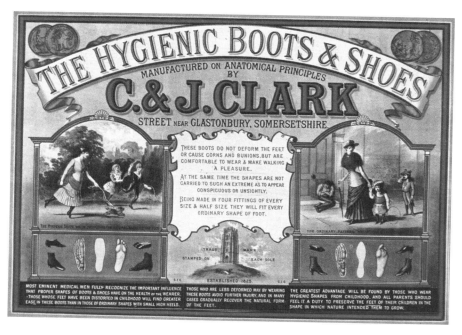

84. Advertising for Clarks Hygienic Boots and Shoes.

154

Most of the collections held by the archive are open to view by researchers but an appointment is necessary with the company archivist. Alfred Gillet Trust, Box 1, 40 High Street, Street, Somerset, BA16 0EQ.

Lotus Shoes Ltd Archives 1835-1992

The history of Lotus Ltd is closely connected to the history of the Bostock family, who owned the firm and many of its predecessor companies. Thomas Bostock established the company in 1814 at Stafford joined later by three of his sons. Edwin continued the Stafford business; Thomas started manufacturing in Stone and Frederick started a business in College Street Northampton in 1835 and later moved to Victoria Street, Northampton. Lotus Shoe Makers Ltd was incorporated in 1903, as a subsidiary company of Edwin Bostock & Co Ltd. Its purpose was to sell ready-made shoes manufactured by its parent company. It was amongst the first shoe manufacturers to mass produce rather than manufacture shoes to order. The company's name was shortened to Lotus Ltd in 1914. At the end of the First World War the three businesses amalgamated and were known as Lotus Ltd. The Company not only manufactured shoes but also had large warehouses, made its own lasts, components and cardboard boxes. It also had a joiner's shop which made packing cases used to export the shoes. It operated its transport fleet and developed staff canteens and welfare facilities.

The early 1920s saw the development of the retail side of the business. The company also owned houses in Stafford which it rented to employees.

The Bostock family severed connection with the company in 1970 when the last Bostocks retired from the company. It subsequently became part of the Debenhams/ Burton group in 1973 and by the end of 1987 it was the second largest footwear manufacturer in Britain.

The records of interest to family historians include:

Pension scheme records: The company established a non-contributory pension and life insurance scheme for its staff in 1948.

War savings records: The National War Savings Committee encouraged people to invest their savings in National Savings Certificates. The Bostock Employees War Savings Association was formed in 1916 and later it became the Lotus Ltd Savings Group listing members and prize winners.

Salary records: Income tax returns for E Bostock & Co Ltd 1907-1919; Lotus Shoe Makers Ltd 1907-1914; Lotus Ltd 1915-1923; and Patent Non-Splitting Wood Heel Co Ltd 1917-1922 exist and the returns contain the employee's name, address, position and salary. The files also contains a list of staff at Lotus Ltd 1921-1922; details of bonus payments, salary revisions and commercial travellers' commissions.

The Grapevine: was the staff magazine first issued in 1960. Like most staff magazines it contains news for and about employees.

Corporate and site records: factory plans, visitors books, catalogues, accounts returns etc.

The archive is held by Staffordshire Archive Service.

Boot and shoe industry

J R Tyler & Sons, boot & shoe manufacturers, Leicester

1817-1979. Tylers, originally a family based company best known for their 'Relyt' brand-name, had premises throughout the UK, the Irish Republic and Channel Islands.

Records include the advertising scrapbooks and photographs 1890-1979, establishment of the company, 1889-1925, financial records, 1885-1979 employees, 1932-1973, property, owned and rented, 1817-1979. Held at Leicestershire and Rutland Archives.

Horace Dyson, shoe factor of Farnham Street, Leicester

1905-1909 ledger and day book. Held at Leicestershire and Rutland Archives.

Equity Shoes Ltd, formerly Leicester Co-Operative Boot and Shoe Manufacturing Society

1887-2009. The Leicester Co-operative Boot and Shoe Manufacturing Society was established by workers of the CWS factory and commenced production in 1887. It was the first co-operative shoe factory in Leicester. The name was changed to Equity Shoe Ltd in 1958. The company closed down in early 2009 and was noted as the last mainstream shoe manufacturer in the city.

Records include workers description books (for each department), Union rules, factory matters, early staff records. Held at Leicestershire and Rutland Archives.

The Gibson Family, saddlers of Eaton

c.1890-1930 accounts and other financial papers. Held at Norfolk County Record Office.

The National Union of Boot & Shoe Operatives

1893-1965. Norwich Branch.
Records include minutes, subscription books, names and addresses of members. Held at Norfolk County Record Office.

Howlett & White (Norvic) Shoe Company

1899-1973. A noted Norwich shoe-making businesses established in 1846 by James Howlett initially as a leather-currying business expanding into a shoe-making empire that became the Norvic Shoe Company. The company began in Elm Hill but after a couple of moves ended up in St George's Plain. John Geoffrey Howlett, son of James, studied the leather trade and by 1859 John was collecting orders at Bourne, Lincolnshire where he met George White who joined the firm as a junior and worked his way to the top. George was instrumental in building the factory and doing away with outworkers.

The St. George's Plain factory was one of the centres of the footwear industry and the building still stands today although is now predominantly residential.

George White became the MP for North-West Norfolk, was knighted in 1907 and became a Freeman of the City of Norwich. A city school was named after him.

Records are at Norfolk County Record Office include deeds, partnerships etc., shares registers, ledgers, bank ledgers, minute books, cash books, wages and salaries, patten and design books, pension fund minutes books 1937-1951, staff wages (pension and superannuation fund) 1956-1962.

Journeyman Boot and Shoemakers' Pension Society

1857-1864. The Society was established in 1850 and it was acquired by the Boot Trade Benevolent Society in 1864.
Directors' minute book.

Boot Trade Benevolent Society

1836-1977. Boot Trade Benevolent Society later the Boot and Shoe Trade Provident and Benevolent Institution and the Master Boot and Shoemakers' Provident and Benevolent Institution.

The Master Boot and Shoemakers' Provident and Benevolent Institution was founded on 17 May 1836 by six master boot makers. The institution was formed for the provision of an asylum for aged and infirm people from the boot and shoe industry and also their widows for whom it also granted annuities.

In 1864 the Master Boot and Shoemakers' Provident and Benevolent Institution acquired the Journeymen Boot and Shoemakers' Pension Society.

The Institution changed its name firstly to the Boot and Shoe Trade Provident and Benevolent Institution in 1890 and then the Boot Trade Benevolent Society in 1900.. Society meetings were held at the Freemasons Tavern, Great Queen Street or at the Mortlake Asylum. Its headquarters moved several times ending up in Old Broad Street in 1961.

Minutes, 1853-1959; financial records, 1836-1977 and news cutting books, 1932-1937.

Peal and Company Limited (bootmaker)

1811-1964. Peal and Company founded by Samuel Peal, a shoe maker from Wirksworth, Derbyshire produced bespoke footwear between 1791 and 1965. Peal had a patent for waterproofing clothing materials by brushing them with a coat of caoutchouc an Indian rubber solution. Peal's boots and shoes became renowned for their comfort and durability.

Peal and Company has been owned by six generations of the Peal family.

The company employed salesmen who, from the 1880s, travelled throughout North and South American, Europe, Asia and the Far East. In addition to taking measurements, the salesmen made outline drawings of every customer's feet. These were kept in a series of Feet Books. Orders were fulfilled at firm's factory in Jeddo Road, Acton Vale, London.

Records consist of administrative records such as account books and ledgers, 'Feet Books' from the 1870s to 1965 when the firm transferred to Brooks in New York.

Worshipful Company of Pattenmakers

1669-1981. The earliest reference is to a guild of patten makers in 1469. A patten was a type of undershoe which was fastened beneath a shoe with a leather strap to make walking more comfortable on the cobbled pavements. The trade died out in the 19th century following the paving of streets.

Records include registers of freedom admissions from 1674; apprentice bindings from 1673; charters; ordinances; Court minute books; lists of masters, wardens, assistants and liverymen; quarterage books; financial accounts; letter books; and brief history of the Company.
Held at the Guildhall Library London.

85. Arms of the Worshipful Company of Patternmakers.

Shoe making glossary

86. Examples of different parts of a shoe with the Lasts.

Ankle Strap: A strap fastening round the ankle.
Apron Front Shoe: Front shaped like an apron.
Awl: Hole making tool, to pierce the skin prior to sewing.
Back Strap: A band covering the back seam of the shoe.
Balmoral Boot: A closed front ankle boot.

Bar: A strap across the instep fastening with a button or buckle added along the length of the foot in the shape of a 'T'.
Bends: The tanned skin sides used mainly for soles of shoes and boots.
Blind eyelet: No metal shown on top of the shoe.
Board Cut: A leather component part of a shoe cut by a clicker by hand round a pattern on a board.
Bottom Stock: Heel and sole cut leather pieces.
Broguing: Punched patterns forming a decorative feature on toe cap, vamp and facings.
Buckle Shoe: One fastened by a buckle and strap.
Cabbages: Off cuts of leather.
Casual Shoe: Slip on shoe with no fastening.
Clicker: A skilled worker who cuts the shapes of the component parts of the uppers of boots and shoes, making the most of each skin.
Closing: The process of sewing the leather parts of a shoe together.

Cobbler: A person who mends shoes.

Comb: A section of a last, corresponding with the instep.

Cordwainer: A shoemaker.

Court Shoe: Slip on high heeled shoe.

Counter: A section added to the back of the shoe covering the back seam and coming forward round the sides of the shoe.

Cuff: The upper ridge around the back of the shoe.

Day Work: An employee paid to do a job of work at an hourly rate.

Derby Boot or Shoe: Eyelet tabs stitched on top of vamp.

Drafting: Pulling uppers into shape over a last.

Drag: For pulling upper leather over the last.

Eyelets: Metal (or plastic) rings crimped onto the edges of the holes for the laces.

Facings: The area of the shoe through which the lace holes or eyelets are cut, usually lined with a layer of leather or fabric.

Fair Stitching: stitching a sole to the projecting edge of the middle sole.

Fellow: One of a matching pair of shoes.

Fetch Out: A process where the clickers knife is ground out (fetched) to the right curve.

Findings: Sundry supplies relevant to the manufacture of footwear including eyelets, etc. possibly a word local to Northamptonshire.

Finishers: Skilled workers who buffed and polished the finished boots and shoes.

Flaming: Adding colour to leather.

Ghille: Lacing through loops instead of eyelets.

Gimping: The edges of the section of the uppers are cut with a fine dentate edge similar to 'pinking'.

Grindery: The nails and tacks that were used in the construction of a boot or shoe.

Heel: A component which lifts the back part of the shoe away from the ground. It can be any height.

Heel Ball: A wax like substance that was used to finish the heels.

Indoor Working: Workers in a factory.

Insole: The inner sole of a shoe.

Instep: The arching portion of the upper foot.

Jodhpur Boots: Ankle high boot buckled at the side. Worn by horse riders.

Last: A wood or metal mould on which a shoe is formed.

Latchet: Straps extending from the front of the quarters across the front of the shoe over the tongue. They can be quite short with a sewn eyelet at the end to take a ribbon to fasten the shoe, or longer to thread through a buckle.

Lining: A thin leather or fabric lining is often included in the shoe. If only the back part of the shoe is lined it is called a half lining.

Loafer: Slip on apron fronted shoe.

Loop: A loop of leather either at the back of a pair of ankle boots, or on either side of the leg of a pair of boots to help in pulling them on.

Outdoor Closing: The stitching of footwear in the homes of the outworkers.

Oxford Shoe: Eyelet tabs stitched under the vamp.

Piece Work: An agreed unit rate of pay, the money paid on each finished article, rather than being paid by the hour to do the same job.

Pressmen: Men who operated the Revolution presses, cutting soles and top pieces out of bends and shoulders, skilfully utilising each piece of leather to the maximum efficiency.

Pullover: A machine which helped stretch the leather of the upper over the last and applied pressure to join the upper to the insole of the shoe (bottoming).

Quarters: The back part of the uppers. There are usually two quarters joined by a seam centre back.

Rand: A strip of leather, often white, placed between the upper and the sole and visible on the outside of the shoe. Now obsolete, it was common on shoes made from about 1650 to 1750.

Revolution Press: A machine that consists of a bed of wood blocks on which a bend or shoulder is placed, and knives in the shape and size of soles and heels are placed on the leather, when the operative taps the bar at his feet the machine comes down onto the knife and cuts out the shape required.

Riveting: Metal pins being used to join two or more pieces of leather together as in the case of soles of shoes.

Rough Stuff: Leather for the bottom of a shoe.

Safety Shoe: A shoe having a reinforced or steel toe cap. A system devised by Totectors.

Sewing: By hand or machines joining the various component parts of the shoe together.

Shank: The narrowing portion of the sole, under the instep, also the material used to reinforce this arch.

Shoetree: A wooden or metal form inserted into a shoe or boot to stretch it or preserve its shape.

Skiver: Pared edge of shoe components to prepare for stitching.

Sling Back: High heeled shoe with a strap enclosing the heel.

Slugging: Wire.

Snob: Shoemaker.

Sock: The lining in the base of the shoe covering up the roughness left during making. Often the maker's name and trade mark are stamped on the sock.

Sole: The hard leather of the boot or shoe, which makes contact with the ground.

Stiffener: An extra layer inside the back of the quarters to help prevent the back of the shoe being trodden down.

Straights: Shoes which do not have any difference in shape between the left and right foot.

Swab: A sample shoe used by salesman and commercial travellers as examples.

Tab or Tag: The binding on the end of a lace, to enable it to be threaded through the holes.

Thread: A strengthened cotton or flax fibre, usually waxed, with which to sew a shoe together.

Toe Cap: A cover applied to the front or toe area of the vamp, giving extra strength and protection.

Toe puff: Insert in the toe area to support the toecap of the shoe.

Tongue: An extension of the vamp under the facings of laced shoes/boots.

Top Edge: The top edge of the upper, around the ankle opening.

Top Piece: The layer of the heel which is in contact with the ground. As shoes are made upside down this is the last piece to be added.

Uppers: The top part of the shoe above the sole.

Vamp: The front part of the upper covering the toes and front of the foot.

Vulcanising: A process of heat bonding of the sole to the rest of the shoe using an adhesive.

Welts: A thin strip of leather between the outer and inner sole.

CHAPTER THREE
Saddle and Harness Makers

S addlery and harness making were once two separate crafts especially
in the towns. In the villages both the saddler and harness maker were
much valued as most of the work related to farm horses and the
making of their harnesses. Mechanisation began to reduce the need for both
crafts towards the end of the 19th century but the industry was kept very
much alive after a lull of about fifty years by those engaged in buses, cabs
and delivery vehicles all of which needed the horse. The peak of the harness
trade is considered to be around 1903-1905.

87. A saddler's business advertisement.

Besides making harness, saddles and collars, the saddler was often called upon
to make or repair anything in leather including occasionally boots and shoes if,
in the village there was no shoemaker or cobbler. This is how the diversification
to fancy goods such as purses, wallets and other riding accoutrements occurred.

Leonard Aldous was a saddle maker born in Debenham, Suffolk and an account from his journal appears in *The Farm and The Village* by Ewart Evans:

'We used to go round the farms to collect the harness work and bring back sets of harness for repair. But in my early days it was quite common for some of the old horsemen to walk anything up to three or four miles and sometimes more to bring harness down to the shop. They came down in their own time after they left work and they'd have a small job done and then take it back ready for the next morning. The main reason was that these horsemen were so jealous and particular about their horses that they wouldn't put another piece of harness on belonging to another horse. Each horse had its own harness and if it couldn't be spared to be sent down to the shop for repair the horseman brought it himself, got it seen to and took it back ready for the next day's work.'

This was typical in many rural communities right up to the early 1900s.

Although most of our ancestors would have been involved with the rural trade a few towns established factories for mass production. Perhaps the centre of the trade was Walsall in the West Midlands. Making saddles and harness on a large scale met a need for the many horses employed on the land, roads and within the army. Factory production necessitated the division of labour so our ancestors may have followed a specific occupation such as a cutter, stuffer or stitcher. Factories also separated new work from repairs. Throughout the trade, a harness used for draught and farm horses was known as a 'black' harness and for riding horses a 'brown' harness. Workers in the factories took as much pride in their work as the village saddlers and because of their skills the saddles and harness were of equally high quality. Because of the production techniques it was possible to offer cheaper saddles without cheapening the quality.

It was suggested that some of the best harness makers lived in towns and alongside this so many of the town horses were fine specimens, well groomed and almost show animals. The van men would have polished their horse brasses and oiled the leathers etc.

The First World War saw the demise of the horse from the field and the road together with the cabs in the major cities which were gradually replaced by motor transport. With this there was a decline in horse keepers, grooms, harness makers, horse dealers, saddlers, farriers and other people whose lives, to that time were totally dependent upon the horse. Within twenty five years the horse had all but vanished as a working animal and the associated trades along with it.

88. Like shoe factories, saddlers' factories were part of a street landscape.

Saddlers' workshops were frequently quite large and light, compared to a cobbler or shoemaker's shop which was often dingy and cramped. Saddlers chose the good quality leathers using, in the main, cattle-hide butts which were vegetable tanned and curried and finished to a high standard. Strength and resistance to wear were essential qualities for all elements of the saddle and harness, a paramount safety requirement. It is said the slogan 'there is no substitute for leather' originated in a saddler's workshop in Derbyshire.

165

89. The workings within a saddler's workshop.

Because of the age of the trade it was possible to formulate standard patterns and tables for the making of saddles and harness but it still required the skill of the craftsman to produce the goods that looked the part and fitted both the horse and rider. It took around 2-3 days to make a saddle and in some cases longer. Some craftsmen needed about a week. Some artistic skills were also needed as saddlers had to recognise a line and a curve so as not to make the saddle lop-sided. Every saddle had its own style and saddlers could recognise one they made or one made by one of their apprentices when they became fully fledged craftsmen.

Making a saddle required certain stages which are described later, namely, preparing the tree, webbing the tree, blocking the seat, making and fitting the skirts and seaming them in, setting the seat, making and blocking the flaps, fitting the panel and stuffing the seat.

During the 1920s there was again a serious slump of the trades in both the towns and the villages but a slight revival occurred with the rise in popularity of fox hunting, riding and horse racing. Once trade levelled out there were about 1800 saddlers and harness makers in the country whereas just twenty years earlier that figure was more than double. The making of neck collards for horses never seemed to be subject to slumps and depressions as the need was always there. In order to survive, the saddlers and harness makers who did not engage in collar making were forced to diversify into making luggage and sports goods including leather footballs and cricket balls.

Although man first tamed horses thousands of years ago it had taken a long time for the recognisable saddle to develop. Saddle and harness-making has had a dramatic effect on horse usage over the years and has evolved because of the many different tasks performed by various breeds of horses.

The modern English saddle is generally light and strong. Some of the more ornate heavy saddles are still very much in evidence but mainly on the backs of police or army horses in ceremonial parades.

Today's general purpose saddles normally weigh about four kilogrammes (without the stirrups and their straps). A few are still 'made-to-measure', by a small band of master saddlers and are very expensive. Most modern saddles come in six standard lengths each with three different widths.

Like all skilled crafts, specialist tools were required for each trade as was the need to qualify through apprenticeship, many working long hours for a minimal financial return. Much of the work in both trades was intricate.

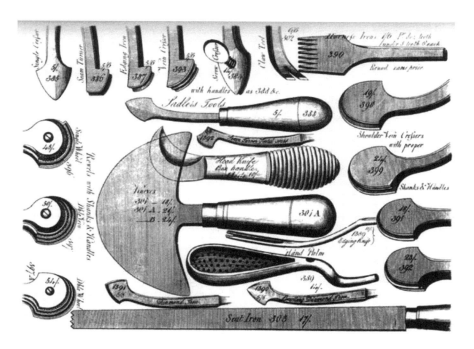

90. Tools used in saddle making.

The saddler's art was very specialist and involved skilled craftsmen in many different aspects during its construction. Different patterns of saddle existed for different purposes. The hunting saddle was different to a military saddle or riding saddle and different again to a dressage saddle. In England the saddle is based on a solid tree, normally made by a loriner (see later), over which webbing, leather and padding materials are added. Traditionally, the tree was made of laminated layers of high quality wood, usually beech, reinforced with steel underneath the front arch and around the rear underside. The sides of the tree that run horizontally along the horse's back are known as bars. Modern saddles (from the early 20th century) are manufactured using various materials to replace wood and create a synthetic moulded tree (some still using spring steel and a steel gullet plate). Synthetic materials vary widely in quality, polyurethane being the most durable.

Leather is added on all sides of the tree to create the seat, flaps and panels. Cowhide is usually used, though pigskin is considered a good medium. The panels on the underside of the saddle traditionally are stuffed with wool flock. The brackets were open-ended so that if a rider was thrown and his foot became tangled in one of the stirrups, the leathers would come apart and he would not be dragged along the ground.

91. A small saddler's workshop typical of the mid Victorian era.

For the individual or small company saddle makers the first stage was to build the tree which was usually undertaken after measurements of the horse and rider had been taken. Some saddles were built to standard sizes such as military saddles because the cavalry horses were usually of a similar size. Metal elements were then added, such as the stirrup bar and the gullet. Component parts were often manufactured by specialist companies and bought in by the saddlers.

The part of a saddle which provides cushioning between the horse's back and the saddle, and allows adjustment in fitting the saddle to the horse is known as the panel which is also an important element in keeping the saddle balanced for the rider. The two panels, one at the front and one at the rear were usually stuffed with wool. Today foam is frequently used. The saddle has two sets of panels one on each side of the horse's spine.

The use of leather in the saddle involved various other elements and processes.

The skirt sometimes known as the jockey was a piece of leather that went over the stirrup bar, to help prevent the rider's leg from rubbing on the buckle of the stirrup leather. It also helped to keep the buckle of the stirrup leather from unbuckling and sliding down. The skirt was small to allow easy access to the stirrup leather.

The saddle flap was a large piece of leather on the exterior of a saddle that fitted between the rider's leg and the billets and girth buckles. The shape and length of the saddle flap was directly related to the intended use of the saddle because it needed to mirror the rider's leg position.

The second flap used was known as the sweat flap which was a large piece of leather on the underside of the saddle between the billets and the horse. This protected the saddle from the horse sweat and also prevented the horse's skin from being pinched by the girth straps and buckles.

Billet straps were secured over the saddle tree on stout webbing and hung down, so the girth could be buckled to it. Like a belt they hadseveral holes in them to adjust the tightness of the girth. There were normally three billets. Some saddles, particularly those used for military saddles, had very long billets to buckle the girth below the saddle flap to reduce the bulk underneath the rider's leg, allowing for closer contact with the horse.

Leathers were the part of the stirrup which attach the stirrup iron to the stirrup bar of the saddle. It could be adjusted to change the lengths of stirrups. Leathers is in fact a plural because a saddle always has two - one for each stirrup. The most suitable leather for saddle work was soft calf or sheep-skin. In fact, three types of leather were normally found in a saddler's workshop, calf or sheep-skin, tough cow hide, and the best quality pig skin for the actual seats. Whole hides were bought ready-greased.

The more thoroughly greased the hides were, the easier the leather was to work with and the longer it lasted. Each hide consisted of almost the whole animal skin, but the quality of leather was by no means the same all over.

The first saddles used were animal skins or cloths thrown over the backs of horses, which gave little comfort to either rider or horse. Around 12AD, the Sarmatians, a nomadic tribe from the Black Sea area introduced a saddle on which the modern 'tree' was based. The tree had front and rear arches joined by wooden bars on each side of the horse's spine. This design was improved during medieval times particularly amongst the knights with the use of the dip-seated saddle.

Ideally, the tree should be built to fit the back of the horse for which the saddle was intended. Most of the time, however, saddles were manufactured for certain sizes and shapes and fitted most horses of equivalent sizes and shapes. Trees were usually made in three width fittings: narrow, medium, and broad, and four lengths: 15 inches, 16 inches, 16½ inches and 17½ inches.

Panels were cushions divided by a channel that gave a comfortable padded surface to the horse's back while raising the tree high enough to give easy clearance of the animal's spine. The panels also disperse the rider's weight over a larger surface, thereby protecting the horse from the weight of the rider. These panels also protected the horse's back from the hardness of the saddle. The purpose of the skirts was to protect the rider's legs from the sweat of the horse, and to cover the girths and girth straps. Saddles also included D-rings, small leather straps with strings attached that could hold canteens, jackets, food pouches, and other items.

In England, foxhunting grew in popularity and this pastime required a new method of riding, as horse and rider had to tackle fences, hedges, ditches and banks head-on if they wished to keep up with the hounds. The old style saddle was cumbersome and somewhat uncomfortable while hunting. The cantle would get in the way of the riders when they had to lean back to keep their balance when going over the fence, and the high pommel created pain as the rider went over jumps. The resulting saddle developed for foxhunting had a very low pommel and cantle with a flat seat, and no padding under the leg, therefore providing the rider with little, if any, support.

The English hunting saddle was the predecessor of the riding saddles. As the sports of polo, show jumping and eventing became more popular from mid Victorian times the saddle shape changed. The 'forward seat,' was developed in which the rider used shorter stirrups and kept his legs under him as he rode with his seat bones hovering above the saddle.

The differences between the styles of English saddle were small but significant, however saddlers tended to specialise in making various styles by the 1860s. The most important distinctions are the location and balance of the seat, and the flap length and shape.

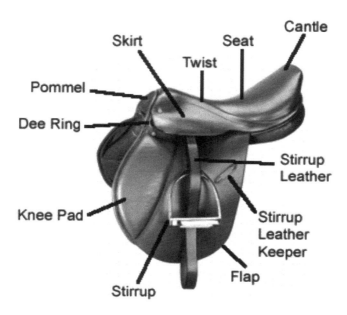

Skirt

Seat

Cantle

Twist

Pommel

Dee Ring

Stirrup
Leather

Knee Pad

Stirrup
Leather
Keeper

Flap

Stirrup

92. The complex saddle.

Supportive padding in the seat, size and shape of knee rolls and the use of additional blocks behind the leg was also considered when developing a saddle. A polo saddle was constructed with a minimum of padding so as to allow the polo player greater freedom to twist and reach for his shot. A saddle used for jumping or eventing may have more padding to help give the rider support over fences. In all cases it was necessary to protect the horse's skin from being chaffed by the ride.

Apart from cutting the leather to the required size and shape, the saddler also had to wax his own thread with beeswax to stop it rotting. He also made his own cord by twisting up to six threads together. This six-cord string was normally used when lacing the parts of a saddle together. Some saddlers also mixed their own special stain to colour and preserve the cut edges of leather.

Harnesses made for light work and for horses drawing smaller vehicles differed from those used in pulling drays and larger wagons. Bridles and head pieces for heavy draught work were much sturdier than those needed for riding purposes. Blinkers were also needed for horses pulling the heavier vehicles. Most harnesses were made of three component parts, the collar, the pads and the straps or breachings.

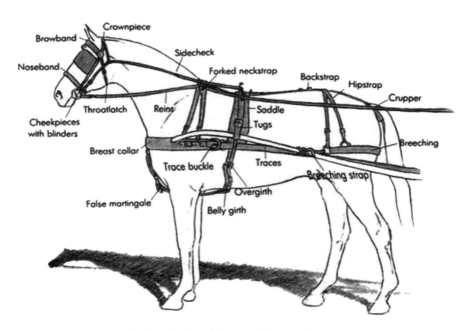

93. Identification of the parts of a typical harness.

The pad took the weight of the draught gear and the shafts, the straps prevented the load straining the hind quarters of the horse particularly when going downhill and the collar allowed the horse to pull evenly.

The most common collar was the draught collar but in the military the 'breast collar' was used. Each collar was made to suit the breed of horse with great care taken in the fitting and adjustment. Some collars were even bespoke made for a particular horse.

A breeching strap around the horse's haunches allowed it to set back and slow a vehicle and was usually hooked to the shafts or pole and was used for a single horse, a pair, or in a larger team, for the wheelers. The lead horses in a team do not have breeching, as they are in front of the shafts or pole and so cannot slow the vehicle. Breeching acting as a type of brake may not have existed if a cart was very light or had efficient brakes on the wheels.

On two-wheeled vehicles the tugs were stiff leather loops, fitting loosely around the shafts to allow flexibility as the animal and the vehicle moved against each other. On four-wheeled vehicles with independently hinged shafts, the tugs were leather straps buckled tightly around the shafts so they moved with the animal.

Reins were the long leather straps running from the bit to the driver's hands, to guide the horses. In teams these were joined together so the driver only needed to hold one pair. Bits for harness were similar to those used for riding, particularly in the mouthpiece, usually operating with adjustable leverage to help balance the effect of the reins on different horses in a team. The bridles of the rear or middle horses in a team of either four or six horses, known as the wheelers, had rings at each end of the brow band, through which the reins of the forward horses passed. Terrets were also included and these were metal loops on the saddle and collar to support the reins. The bridles of the rear animals of a large team may also have had terrets to take the reins of the animals to the front of them.

When working in harness, most horses wore a specialised bridle. These usually included blinkers around the horse's eyes, to prevent it from being distracted by the cart and other activity behind it.

Head Collar with Bit and Bridlehead

1. Crown piece
2. Brow band
3. Brow band tab
4. Throat lash
5. Nose band
6. Back stay
7. Jowl piece
8. Head piece
9. Cheek piece
10. Long piece of heads, bridle
11. Short piece of heads, bridle
12. Bit, P.M.R.
13. Chains, curb
14. Reins, bit
15. Reins, bit for curb

94. A typical head collar used by a draft horse.

Some horses pulling lighter vehicles may have had an overcheck to assist them in holding a desired head position, and for safety reasons (to avoid the horse's head and neck going under the shaft in a stumble).

Horse brasses were the brass plaques mounted on leather straps, used for decoration, especially on working harness.

A collar was a part of a harness used to distribute load around a horse's neck and shoulders when pulling a wagon or plough or dray vehicle. The collar often supported a pair of curved metal hames, to which traces were attached. The collar allowed a horse to use its full strength when pulling by pushing forward with its hindquarters into the collar. From the time of invention of the horse collar, horses became extremely valuable for agricultural work and for pulling heavy vehicles.

Walsall - the centre for saddlery and harness making

As Northamptonshire was the centre of the shoe trade, so Walsall was the centre for saddlery and harness making business. At the turn of the 20th century Walsall was home to nearly a third of Britain's saddlers and harness makers. However as the age of the horse declined Walsall had to adapt. Some firms had been actively producing other leather fancy goods such as cases, bags, wallets and writing cases since the 1870s but by the outcome of the First World War most companies who had built their trade as saddlers were no longer doing so as their prime trade, most making saddles and harness to order, a trade which continues to this day.

Within the town's early records there are references to leather workers but generally the centre was built on saddlers' ironmongers or loriners. The loriners who made the metal parts of the horse harnesses needed high grade iron, charcoal, coal and limestone all of which were available close to the town.

It was not until the early 19th century that leather working became an important local trade. The establishers of the town's leather goods trade were said to have been 'bridle cutters' who could resource the skills of local loriners for the metal parts.

The leather working industry grew significantly after 1840, boosted by the building of the South Staffordshire Railway through Walsall in 1847.

The Victorians needed horses for both economic and social reasons and it is said there were over three million horses in England at the height. Certainly the working horse was the chief means of power on most farms.

The latter half of the 19th century was, for Walsall, considered to be the 'Golden Age' of prosperity. Walsall leather firms were sending their products to most parts of the British Empire and the Victorian wars helped to provide a lucrative trade.

The industry however remained a mass of independent, small and often basic backyard workshops although a few larger factories existed employing around two or three hundred people. Unfortunately the hours for even highly skilled workers

HOBDAY & SMITH,

WHOLESALE SADDLERS & HARNESS MAKERS, WALSALL.

*Every style of **Riding Saddles** made for all markets, and orders executed with promptness through any Merchants.*

95. Large scale saddle manufacture occurred in Walsall.

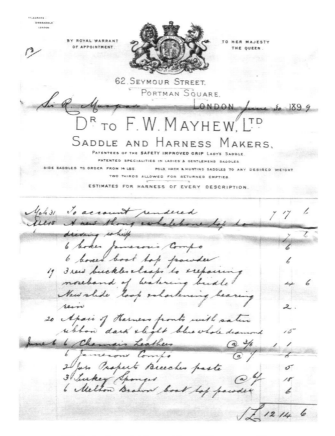

96. Typical receipt for saddle and harness making.

were long, wages poor and conditions below standard as identified by the Sweated Trade Commission.

A male saddle maker would earn about 28s. for a 55/60 hour week and women in the industry would only earn about a third of this. Male employees were usually paid by the hour but most women were paid on the completed item and if there was no work the women were the first to be laid off.

In many of the larger and modern factories in the town, deductions were made from wages for utilities such as heating, lighting and even 'rent' for the space in which the employees worked. Around the turn of the 20th century about 10,000 people were employed locally in the various leather industries.

Worshipful Company of Saddlers

The earliest known document referring to saddlers of London is a parchment in the Westminster Abbey library but was known to originate in records of the Church of St Martin-le-Grand and is an agreement between that church and the Guild of Saddlers. It dates somewhere between 1160 and 1193 but it is thought the Saddlers' Guild may have existed in Anglo-Saxon times but there is no evidence to prove this.

97. The Worshipful Company of Saddlers.

By the early 16th century there was a distinct move away from crafts to merchants within the City of London and at this time the City Court of Aldermen established an order of precedence of Livery companies in 1515, the Saddlers being allocated 25th place.

In the early middle ages, the Worshipful Company of Saddlers had jurisdiction over all saddlers within a two-mile radius of the City: apprenticeships, admissions to the Freedom, wages, working conditions and the quality of goods offered for sale were among the most important matters dealt with by the company which also regulated its members and imposed fines or imprisonment for any contravention of its ordinances and bye-laws.

During the 19th century the Saddlers' Company declined in both influence and membership. Much of this period was spent fending off attempts to abolish the ancient institutions of the City of London, as they were perceived as being founded on privilege thus making no contribution to the community as a whole.

The survival of the company and others is attributed to the master of the Saddlers' Company, Sir Richmond Cotton, who also became a Mayor of London.

The majority of the archives of the Saddlers' Company were destroyed by fire in 1940 when the Company's third hall was bombed. Nevertheless, the Company still holds a limited but valuable collection of historical records. The collection includes the following:

Charter of James I, 1607.
Charter of Charles II, 1684.
Charter of Elizabeth II, 1995.
Record/Testament Book, 1434-1698.
Freedom Roll, 1560-date.
Court Minute Book, 1606-65 original, Ms 05385, held in the Guildhall Library, copy available at Saddlers' Hall.
Audit Book, 1555-1822 original, Ms 05384, held in the Guildhall Library, copy available at Saddlers' Hall.
Apprentice Binding Register, 1800-1962.
Alphabetical list of pensioners, 1831-1929.
Minutes, 1892-date.
Account Books, 1904-date.
Index of all known members of the Company (compiled since the 1950's from various sources, which include the records listed above and the Corporation of London City Freedom papers).
A Guide to the Archives is available at Saddlers' Hall.

Military saddlers

Throughout the history of the British army the cavalry and artillery regiments have employed saddlers and indeed it is a recognised rank within those regiments. The Army Service Corp instigated the Corps of Waggoners in 1794 and saddlers were part of the Corps whose main responsibility was the organisation of transport which at the time was horse drawn. Our ancestors may have enlisted and served in the army and would have held a rank associated with saddler.

Normally an artillery brigade included two saddlers whose role was to attend to all the needs of the brigade in regard to both saddle and harness ware. The making and repair of tack occurred both at the barracks and in the field. All leather work on military harness is hand sewn. Within the cavalry regiments (Lancers and Hussars) there was a Saddler Sergeant attached to each regimental headquarters and any number of saddlers within the ranks, usually around four or five. Each cavalry regiment had 528 riding horses for which each had its own tack, 48 reinforcements, 74 draught horses and 6-8 pack horses. Different saddles existed for troopers, officers, drivers and as pack saddles. Head collars also varied depending upon use.

98. Handbook used by Military Artificers relating to saddles and harness.

Records for our ancestors who served in such capacity will be amongst the records of enlisted army personnel up to the rank of non-commissioned officers.

The term 'pattern' refers to a specification as laid down by the British War Department to govern the manufacture of equipment for her armed forces. These patterns ensured that the various companies contracted to manufacture this equipment supply items of a known and compatible standard.

In 1796 the first 'Universal Pattern' for the manufacture of cavalry saddles was issued. The 'UP' saddle was developed at the height of cavalry as a mounted force and continued to evolve until its final days.

99. British Universal Military saddle used in First World War.

British Universal Pattern military saddles were used by the mounted forces from Britain and within our colonial forces. In India saddles were made in that country for the use of British, European and native regiments. British saddlers, would have resided and worked in India either attached to the regiments or as civilians supplying the military.

Various styles of saddle were made for military use. The Steel Arch Universal Pattern saddle Mark I was issued in 1891 but this was found to irritate riders so in 1893 it was modified and became known as the Mark II. In 1898 still further modifications were made and the Mark III appeared which had the addition of a V-shaped arrangement of strap billets on the sideboards for the attachment of the girth. This girthing system could be moved forward or back to obtain an optimum fit on a wide range of horses.

From 1902 the Universal Military Saddle was manufactured with a fixed tree, broad panels to spread the load, and initially a front arch in three sizes. The advantage of this saddle was its lightness, ease of repair and comfort for horse and rider. From 1912 the saddle was built on an adjustable tree and consequently only one size was needed. Its advantage over the fixed tree 1902 pattern was its ability to maintain a better fit on the horse's back as the horse gained or lost weight. This saddle was made using traditional methods and featured a seat blocked from sole leather, which maintained its shape well. Military saddles were fitted with metal staples and dees to carry a sword, spare horse shoes and other necessary equipment.

During the Boer War the Imperial Yeomanry employed numerous saddlers such as Arthur Ernest Berry (regt. no. 38467). Within the month of April 1902 Walsall firms filled the following orders form the War Office to supply the mounted regiments (including the Imperial Yeomanry) serving in South Africa:

31,000 bridles
15,000 breast plates
56,000 girths
34,000 reins
52,000 stirrups
15,500 saddles
28,000 rifle buckets
16,000 horse shoe cases
26,000 head collars

During the First World War and within cavalry and artillery regiments, civilian saddlers and harness makers were also employed to provide and maintain harness for gun carriages, cannon, field ambulances etc. Each saddler would be equipped with a chest.

A military saddler's chest contained the detachable tong and the saddler's tool roll. The tool roll itself had each pocket numbered to identify what tool is to be kept in which numbered pocket. Approximately 75 different tools ranging from gauge, knives, rawhide head hammer, prickers, saddler's palm to packets of needles were included.

It would also have contained the following:

nail bag with assorted nails
brace (hand drill)
burr, rivet
needle case
saddler's clamp
dee
drawing knife
leather, latigo,
nails, rivets
Civilian harness makers also joined the ranks.

Herbert James Leech became a military saddler in the First World War. He was born in 1895 at Chingford the son of William James Leech born 1868 also at Chingford who also became a military saddler. Herbert worked for James Brothers of Chingford before joining the Army Service Corps (regt. no. 4893) and serving in France. His father William joined the Royal Artillery (regt. no. 82681), also serving in France. Saddle manufacturers in Walsall supplied over 100,000 saddles to the British army throughout the First World War.

Coach harness makers

The coach harness was different to that of a horse harness and was a specialist trade. Coach harnesses were used where the coach or carriage was driven by a coachman sitting on the carriage itself rather than on the horse. The coach harness maker made the harness and gears for pulling coaches and carriages and frequently did so at the time that his counterparts were building the coach. In effect the coach harness was individually made for the coach and not the team of horses. Thus many coach makers/builders were also coach harness makers which is why the apprenticeships were served under the Worshipful Company of Coach and Coach Harness makers to which they ultimately belonged.

The coach harness unlike the horse harness did not include the bridle or any form of saddle and usually included a much larger and stronger collar. Independent of the coach builder the coach harness maker may well have practiced the trade of 'saddle and harness makers.' If the coach or carriage was to be postilion driven then a saddle would have been made for the postilion horses (usually the left hand horse of a team) and a special type of harness would be made with bridle and bits etc.

Closely associated with coach harness making is the craft of the coach trimmer and many coach harness makers also carried out trimming. Coach trimmers were responsible for making and fitting the upholstery and the internal furniture of the carriage or coach

The coach trimmer needed special attributes to enable him to be successful. Most seats in coaches were leather covered so he had to quilt like an upholsterer, stitch like a harness maker, sew like a tailor and also be able, with a keen eye, to make upholstery well-padded and comfortable. He also needed a keen eye for design and colour matching.

Many of the materials used included top quality leathers and these were often the most expensive materials used in the coach builder's premises. It was important that the trimmer utilised as much of the leather as he could. The trimmer served an apprenticeship like most others for a term of seven years. Some coach trimmers actually served apprenticeships with the Upholders Company and progressed into the trade. Others served through the Coachbuilders and Coach Harness Makers Company. The trimmer used much the same tools as others such as awls, knives, pliers etc. specialist clamps, stretching tools etc. which were part of his everyday tool kit.

The Coach Makers and Coach Harness Makers Company

The Company existed before it received a charter in 1677. It had petitioned the Court of Aldermen in 1631, jointly with the Wheelwrights to procure Letters Patent from the King so they could control their members. By the charter, Edmund Awbry, coach maker, Charles Nevill, coach harness maker, Thomas Brigham, coach maker and others became the Master, Wardens, Assistants and with the rest of the members at the time became the Company of Coach Makers and Coach Harness Makers.

Within ten years of the grant, in October 1686, the Company was forced to surrender back to the King the powers conferred by Charter. In May 1687 a second Charter was granted. The chief change was that the King, by Order in Council, might displace the Master, Wardens, Assistants and Clerks, or any of them, and require the Company to elect others.

No freedom records survive before 1803 as much of the archive was destroyed by enemy bombing in 1940. Surviving records are held at the Guildhall Library in London and comprise:

Alphabetical List of Freemen 1803-1893.
List of masters of Apprentices 1722-1822.

Like other companies where records do not survive in their entirety it would be useful to search the City Poll Books which list the Livery men for the period 1700-1796. Alphabetical List of Apprentices 1677-1893 (gap 1800-1803).

The Society of Genealogists publication compiled by Cliff Webb, *London Livery Company Apprenticeship Registers, Vol. 23 Coachmakers and Coach Harness Makers' Company 1677-1800* should also be consulted. The Society Library also holds a typescript index made from the then surviving apprentice binding book.

Court Minutes 1830-1893, 1914-1997 (The earlier volumes contain an index to Freemen).

Loriners

The Loriner makes and sells bits, bridles, spurs, stirrups, saddle trees and the minor metal items of a horse's harness. The word loriner is derived from the Latin 'lorum', a thong, bridle or reins. The craft and the design of bits has not altered much over the years.

The craft has unfortunately disappeared from the City of London. The last working loriner in London existed until around the late 19th century. The craft continues mainly in and around Walsall.

The loriners, alongside painters and fusters or joiners, were trades subordinate to the saddlers.

At the height of the loriners trade, throughout the 19th century the market for such goods was booming. As a result of the Industrial Revolution and the improvement in the road systems in both urban and rural areas there was a huge increase in horse-drawn traffic of all types from stage coaches to heavy wagons and lighter commercial carts all of which needed either a horse or a team of horses.

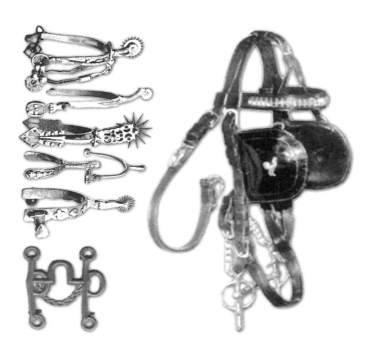

100. Parts made by the Loriner associated with harness.

Private driving turnouts were very common within the wealthier classes and riding horses were used both for business and pleasure. Hunting also became one of the most popular rural pursuits. The Army also used a phenomenal number of horses both in cavalry regiments and for artillery transportation. The saddle, harness and loriner businesses were developed to meet all these different requirements.

A large variety of bits were made to prevent horses from pulling, rearing or getting their tongue over the bit. Different designs also existed for horses with soft mouths and others to control those with hard mouths and many were ornamental for use with carriage horses. Spurs were always small with a disc at the end of the spur arm and were usually of best quality hand forged steel. Stirrups were designed both for appearance and for safety.

Britain's expanding overseas empire and its involvement in the Victorian Wars had a considerable effect on the types of loriners' products made in the town. For example the Walsall Pearce's 1813 Directory lists those employed in the diversified loriner and allied trades as follows:

10 Bridle bit makers

1 Brass coach founder

10 Buckle makers

4 Saddle Tree makers

23 Stirrup makers

14 Saddlers' ironmongers

3 Stay makers

6 Spur makers

23 Bit makers

as well as other closely associated industries. It is also interesting to note the specialism of many of these craftsmen.

The Industrial Revolution had an effect on the loriner trade in Walsall. One major development which made Walsall renowned within the trade was a system, developed in Birmingham in 1811, of making malleable iron castings without them becoming brittle, by placing them in annealing ovens after casting. Nickel, both malleable and as plating, became widely used in the trade. These two advances also made it more economical to produce goods in factories as opposed to the earlier established small workshops. Plating and drop forging quickly took the place of hand forging.

There is a slight 'chicken and egg' situation with regard to the loriner trade in Walsall. It is thought that the establishment of saddlers' ironmongery as a major trade in Walsall was responsible for the growth of the kindred leather and saddlery trades, but it could easily have been the other way round. Walsall developed a worldwide reputation for high class saddlery, harness and leather goods, due possibly to a flourishing saddlers' ironmongery trade.

Worshipful Company of Loriners

The Worshipful Company of Loriners was originally a trade association for makers of metal parts for bridles, harnesses, spurs and horse apparel such as brasses.

The company was established in 1261, and its ordinances predate those of any other existing livery company. The company's Royal Charter was granted by Queen Anne in 1711.

Originally being a 'loriner' applied to those who hand forged their products. However, with the advances in metal casting, drop forging and electro-plating processes very little hand forging is now used and in modern terms 'loriner' applies to anyone who is engaged in the production of saddlers' ironmongery.

Until the end of the 18th century, bits, spurs, stirrups and other harness parts were forged in wrought iron. Steel then became the preferred material. Similar processes to that used by blacksmiths were used with pieces being hand forged, using heat, anvil and hammer, finished by filing smooth and burnishing.

The tools used by loriners for hand forging and burnishing are generally the same as those used by all types of metal smiths. A good description of the process and some of the tools involved can be found in R A Salaman's 'Dictionary of Leather-working Tools'.

Casting became a more viable alternative to forging from around 1811. Brass and nickel were also cast in the same way. The metal was usually heated in a crucible and then poured into a prepared mould. Each casting was then filed and polished in the same way as hand forged items. Where mass production in factories was undertaken the castings were polished in 'mopping' and 'bobbing' shops using mechanical polishing machines.

From the mid 19th century the plating of cast iron bits with either brass, silver, nickel alloy or tin was common. Much of the harness furniture was brass plated.

The stamping of sheet brass to make harness and harness decorations was also a common process and in 1892 caused an outcry amongst the hand forgers because they wanted to prevent stamped bits being sold as cheaply as forged bits. Manufacturers competed with each other to produce a rust free alloy from which to make horse furniture, some even advocating in publicity material that they would never rust. In the 1890s many different patents were taken out for furnishing designs.

During the whole of the 19th century the overseas market was increasingly important for the survival of businesses engaged in the saddlery and harness making trade particularly in the major production centres such as Walsall. Many companies had an overseas marketing campaign with 'export brochures' and even foreign agents / representatives. Large consignments were regularly sent all over the globe by some manufacturers. Britain's colonies such as India and Canada were among the best customers. The South American countries, particularly Peru relied largely on Britain for saddlery and harness.

Walsall prided itself in having made sets of harness for foreign royalty which led to firms specialising in harness decoration. One individual was Harry Gill of Vicarage Street, Walsall who specialised in heraldic work for the harness, one of which was used in a 1902 Coronation in Delhi.

The decline in the saddlery trade commenced around 1880, and the interruption of exports during the South African War led to the colonies starting to produce their own saddles and harness.

Records of the Loriners Company

Records of the Worshipful Company of Loriners are held at the Guildhall Library and comprise:

Constitutional records, 1711-42
Court records, 1722-31, 1759-1811, Court minutes only 1940-2005
Membership records, 1424, 1723-1949 (some gaps) Freedoms from 1784,
Apprenticeships from 1883
Financial records, 1723-1837, 1940-99 Clerk's records, 1901-2005

Trade and Craft Guilds

Saddlers are recorded in Chester from 1392. In 1472, their company was given a monopoly by Edward IV to last for 40 years. In 1639, the company was granted a charter by the City. The saddlers company amalgamated with the curriers and leather dressers and was one of the three responsible for presenting prizes for the Shrove Tuesday races held on the Roodee after 1540.

During the 16th and 17th centuries, they fought to protect their craft against the shoemakers and the cutlers, their dispute with the latter being over the sale of spurs.

The Saddlers originally had their own meeting place in Chester - the Saddler's Tower on the city walls at the east end of Abbey Street but this was demolished in 1774. By 1835, in spite of the continuing demand for saddlery the Company was reduced to just five members.

Trade journals

Saddlery and Harness was a monthly trade journal published by T Kirby and Sons of Bradford Street, Walsall from July 1891 onwards. Copies are available for research at the British Newspaper Library in Colindale and at Walsall Library. Its stated aim was to become 'the authorised and duly acknowledged organ of the Saddlery and Harness Trades'. Being published in Walsall the journal tends to be biased towards the town but it was successful in becoming the recognised national trade journal alongside the *Saddlers, Harness Makers and Carriage Builders Gazette* published from 1871.

The journal contains some interesting information about the state of the saddler trade and also includes details of both manufacturing companies and individuals. If you have saddlers and harness makers amongst your ancestry both journals are worth investigating.

The following are some examples from *Saddlery and Harness* in 1902:

'Trade exceptionally good, the war in South Africa undoubtedly the main cause. The price of labour has increased. This has had a damaging effect on exports to other countries, as prices have increased'.

'War Office tenders invited for 10,000 horse collars, 20,000 leather aprons, tool bags and cases, and regular saddlery and harness. Quantities so great that the Woolwich Dockyard (where munitions are inspected) has to be reorganised. The ships which have been used for the purpose for last 160 years are being removed'.

'Cawnpore, May 5th 1902, sent by J K Urquhart. 'Cawnpore is to the Indian saddlery trade what Walsall is to the home. Here we turn out all sorts and conditions of saddlery. Products include strapping for elephants and camels. The Indian trade has its difficulties. The climate is very bad for leather and it becomes very brittle'.

'Mr JA Barnsby is 80 years old on Nov 1st. commenced in work at an earlier age than is now the custom and was actively engaged in the business until 3 years ago. The business was founded by Mr Barnsby over 30 years ago and 'the firm now is probably the largest brown saddle makers in England'. Riding saddle dept. employs 80 journeymen 'when in full swing', producing several hundred saddles a week. JAB served an apprenticeship in Macclesfield. After unsuccessful attempt to find employment in London he came to Walsall in 1854, finding employment with Chawner and Newman. 'Here it was that he perfected his knowledge, and after remaining with the firm many years, he commenced business himself.' Business was so successful that the Lichfield Street factory was inadequate and the Globe Works was erected a few years ago. The business is now run by his three sons.'

'Moss, Stone & Company of Imperial Leather Works, Butts Road was founded in 1898 by Mr Alfred Moss. The firm manufactured saddlery of all kinds and specialised in light saddlery for racing, steeple-chasing, exercising, and polo, which was used in the principal races and polo clubs. Another product, solely manufactured by the company was the patent ventilated, extremely light saddle invented by Robson of York.

In 1913 the company acquired the old established business of the late Mr Thomas Ash, Paragon Works, Walsall, together with the goodwill, patents, trademarks and manufacturing rights. The company also produced fancy leather goods including purses, pocket books, jewel cases, music cases, camera cases, attaché cases, suit cases, watch guards, wristlets, braces and men's belts, blotters, dog collars, leads, and dog sheets.

The firm was also a large Government contractor, making all kinds of military saddlery, harness, and equipment for the War Office, and patented a side saddle called the 'Climax', and a saddle called the 'Eldonian'. The firm was bought by Jeffries in 1987. The London Offices were at 63, Queen Victoria Street.'

Saddle and harness makers

Merry and Company (saddlemakers)

1883-1951 Records include letter books, ledgers, account books, wages books, order books containing clients' names, notes of their requirements (whips, racing equipment, sporting gear, etc.) and correspondence.

Walker & Aldridge Saddle Makers, Huddersfield

1919-1940 Financial records. Held at West Yorkshire Archives.

Samuel Nash, saddle tree maker and grocer, Great Missenden

1829-1842 Large ledger also used as maths exercise book with additional memoranda of sermons given at Great Missenden, Kingshill and Aylesbury gaol chapels, 1839-42, with other religious notes, memoranda and books.
Held at the Centre for Buckinghamshire Studies. Aylesbury.

Thomas Bradford, harness and saddle maker, Aylesbury

1830-1834 Business records. Held at the Centre for Buckinghamshire Studies. Aylesbury.

101. Raban & Co Trade Journal advertisement.

CHAPTER FOUR
Glove Making

The word glove is thought to come from Old Norse because gloves were first used by Vikings. Leather gloves have been worn for thousands of years. The unique properties of the leather allow for both a comfortable fit and useful grip for the wearer. The grain present on the leather and the pores present in the leather gives the gloves the unique ability to assist the wearer as he or she grips an object. As soft as a leather glove may be, its pores and grain provide a level of friction when 'gripped' against an item or surface.

Purpose of gloves

Gloves were invented out of a necessity to fulfil a specific function which has changed little as we reach modern times. It is thought that early cavemen used them as a crude mitten type of covering to complete an awkward or uncomfortable task. Since Roman times people have worn gloves initially made of linen and silk to eat meat to keep their hands clean and free of grease and juices. Insulation from the heat or cold or to prevent scratched hands while working with hostile materials, flint, stone or iron, meant gloves became a popular item and eventually became a fashionable one. Over the centuries uses for gloves increased and were used by many different people, in differing occupations. As the practice of falconry, archery and other occupations and sporting interests became popular in England, leather gloves began to be utilised and become an essential clothing accessory for protection. Today gloves are still manufactured along similar processes to those centuries earlier differing little in terms of shape and design to the first gloves made.

The popularity of gloves increased greatly when they became more of a fashion statement considered to be an essential accessory by members of the aristocracy and gentry. As royalty and the clergy started to wear gloves, initially in a symbolic nature, gloves started to become a statement of wealth and power.

The Dictionary of Etiquette published in the 19th century states:

> 'Gloves should be worn by a lady when walking out or driving, at tea dances, balls, dinner parties, the opera or theatre. Men should wear gloves in the street or at a ball, when paying a call, driving, riding and in church.'

In England the skins chiefly used in glove making were from sheep and goats. Leather used for glove making needed to be strong and tough yet supple enough to be comfortable to the wearer. Dressing of leathers for gloving took a fair amount of time. At one time the glovers themselves dressed the leather, hence in some areas we see evidence of leather dressers and glovers. Since the end of the 18th century, dressing has been undertaken mainly by curriers as a separate process.

Inventor of gloves

No one really knows who invented gloves as it is thought their inception came about through several inventors at around the same time. Necessity was probably the 'mother of invention'.

Gloves 12th - 16th century

It was not really until the late 11th early 12th century that glove making began to develop as a trade. Gloves started to evolve as different materials and designs were employed. It was after the Norman Conquest in England that gloves became a more popular clothing accessory.

The period between the 12th and 16th centuries saw the humble glove take on symbolic importance as well as practical significance in Britain.

In Britain when the glove making industry started they were made from local deer, sheep, or imported kidskins. Iron or chain mail gloves were also developed and used by Knights in warfare. Leather gloves were also used in both falconry and archery. Queen Elizabeth I made leather gloves fashionable for ladies in the 16th century.

Glove styles

Glove styles tended to be defined by social standing and earlier gloves were made in three and five fingered designs. three finger glove designs were referred to as 'country man's gloves' as early as the 15th century. The wearing of sheepskin gloves for protection has been documented in the middle ages as being worn by stone masons who used dangerous tools. Shepherds also wore three finger gloves known as split mittens.

Gloves and symbolism

The wearing of gloves also began to develop symbolic meanings. It was good social etiquette when approaching a person of high authority to remove the right hand glove as a mark of respect. A lady could show her affection or favouritism to a man by taking off her glove and offering her hand to him. In Freemasonry the glove plays an important symbolic role. Freemasons believe that the glove alludes to the purification of life. The tradition of wearing gloves for Holy Sacrament by Roman Catholic bishops became a religious ritual and as early as the 10th century for which purpose popes, cardinals and bishops wore gloves.

Glove making

The earliest forms of gloves were most likely a 'mitten like' design made from animal skins and seem to have originated in the Northern Hemisphere to protect its wearer from the cold winters or to protect their hands from cuts, grazes and blisters when using crude flint tools. Gloves have also been found in Egyptian pyramids being a linen pair discovered in the tomb of King Tutankhamen dating back to 1,400 years BC. Pharaohs are known to have worn gloves as a symbol of their power and position and some Egyptian women wore gloves as part of their beauty enhancement. They used fragrant oils and honey on their hands before wearing silk gloves to protect them.

As time progressed glove making became an art and the mitten designs were improved incorporating the use of fingers to provide greater freedom and control of the hands while wearing them. As early as the 11th century the glove industry was started in Britain with the earliest trade guild being established and preceding the Worshipful Company of Glovers.

Glove making has always required the skilled hand and eye of the craftsman. The craft did not undergo mechanisation in the 19th century unlike so many other textile industries. Even today the most important elements of glove making remain almost entirely dependent on the dexterity of the skilled artisan.

The component parts in a leather glove are one pair of tranks, one pair of thumbs, four whole fourchettes, four half fourchettes, two gussets, and six quirks. Depending on the style of the glove there may also be roller pieces, straps, rollers, eyelets, studs, sockets and domes. Finally, linings will themselves consist of tranks, thumbs and fourchettes.

A skilled glove cutter normally served a seven year apprenticeship under the guidance of a master cutter. A glove cutter required two essential characteristics; a keen eye and dexterous hands. Many of the skills our ancestors would have practiced are still required today. To make a glove requires over thirty different processes many of which are still undertaken by hand.

It all starts with the selection of the correct type of leather. No two pieces of leather are the same and contain subtle variations in shading, markings etc. The glover would have chosen carefully for each pair of gloves, the quality depending upon the eventual use. The selection process needed a keen eye as things like grain, texture, thickness and strength had to be determined. When the skins first came from the leather dressers they were washed in cold water and then in warm water mixed with egg yolks after which a barelegged man physically entered the tub and trod on the leather for a period of about two hours. The leathers were then taken out of the tubs and spread out to dry. This made the leather hard following which they were 'staked' to smooth and soften them so they could be used to make the gloves.

Gloves needed to fit correctly and hands were measured so that the cutting was finite. The glover had to be aware of careful shaping and stretching of the leather so the gloves fitted perfectly when finished. The leather was preliminary stretched and manipulated so it could be cut correctly to form the glove. To do this the skins were slightly dampened by laying between layers of damp sawdust and then pulled to the maximum length of give. When the skin was pulled tight the cutter used his skill to use the most economical widths.

Intuition from experience and the cutters' skills in manipulating the leathers were considered to be the essentials of a cutter's art. If this was not undertaken correctly it was said in the trade that he 'loses all and the shears have dined before the master'. It is only when this process has taken place that the glove can be 'tranked' or cut.

Gloves were made to a pattern which was a thick flat piece of card shaped to fit the hand to which the finished glove was to be applied. The patterns varied according to the type of leather being used. All leathers have a natural stretch so the patterns were adapted as such. Many patterns used originally have been adapted to around 20 different modern sizes used today. Up to the mid-1840s gloves were generally sewn by hand using the wooden donkey. The invention of the gloving donkey by James

Winter of Stoke Sub Hamden, Somerset in 1807 revolutionised the process. The gloving donkey consisted of a clamp with evenly spaced brass teeth which held the glove and enabled the sewer to sew evenly and more quickly. It was an ingenious invention which gave consistency and quality to gloves only to be superseded after 1845 by a machine invented by Elias Howe which replaced the 'donkey' and undertook mechanical sewing. However the skill of the glover was still needed in its operation and more importantly in the initial hand cutting.

102. Women seemstresses employed by glove makers.

Stitching of gloves whether by hand or machine depended upon the style and weight of the leather used. The two most common methods of stitching were the prickseam whereby the sewing is exposed on the outside of the glove, or the inseam where the sewing is on the inside so the stitching is invisible when worn.

As a fashion item gloves were not always plain and decoration to the back of the glove and the upper side was needed. Fancy stitching and/or embroidery, the incorporation of buttons or brass fittings and other trimmings had to be incorporated.

Most gloves also needed to be lined and the way in which linings were incorporated affected the final appearance of the glove. Silks, cashmere and sheepskins were the most common linings used. Many glovers made the linings as a second pair of gloves before inserting them in the actual glove. The lining was inserted using a former.

When the glove was complete it had to be ironed known as 'laying out'. This was another hand process which could either make or spoil a pair of gloves. To aid the process 'dolly sticks' were inserted into the glove with a damp cloth before a special iron was applied. In later years machinery took over the laying out process and instead of the dolly stick being used the gloves are placed over an electrically heated brass hand (hence the standardisation to about 20 sizes in modern glove production). Once ironed the gloves are ready to be used.

103. Modern gloves made using a glove mould/press.

Ladies' glove styles

Ladies' gloves for formal and semi-formal wear came in three lengths: matinee or wrist, elbow, or opera or evening gloves. Leather gloves for women became an integral piece of women's clothing. The longer ladies leather gloves that reached beyond the elbow were popular at the opera (hence their name) where they could be shown off and were also termed as evening gloves. One peculiarity was that women tried to fit their hands into gloves a size too small. Gloves became so popular that it was considered bad manners to be seen without wearing gloves.

Different leathers were used for different gloves:

Cowhide: was often used for lower quality gloves. This leather was generally considered too thick and bulky for the majority of fashion glove styles; it was used for falconry and archery gloves.

Deerskin: had the benefit of great strength and elasticity, but had a more rugged appearance, with more grain on the surface,

Goatskin: was occasionally used for gloves. It was hard-wearing but coarser than other leathers and was normally used for cheaper gloves.

Hairsheep: originates from species of sheep that grow hair, not wool. The leather was finer and less bulky than many other leathers. Its major benefits were softness of touch, suppleness, strength, and lasting comfort. It was very durable and is frequently used for dress gloves.

*Peccary: wa*s the rarest and most luxurious glove leather. It was very soft, difficult to sew, but extremely hard-wearing.

Sheepskin was widely used for casual and country gloves.

Slink lamb was used only in the most expensive lambskin gloves.

Materials used for lining gloves included:

Cashmere: was warm, light in weight, and very comfortable to wear. Cashmere came from the hair of mountain goats, whose fleece is mellowed by exposure to extreme weather conditions.

Silk: was warm in winter and cool in summer and was used both in men's and women's gloves, but was more popular in women's.

Wool: was well known for its natural warmth and comfort, as well as having a natural elasticity.

Did your ancestor commit a crime?

Criminals have also been known to wear leather gloves whilst carrying out their crimes. The gloves were worn by criminals for the same reason that people wear them as a fashion item or for work; because the tactile properties of the leather allow for good grip and dexterity. The grain present on the surface of leather makes the surface of the leather as random as human skin since leather is also skin; forensic scientists were able to dust for the glove prints left behind from the leather the same way in which they dust for fingerprints today. In the early police forces of the Victorian period and before the invention of fingerprints this process detected many crimes and was thought to be the forerunner of fingerprint detection processes.

The Worshipful Company of Glovers

A guild existed well before 1349, the date when the company's first formal ordinances were made. No glove maker was to be admitted to the Freedom of the City without consent of the Wardens. The ordinances also fixed the price of sheepskin gloves at a penny per pair and ordained that gloves must not be sold by candlelight as 'folk could not tell whether they were of good or bad leather or lawfully or falsely made'. The latter, described in another document as '*naughtie and deceitefulle gloves*' could be confiscated or destroyed by order of the Wardens.

104. Worshipful Company of Glovers.

With the decline in trade, the Glovers amalgamated with the Pursers in 1501 and were taken over by the Leathersellers Company in 1502. The changes in fashion during the reign of Elizabeth I and later in the 17th century allowed the Glovers to prosper so they became an independent company again and their status was confirmed by a new charter granted in 1639 by Charles II. Their hall was established in 1662 at Beech Lane, Cripplegate.

The next couple of centuries saw many social and economic changes. The move to the suburbs by the middle classes and the Industrial Revolution meant that the glovers' workshops of the City were being replaced by factories away from the City so much so that the livery fell significantly during the latter part of the 18th century and the hall was surrendered as the company was unable to maintain it.

These changes and declines in wealth affected most of the City livery companies. Today they maintain strong links with their trade, provide educational bursaries and are heavily involved in charity programmes. It maintains a collection of gloves dating from the 16th century to the modern day.

Records of the Worshipful Company of Glovers

Records are held by the City of London Joint Archive Service at the Guildhall Library and comprise:

Freedom Registers 1738-1851 (unindexed).

No freedom records available for the years 1680-1737 and 1852-1940. It may be worth looking at the City poll books, listing liverymen, and covering a number of years from 1700 to 1734.

Apprenticeship Bindings 1694-1794 (includes Orphans Tax Book).

Apprenticeships 1675-1679, 1735-1748, 1766-1804.

This listing also exists in printed format *London Livery Company Apprenticeship Registers Vol. 4* published by the Society of Genealogists.

Court Minutes 1675-1679, 1773-1804, 1941-1970 (the earlier volumes include quarterage books).

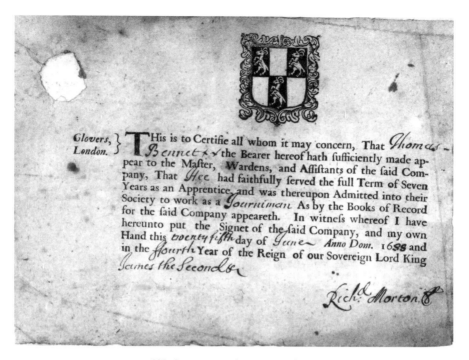

Glovers, London. THis is to Certifie all whom it may concern, That *Thomas Bennet* the Bearer hereof hath sufficiently made appear to the Master, Wardens, and Assistants of the said Company, That *Hee* had faithfully served the full Term of Seven Years as an Apprentice, and was thereupon Admitted into their Society to work as a *Journiman* As by the Books of Record for the said Company appeareth. In witness whereof I have hereunto put the Signet of the said Company, and my own Hand this *twenty fifth* day of *June* Anno Dom. 1688 and in the *fourth* Year of the Reign of our Sovereign Lord King *James the Second &*

Rich: Morton

105. Journeyman admission certificate.

The Skinners and Glovers Company of Newcastle upon Tyne

The establishment of the Skinners Company was January 1437. The society was to meet on a Tuesday after Michaelmas every year to choose their stewards and pass their accounts.

The Glovers' Society records commence in 1648 noted by renting part of the Skinners' meeting-house, at the annual rent of five shillings. The Glovers appear to have been incorporated with the Skinners around 1703-1705.

The first official notification of them joining the Skinners was when in 1712, the meeting-house, on the west side of the Blackfriars, was repaired at their joint expense. The Ordinances of the Glovers' Society, dated January 1436, enjoined them to go together in procession at the feast of Corpus Christi, in a livery, and play their part at their own charge; to choose annually three stewards; that apprentices should serve seven years, on pain of forfeiting 6s.8d. 'to the light of the said craft;' that no Scotsman born should be taken apprentice, nor allowed to work in the town, under penalty of 40s.

On 12 April 1643, at the quarter sessions held at the Guild Hall at Newcastle upon Tyne, information was made against William Ramsey, button-maker, for tagging of points, which was proved to be part of the glovers' trade, and he was tried by jury. Ramsey was fined forty shillings, and the charges of the court.

Records of the Skinners and Glovers Company

These are held at the Tyne and Wear Archives and comprise:

Order Books including some lists of members 1471-1783, 1901-1958.
Court Minutes 1813-1868..
Apprenticeship Bonds 1624-176.
Membership and Quarterage Books 1741-1742.

Glove Maker Trade Guilds

Chester Glovers Guild

Chester has had trade guilds for 800 years. In a document dated 1190-1193, the Earl of Chester confirmed the citizens' Guild Merchant. Individual craft companies, or guilds, later developed to protect the interests and welfare of the merchants and craftsmen of Chester.

Among the earliest guilds to emerge were the Tanners, who are first mentioned in 1361 but 19 Guilds are listed in a book of 1475-1476.

Originally there was only one Guild, the Guild Merchant. During the Middle Ages each craft gradually set up its own guild, to protect the interests of its own craftsmen.

The Guilds reflect the economic life of Chester in the Medieval and Tudor periods. Leather work formed the largest group of occupations and many guilds were associated with the leather trade (tanners, skinners, glovers, saddlers, cordwainers).

Sometimes craftsmen involved in the same trade worked in the same part of town. Shoemakers Row was in Northgate Street, Mercer's Row in Bridge Street Row East and the Skinner's Houses were between the Castle and the River Dee.

No craftsman or trader could work in Chester unless he was a freeman and a member of the relevant guild.

Apprentices served at least seven years to learn their trade. They could then become freemen of the City and then seek admission to the appropriate craft guild.

To become a freeman, a man had to be the son of a freeman, have served his apprenticeship to a freeman or be admitted by order of the City Assembly.

The guilds were always quite small, varying in size from 20 to 60 members. Women could not become freemen, but widows of guild members who carried on the family business could be admitted to a guild.

The guilds controlled the economic life of Chester. A craftsman had to be a member of a guild to set himself up in business and he could practice no other craft than his own. Outsiders could only trade in the City, if they paid tolls or came to the special fairs held in the summer and autumn.

Glovers are recorded in Chester from 1380 and stewards of their company are named in a Pentice Court roll in 1445.

In October 1562, when one of their members, John Harvey, was elected a Sherriff of Chester, they were involved in a serious dispute; some of the company were summoned to Ludlow to appear before the Council in the Marches of Wales.

Glove making was long said to have been one of Chester's staple industries and survived the destruction of all the glovers' houses under the walls of the City in the siege during the Civil War.

The Company had its own meeting house by the City walls at the east end of Duke Street. By 1835 it had 22 members.

Wet glovers produced their gloves in leather; dry glovers used other materials, such as cloth.

Records of glovers held by Cheshire Archives include oaths and orders; accounts, 1630-1792; admissions of new members, 1630-1799; enrolments of apprenticeship indentures, 1630-1720.

Oxford Glovers Guild

The glovers' guild was in existence in 1461, when it was paying for lights in Trinity Chapel in All Saints' Church; the glovers' mass on Trinity Monday continued until the 1520s. In 1531 the university included the glove makers in a list of guilds which, it claimed, were upheld by the town illegally.

The glovers were incorporated by the city with the approval of the assizes in 1562. The cause of that action was said to be the recent import into the city of gloves of inferior quality apparently sold as Oxford gloves, to the 'infamy and disworship' of the city. In future only gloves sown and cut in the city and suburbs were to be sold there. Only freemen of the city and company were to make gloves or trade in the raw materials. Imported gloves discovered during guild searches were confiscated.

Glovers were forbidden to work anywhere else except at a company member's house or shop. None were to keep more than three or four apprentices, who should first be presented to the company's officers. There were fines for non-attendance at meetings and for verbal abuse and imprisonment and fines for disobeying officers, who in turn could be fined for negligence or partiality. Quarterage was 4d. for each member. Disputes arising out of the ordinances, or changes to them, were to be dealt with at the assizes.

In 1594 the city council agreed that for ten years no foreign glover would be admitted free for less than £5.4s.6d. and only then with the company's approval; further agreements relating to foreign glovers were made in 1617, 1630 and 1647. The council allowed the company to apply to the justices for new ordinances in 1604 and 1669. The company was permitted in 1714 to invoke the city by-laws against foreign glovers and was last mentioned in 1728. A sermon in All Saints' Church, known as the glovers' sermon was preached annually and was still preached in 1844.

Glove Making as a Cottage Industry

Worcester's gloving industry reached its peak between 1790 and 1820 when 150 manufacturers of gloves employed over 30,000 people in and around Worcester. At this time nearly half of all glovers in Britain were based in and around the city of Worcester.

The glove making trade was very much a cottage industry in the areas around Worcestershire, Herefordshire, Yeovil in Somerset and Woodstock in Oxfordshire mainly involving women and children. In many cases glove making bore resemblances to all the other cottage industries practiced around the country. In the Worcester area it was common for the children to work with their mother at home rather than to attend a gloving school. A girl from Evesham was interviewed in connection with the Children's Employment Commission in 1864, stating that she had been gloving for more than six years and she worked at home with mother. They usually worked from 8am to dusk but never worked by candlelight At another house in Evesham a mother and two daughters were similarly employed. As a group the workers made six pairs of best men's gloves a day and were paid at the rate of 3s.6d. or 3s.9d. a dozen, with 7d. a dozen if they did the pointing as well.

In the Woodstock area of Oxfordshire the girls worked in either the cottage industry at home or in one of the local glove factories. The factory children in the late 19th century worked generally from the age of ten from 8am to 8pm on simple tasks with a weekly wage of about 2s.6d. In order to keep their sewing neat the girls used a brass machine which held the gloves in a vice, and had a row of little holes through which the needle passes keeping the stitches uniformed.

In East Chinnock, the glove making was slightly different and done on a 'school' basis where girls were at work at their machines. The cottages were clean but slightly stuffy and in the main belonged to respectable women. It is unlikely that all of the employers however treated the children well. There were frequent complaints that eyes had suffered, many being able to see well at the start of the week but by the end of the week the eyes had become tired. In one case when a girl's eyes felt bad, the woman would not let her look up from her work and thought it was laziness, so she used to slap her on the head in order to keep her at her work.

At the time of the 1851 Census of Population there had been 1,683 female glove makers aged five to fourteen in full time employment mostly in cottages. By 1871 their numbers had fallen by more than half to 764 and the trend continued downward as the century progressed.

Records of glove making existed at Ilchester from around 1212. It was a major occupation in the Yeovil area from at least the 4th century. In 1378 an Act of Parliament allowed leather gloves to be exported. Then in 1382 gloves were permitted to be exported from Bristol free of taxes. By 1793 gloving had become 'a great trade' and around 1834, three hundred thousand pairs of gloves were made annually in the Yeovil area.

The effects of the Victorian wars, the coming of the railways and the Agricultural depression of the 1870s, which released labourers from the land to work in the factories, meant a period of considerable expansion within the local industry. In the early 9th century around 20,000 people were employed in gloving in and around Yeovil. In 1822 the majority of families in Yeovil earned their living from glove making which remained the town's principal industry until the end of the 19th century and continued to thrive until the outbreak of the Second World War. In 1952 the area was still responsible for half of England's glove production.

During the 19th century the trade involved all the family. The father was a pattern maker and cutter. Sons were frequently formally apprenticed to him or another as cutters and the females of the family were sewers. Girls frequently sewed from the age of seven or eight and were often employed before that to 'tie off the threads'. It was traditionally a trade that relied heavily on women, many working part time from home as a cottage industry to produce the goods. Homes were supplied by a 'bagwoman' who distributed raw materials and collected the finished items.

In areas where factories came into existence, boys from the age of ten were employed in the workshops pressing out the thumb pieces or packing. Then from the age of 12-13 years they were apprenticed to the factory cutters rather than their own fathers.

By 1856 fully employed glove cutters earned 25s.0d. to 30s.0d. per week, Women sewers earned 4s.0d. to 6s.0d. per week mainly part time and girls under 14 years earned around 2s.6d. per week. Apprentice cutters were paid around 17s.0d. per week.

During the First World War many glove factories were engaged to manufacture officer's gloves and khaki puttees.

The process used in the cottage industry varied little from that in the factories. Leather was delivered to the cottage with instructions as to the type of glove to be made and the size. An oblong piece of leather was cut and inserted into a punch of the appropriate size, driven by a hand press. The same punch marked the stitching holes for the 'points', the three rows of stitching running down the back of each glove. The glove was then cut and the men's work was then finished at which point the women and girls stepped in, sewing together the completed item. Finally the gloves were put on a hot last, finished off, ironed, polished and packed in boxes in dozens.

Historically, the mortality rate in the industry was fairly high and consumption was the main disease that women and children suffered from because of conditions in which they worked. The hours were also long and not conducive to good health. Even as late as the 1920s girls worked from 5am to 8pm, with an hour for lunch, and then often had to take ten dozen gloves home to 'tie off' the ends and all for 21s.2d. per dozen.

Men were the mainstay of the work force, even though it was heavily dependent on the women for the sewing. The male 'cutters' were frequently self-employed, working in a dedicated room or a shed in the back yards of their homes. This was an experienced job and initially cutters served a seven year apprenticeship. By 1934 the term for an apprenticeship had been reduced to four years.

There is a record of glove-making in Dorset as early as the 14th century and the industry was certainly an established trade in Bridport in the 15th and 16th centuries. Glovers were also working in Beaminster, Cerne Abbas, Bere Regis and Sturminster.

Until the industrial revolution however, glove making in Dorset was like elsewhere, a cottage or home-based occupation. Demand for the product was seasonal. By the early 19th century the leatherworks in Yeovil were dispatching leather to women glovers in Sherborne for sewing. It is likely that the town acted as a distribution centre, sending leather to cottage workers living in the surrounding villages. At Cerne skins were also prepared for parchment and other leather goods.

In 1851 the census showed 1,686 people in Dorset as glovers. The 1891 census shows the number of glovers recorded in the county had fallen to 422 of whom only 31 were men, a similar downward trend to that elsewhere in the country.

In the 1930s there was still a glove-making industry in Sherborne with H Blake & Sons, Seager Bros and Stewart Adams & Sons as the prominent manufacturers. Chester Jefferies and Fownes Bros were at Gillingham in the 1930s and George Baker was in Beaminster in 1922. Dent, Allcroft and the Goldcroft Glove Company were also operating in Sturminster at the time. On the Hampshire/Dorset border, cottagers were still making gloves only instead of using leather were making 'Ringwood Gloves' knitted from soft string.

In Walsall the glove industry developed after the First World War to combat the decline in the saddlery and harness trade. The first specialist glove manufacturer in the town was D Power and Sons. Many of the glove cutters were recruited from Yeovil in Somerset and by 1940 there were six glove manufacturers in the town.

The industry was an important source of local employment for women particularly up to the 1960s but increasing foreign competition forced the remaining glove makers either to close down or build 'niche' markets for such items as golf and cycling gloves.

Glovers records in archives

Throughout the United Kingdom various records exist in local record offices. The use of on-line catalogues will enable searches to be made before a visit. The following is a brief sample selection of records available so it is important to contact the local record office covering the area of origin of your glove making ancestors.

Dorset History Centre
Gillingham Glove Factory - photographs mid-20th century.
Business records of William Bide, glover of Yeovil c.1805-1892.

Oxfordshire County Record Office
Apprenticeship records, Recognisances, various deeds relating to glovers (principally of Woodstock).

Bicester glove industry c.1865.

Records relating to Woodstock glove makers including Josiah Nutt Godden, Thomas Osborne and the Buckingham family.

Somerset Record Office

Patter book of Harold Lilley, glove maker c.1930.

Clark Son & Morland, Street and Glastonbury, business records.

Worcestershire Archives

1810 licence to Jacob Parker and John Parker glovers.

Bankruptcy discharge papers for Richard Lane & Son glove manufacturers Worcester c.1838.

Records of the Worcestershire Association of Glove Manufacturers 1918-1947.

Cheshire Archives

Records of the Company of Glovers Chester.

Harold Ashley, Shepton Mallet, glove maker

1919-1939 Order and Pattern Book. Held at Somerset Archives

Oral history recording of Marjorie Wilkes of Tintinhull, glove-maker

Includes details on her work as a glover, her apprenticeship, making gloves and instructing other girls how to make them, working for the firm of Southcombes, working as an outworker, looking after her family while working, and making gloves to supply the Army and RAF during World War Two.

Somerset Heritage Centre

Worcester Glovers' Company

1571-1786 Also includes the following trades: Glovers, Whitlawers, Pouchmakers, Pursers, Saddlers, Pewterers, Brasiers and Plummers.

Volume containing the minutes of annual and quarterly meetings, 1571-1662, including the election of officers and accounts; apprentice bindings 1571 - 1660; fines for non-attendance at meetings 1626-1641; lists of journeymen, 1592 and 1605; admittances of Freemen 1614-1662; ordinance passed at the annual assembly in 1642 forbidding the making of gloves from linen cloth or fustian; and a note that no meetings were held in 1637 due to an outbreak of plague.

CHAPTER FIVE
Other Leather Trades

L eather was also used in a variety of other trades and for the manufacture of balls, hats, drive belts, sporrans etc. Our ancestors may have been involved in the manufacture of such commodities and this chapter explains some of the processes they may well have been involved with.

Cricket ball makers

The manufacture of cricket balls was one of the oldest industries in Tonbridge, Kent and appears to have begun following the decline in the saddle making industry. The River Medway was good for tanning the leather, hence the area had a natural resource. In the early years of the 19th century Thomas Martin first made cricket balls in a workshop above Teston post office. The business was taken over by Alfred Reader who opened the factory in the 1820s that produced 1,400 balls per week. The workers of the Reader factory formed one of the smallest trade unions in the country.

106. Thomas Martin later Alfred Reader possibly the oldest cricket ball maker.

Cricket balls have a core of cork known as a quilt, layered with tightly wound string and further strips of cork in layers. At each point the quilt is placed in a metal mould and hammered into shape. The leather is then applied cut into quarters and the edges of each quarter are bevelled to prevent the seam from standing proud and these are lapped and sewn together. The leather covering is made of four pieces of leather segmented like the shape of the peel of a quartered orange, but one half is rotated by 90 degrees. The half covers are fitted into a powerful vice thus temporarily compressing the ball after which it is placed in a horn for final sewing. All cricket balls have six rows of stitching around the main circumference with the remaining two joints between the leather pieces left unstitched. This stitching is said to provide a better grip for the bowler.

Each and every manufacturer had its secret process as it was thought the way the balls were structured affected their performance. Most cricket ball used best cowhide as a covering. Often soft items like feathers or worsted were included with the cork to provide greater spin and bounce. Cricket ball makers on the shop floor who also often played the game frequently disputed this and many other theories. However cricketers had a preference for and used a particular type of ball when playing matches.

It was not unusual for cricket ball makers to make and use their own tools. Often cog wheels from clocks were used to set the stitching intervals to give a ball a perfect stitch. Seam stitching used multiple pieces of thread and boars' hair tied together impregnated with bees' wax and hooked over a nail. Bees' wax was run up and down the thread.

Some of the Tonbridge ball makers amalgamated to fight off competition from foreign makers and other companies setting up elsewhere in England. They became Tonbridge Sports Industries and included local established firms such as Dukes, Surridge, Wisden, and Tworts. The company, Readers, did not become part of the organisation.

107. Trade advertisement for Ives & Son.

Dukes was thought to be the oldest company to make balls. The origins of Dukes cricket ball making can be traced back to the year 1760 when production started in the Tonbridge area of Kent. Dukes' cricket balls have a distinctive dark red colour. Making cricket balls was a highly skilled job and the skills were refined and handed down through the generations. Craftsmen at Dukes who nearly always learned their craft having served apprenticeships, used only the best raw materials. Although modern cricket balls use new technological processes the same traditional processes are still used with many still being hand sewn.

Cricket balls are manufactured in various designs. Four of the main cricket balls designs in the UK are Kookaburra, Slazenger, Readers and Gunn and Moore. All manufactured balls are suitable for training and matches.

108. Section through a cricket ball.

Alfred Reader, have been manufacturing cricket balls for over 200 years. They now make about 29 different styles all with variations on colours and sizes. Hard balls are used for both matches and training while soft balls are solely for training.

Trade union membership in this highly specialised field was never very great and had largely been confined to one factory in Kent. Cricket balls were made in the area around Tonbridge from around 1760 to 1994, and the history of trade unionism among the skilled leather workers who made the balls began in 1898, when 180 employees at Alfred Reader formed the Amalgamated Society of Cricket Ball Makers. The last remaining factory in the area is believed to be that of Timothy Duke.

The union originally held its meetings at the Mitre Hotel in Tonbridge, but in the early 20th century moved its gatherings to the Station Tavern. Membership peaked in 1906 when the union strength was 216 members. By 1912 the first surviving annual returns to the Registrar of Friendly Societies recorded membership as 163 and all of them were males. In 1912 the union's largest items of expenditure was in unemployment, travel and emigration pay to 14 members.

This small union played its part in the wider trade union movement as the same return indicates that it was a member of the Tonbridge Trades Council, the General Federation of Trade Unions and the Labour Party. It had also undertaken financial commitments to the Birmingham Trades and Labour Council, to furniture workers and to the Transport Workers Federation in support of the various disputes that they were involved in.

109. Living wage for cricket ball makers - the smallest union.

The union had no branches and only served Readers' employees. It did, however, elect shop stewards who collected subs from members on a monthly basis.

At that time, the return named H M Heath, president, F Boorman secretary with Frederick Wells and Horace Orrom senior as trustees. It is assumed that these were employees of Readers.

The auditors were Fred Belcher and C E Cockerell, both of whom were also shown to be cricket ball makers.

The First World War disrupted the trade union just as much as any other aspect of life at home. The war also caused other problems particularly in relation to the union being unable to fully account for strike money paid during 1914 because many were serving on the front. There was also a dispute relating to poor book-keeping and this could not be clarified with the former secretary and the union's management. These problems led to the formation of the Teston Independent Society of Cricket Ball Makers in 1919, a breakaway group of former members of the original union.

By the time the union was wound up in 1948 it had only eight members left each of whom was required to hold one or other of the union's official positions.

In the early post war years the TUC attempted to facilitate mergers between other unions working throughout the leather goods industry.

The Teston Independent Society of Cricket Ball Makers continued for a further fifty or so years, within which time it attempted to diversify and recruit workers making and distributing sports goods and equipment, a venture which was not completely successful. The Independent Society finally ceased in 2005.

Leather football makers

It is thought that the modern round leather football owes its design to Joseph Pracey who was based in London around the turn of the 20th century. His ball design was centred around six equal sided leather panels so the ball when in use was not misshapen.

In making the football, the sections were stretched and then assembled to be sewn by hand, leaving gaps so the ball could be turned the right way out at which point a tongue was sewn in (like the tongue of a shoe). This was to enable a bladder to be inserted and to hide it when the ball was laced.

A tool known as a ball squeezer was used which incorporated a screw type press to hold the sections together while they were being sewn. This squeeze was adjustable so it could be used for both oval (rugby) and round (foot) balls.

Records in archives

Alfred Reader & Co 1875-1977 staff and business records. These are privately held but access is through the Kent History Centre at Maidstone.
Amalgamated Society of Cricket Ball Makers - various records (early 20th century) held at the People's History Museum.
Cricket Ball Makers Society - member records and annual reports - early 20th century held at People's History Museum.

Leather fancy goods

The development of saddlery and harness stimulated the manufacture of other leather goods from the late 18th century. In 1752 a Walsall saddler began to make leather upholstery and by 1834 four other firms in the town were involved in production. Leather ancillaries for riders and travellers were produced by the saddlers and harness-makers throughout most of the 19th century and they later diversified into making purses and cigar cases. Many bridle-cutters diversified and began to supply straps and bandaleroes for the army during the Napoleonic Wars.

The depression in the saddlery trade in the late 19th century accelerated the manufacture of fancy and light leather goods as an independent trade, and the diversity of products increased to items such as dog collars, razor straps, whips, gaters, blotters, small containers and even early condoms. By 1886 some firms were also making bicycle saddles. The manufacture of fancy leather articles really took off at the beginning of the 20th century. In 1910, 42 firms were making leather goods, and just a decade later the number had more than doubled. The leather goods industry continued to prosper in the 1920s and 1930s, though during the Second World War many leather goods firms seem to have reverted to saddlery.

The change of emphasis from saddlery to other leather goods in the late 19th and early 20th centuries had little effect on the siting of the industry because most firms remained in the same premises due to economic restraints. It is feasible therefore that an ancestor formerly listed as a saddle maker could have become a fancy goods maker or followed a similar occupation.

After the end of the Second World War and through the 1950s the leather goods industry suffered as a result of competition from abroad together with the use of artificial and synthetic substitutes. As such the number of firms producing the goods had fallen significantly.

110. Trade advertisement for a fancy leather goods maker.

Leather crafting was the practice of making leather into craft objects or works of art, using shaping and colouring techniques.

Leather dyeing involved the use of alcohol based dyes where alcohol was absorbed into the moistened leather which carried the dye pigment into the surface, the effect of which was to give contrasts depending upon the tooling or pattern which had been set into the leather. Modern techniques use water based dyes. Shoe polish could also be used to dye and preserve leather as happens in the shoe finishing process although a wax paste frequently serves as a finishing coat. In some cases linseed oil was also applied. Specialist leather workers with a degree of artistic bent were employed in the art. Belts, sporrans, personal drinking flasks and bags alongside other fancy goods were frequently treated in this way.

Leather painting differs from dyeing because paint stays on the surface rather than being absorbed. Leather painting techniques were not used on items that could or must bend or are subject to friction, such as belts and wallets as the paint was likely to crack and flake off.

Leather carvers worked alongside the fancy goods makers and used specialist metal tools to compress moistened leather to give a three dimensional appearance. It was a highly skilled job although it did not usually come about as a result of an apprenticeship, rather than by 'on the job' training for those with a keen eye and an artistic bent.

Leather needed to be prepared a certain way for leather carvers to work the leather. The carver would first 'case' the leather by soaking it in water and then let it dry to the proper moisture level (and that depended upon the type of leather being used), thus making the leather easier to tool. If the leather was too dry the impressions fade over time and would usually not be to a consistent depth. If the leather was too wet, it would not hold its shape or definition. Properly cased leather was cool to the touch, and felt like a firm but wet clay felt. A damp sponge was used to maintain the moisture during the working of the carving.

The carving consisted of three basic procedures using tools to 'carve' leather including a swivel knife used in much the same way as a pencil is used, primarily to cut the initial pattern after which more specialist shaping tools were used such as veiners, bevellers, seeders and shaders. The other tools were struck with a wooden or hide mallet to add further definition to the cut lines.

When the leather had been properly cased, the carver used the swivel knife to make the bold cuts about half the thickness of the leather forming the basis of the carved image but depending on the effect the carver wanted to create.

The carver then used a shader and beveller to compress one side of the cut creating an impression of depth. As a general rule, the outside of curves and the outside edge of anything overlapping another part of the design was beveled.

A process known as dress cutting was the final step in creating a carved design. The swivel knife was used to create intricate and decorative cuts in the design to enhance its appearance.

Leather bottle makers

Leather bottles were commonly in use in Great Britain from the 11th century to the time of the Crimean War. The best leather to use for leather bottles comes from the 'belly of the beast'. This is because belly leather is very stretchy.

Documentation regarding leather bottle making techniques is sketchy but the practices were controlled by guilds dating back to the 13th century. The earliest ordinances associated with the Guild of Cordwainers addressing the various leather-related industries dates to 1272. They mention very specifically the various trades by name including 'tanners, curriers, cordwainers, cofferers, workers in tan leather and workers in alum leather'. By the early 14th century, each of these crafts had developed into a specific guild. The Company of Botellars ordinances date from 1373.

111. Examples of early leather bottles.

English bottles looked like small kegs. Several such bottles were raised from the Mary Rose alongside a number of leather flasks. When bottle makers constructed leather bottles, flasks, and jacks, they used two distinctly different shaping forms: sand and wooden lasts.

Moulded leather vessels may date back to early Egyptian times when some pottery forms followed the shape and style of skin bags. An early Nubian pre-dynastic grave has revealed a leather vessel at the head of the occupant where a pottery one would normally be expected.

A Neolithic beaker was found at West Smithfield, London, made of tanned cowhide with some hair still attached. Britain has been the home of leather vessels for longer and in higher numbers than anywhere else in history. In 1848, near Buxton, a leather cup with a silver lip was found in a Saxon barrow.

In the village of Hallaton, Leicestershire the sport of bottle kicking was very popular. More recently made of wood, the bottle was originally made of leather making one wonder if this was the origin of the leather football.

In the Black Country during the early steel industry, the leather bottle became known as a black jack later called a piggin. A 'black jack' was a leather tankard, usually 5-10 inches in height, and formed by shaping the leather when wet over a wooden mould. The largest, which were used as jugs, were known as bombards which were thought to resemble a cannon in appearance. With a whistle attached to the handle it was used by thirsty steel workers to summon the water boy, hence the name piggin Whistle which became a popular pub name, The Pig and Whistle. In the Yorkshire mining town of Barnsley the same jacks had bells attached to the handle for similar use and were known as jingle boys.

During Elizabethan times, even wealthy merchant families would possess just one wine glass because of the then high cost of Venetian glass. It was used by all the family and would be refilled as needed by a man who stood in the corner of the room with a leather bottle. He was known as the botellar and it is believed that the butler is derived from this act. In the 14th century the makers of leather vessels in London were organised as the 'Guild of Botellars' but unfortunately there are no surviving records.

The leather bottle maker would first build a wooden last and frame, on which to shape the leather for the bottle, he would then sew the leather 'jacks' (leather parts) together when he had removed them from the last and then seal them with pitch and/or wax. The making of flasks does not seem to have used this technique. Instead, flasks were expanded using sand or air. This technique was also used for the shaping of leather for crest helms during the 15th century.

They were not always bottle-shaped - some were a simple tube of leather with the ends stitched up leaving enough of a seam to attach a shoulder strap, others were flask-shaped, and others were dumpy flagons. Originally the insides were treated with black pitch to keep them waterproof, and some had embossed coverings.

Basically the leather bottle, of whatever shape, was made using a simple process. The belly leather from pigs was generally used. The pattern of the bottle was then cut and the sections were over-stitched together. The leather was soaked in water, dried and filled with fine sand which was pounded into the joints and seams and left for a week. When the sand was removed the inside was 'pitched' to make the bottle waterproof. Pitch was made up of 50% beeswax and 50% pine or beech pitch. Hardwood bottle caps were made by hand.

Leather bottle makers became part of the Worshipful Company of Horners in 1475 having previously been an ancient trade guild. The trade has always been associated with London and in particular the area around Southwark.

Records of the Worshipful Company of Horners

Records held at the Guildhall Library include Freedom records from 1847. Apprenticeship records from 1634, Ordinance and Court books from 1373. Some records are restricted and need permission of the Company before being able to be searched.

Driving belt makers

With the advent of the Industrial Revolution and the steam engine in the 18th century, drive belts were the usual method of transmitting power from engine to machine and were necessary to achieve an economical output. The spinning wheel was probably the first machine to use motive power where a belt was needed to run from one wheel to another but these were made on a small scale at the time.

Drive belts were a common sight in the mills and manufacturing factories of the 1800 and 1900s up to the time electricity was used. Shoe factories in Northamptonshire were still using leather drive belts as late as 1960 although the drive belt industry went into decline from the 1930s. They were also common on the farms and were used where steam engines drove threshing and ploughing machines especially around harvest time. Coal mines also used leather belts in the early 1900s for conveyor systems.

Essentially leather drive belts had to be extremely strong but flexible enough to remain attached to both small and large pulley wheels. They needed to not slip and to last a long time. The belts were normally made from ox hide butts and were normally vegetable tanned rather than chrome tanned. They were usually cured with tallow or fish oil. The butts were cut into strips of the required width and length. The ends were tapered and the joints were then glued together and either hand sewn or riveted depending upon the degree of use they were to be exposed to. The edges of the belts were smoothed to prevent chaffing during use. This job required specialist skills and was undertaken by a 'burnisher', an occupation appearing in the Victorian census returns. Belt makers often worked in saddle and harness making companies or in a 'strap shop'.

Belt makers worked at long benches so the complete lengths of leather could be laid out flat. In the making, part of the belt was covered with a steel plate for its entire length. Some of these steel plates were over 40 ft in length. The plate was used as a bed for the belt to be flattened when flat cement could be applied. The joints were then compressed with a heavy mechanical roller. When this process was completed the belt was turned on its edge and laid in a slot which ran along the edge of the bench. This exposed the edges of the belt so that it could be burnished before the ends were joined together to make it continuous.

Leather hat makers

Stevedores, firemen, fishmongers, dustmen and policemen were amongst the occupations who wore leather hats. Alfred Doolittle father of Eliza as depicted in My Fair Lady wore a leather hat with a long leather flap running from the brim to cover the shoulders which was used as padding when carrying heavy or awkward shaped loads. In the 1800s protective hats worn by many trades were made of heavy leather but have now in the main been replaced by metal or plastic helmets. Firemen's helmets are a good example.

Although not a hat, leather was used in hat production to make the sweat bands which were sewn into the inside of the crowns of all men's hats and to some extent in women's hats as well. This helped to ensure a comfortable fit. The comfort of a hat was said to be determined by the quality of the leather used as well as its design and fit.

Beaver hats were made usually with the fur intact. In the 16th century the fur was removed and the beaver skin was used to make what is described as the modern top hat. Stove pipe hats and farm labourers' 'billycocks' were usually made from a combination of leather and beaver pelts. Today top hats are made from a mixture of fibre felts and 'silk'.

The process used by the leather hat maker was not that different from that used by any hat maker irrespective of the material used. The origin of the leather hat was not certain. The top hat became a fashion item around the same time that gloves became fashionable and in some areas the two trades were synonymous. During the latter part of the 18th century the silk topper was becoming common.

A body maker built the foundation of the hat using a pattern in which the leather was cut and treated with shellac or similar preservative. A 'blocker' did most of the build for the hat. A block was used as a mould when building up the sides to the crown of the hat and depended upon whether the hat was soft or hard. The blocker placed this into a spinner to enable the hat to be revolved during its making, varnishing and ironing if needed. When the main shape of the hat was formed the brim or collar was cut and built to form the brim with the crown and brim being married together, jointed and sewn to provide a one piece hat. The brims were shaped using hat irons and dummies as well as a brim gauge. The latter was particularly needed when the brim had to be the same width all around the hat.

The finisher then lined the hat with silk or felt and fitted the 'sweat band' which was cut to the shape of the brim of the crown. The lining was usually fixed using adhesive. In the 'industrial hats' calico or muslin was used as this helped to absorb the perspiration and hair oils rather than silk etc. which did not.

Where a topper was made or the hat required a specific shape to the brim the shaper took over from the finisher and introduced a stylish curl to the brims specifically using a brim shaping tool and hat planes. He also shaped the hat at the brow to fit the customer's head. It was not uncommon to have a head individually measured and a profile taken for a particular hat. Such a process was rarely used for working hats.

If necessary the trimmer covered the edges with braid or other decoration often relating to the particular trade or livery for which the hat was to be used.

Leather bookbinders

Leather used in book binding had many of the same preservation needs as for any other leather. However the leathers needed to be protected from handling damage to prevent the residues from getting on hands, clothes and the text block.

112. Leather has been used for centuries as a book binder.

Today our relations may well be involved in conservation and preservation of leather bound books as well as perhaps the re-covering but in bygone times they would have been binding the book from scratch.

There is no real way to be certain where the leather bookbinding craft originated. It was an evolving art encompassing techniques from a variety of cultures and civilisations.

The craft of bookbinding is believed to have originated in India with the binding of religious sutras which were originally copied on to palm leaves with a metal stylus like tool. The leaves were then dried and rubbed with ink and the finished leaves were given numbers, and bound together using two long twines threaded through each end through wooden boards, making what we today call a palm leaf book. When the book was closed, the excess twine would be wrapped around the boards to protect the manuscript leaves. Buddhist monks possibly pioneered the technique in the first century BC. Similar techniques were also to be found in ancient Egypt and in Spanish Latin America.

The modern English word *book* comes from the Proto-Germanic *'bokiz'*, referring to the beech wood on which early written works were recorded. The book was not used in ancient times, as writings were on scrolls often of considerable length either rolled or folded concertina style.

The origins of leather binding commenced with western books from about the 5th century. They were bound between hard covers with the pages made from parchment folded, sewn with strong cords and attached to wooden boards which were then covered with leather.

The earliest bookbinders used white leather (relating to the process of tawing - tanned leather using allum). Vegetable tanned goatskin and calfskin were later used.

Early books were handwritten on handmade material and their size and style varied considerably. Early and medieval books were bound with flat spines, and it was not until the 15th century that books began to have the 'modern' rounded spines that are still found today. The vellum and parchment pages up to the early 20th century (when paper became the more common medium), would react to humidity which would frequently cause the book to take on a wedge shape or cockle the covers. They were often secured with straps or metal clasps as we sometimes see on original parish registers and other books, used for record keeping.

The earliest known use of paper for pages of books in England occurred around the start of the 1300s but the first paper mill was not established until the end of the 15th century so it presupposes that paper was hand made before that date. From the late 15th century paper was used alongside parchment and generally replaced parchment, unless the books such as parish registers, legal books etc., were considered important documents.

The earliest surviving European bookbinding of this type dates from around 700 AD, known as the St Cuthbert Gospel house in the British Library.

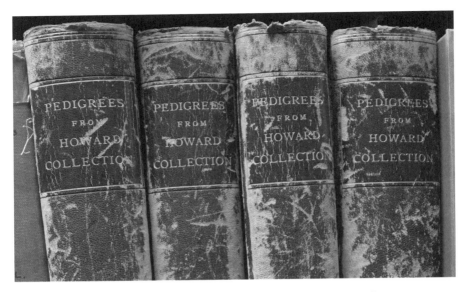

113. Leather showing deterioration which needs conservation skills.

Luxury books for the library had leather covers decorated, often all over, with tooling, blind stamps and small metal pieces of furniture. Until the end of the Elizabethan period, books were not stood end-on on shelves but were frequently laid flat. The most functional books were bound in plain white vellum over boards and had a title hand-written on the spine. We today associate leather bound books with gold leaf which was fixed under the tooling and stamps from the 15th century and thereafter. The gold-tooled leather binding has remained the conventional choice for high quality bindings. Binding and tooling were shared crafts of the leather bookbinder.

The edges of the books required the bookbinder to use his skills as decorator. The prime reason for the smooth finish to books was to protect the book from dirt and dust. Edge finishing was done with a solid colour, the dyes frequently being made from indigo, brazil wood or powdered earth (clays). Marbling became common in the 17-19th centuries and edge gilding became popular by the middle of the 17th century.

Bookbinders would often use dyed, grained or embossed leather for the covers into which 'blind tooling' was used. This was a process of indenting designs or words onto the cover without using gold gilt. Stamps were frequently mass produced and sold to bookbinders so that a design could be impressed into the leather.

114. Early bookbinding process undertaken by hand.

Although the advent of printed books vastly increased the style of bindings they did not change significantly. All that happened was that paper replaced the vellum and parchment.

Commercial bookbinding developed in the late 18th - early-19th centuries when books generally became cheaper as well as smaller. However the techniques used earlier were retained by the commercial binders and still exist today.

Bookbinders used five basic processes to complete their books.

Folding and Pressing: a process where paper inserts were folded, cut and pressed into shape, usually in 'quires'.

Sewing: where the sections were sewn together.

Fitting the Boards: sometimes known as Forwarding (this occupation was sometimes referred to in the census returns as 'Forwarder'). The spine was glued and the backing process was undertaken, the edges levelled and the cover boards were cut.

Covering: the leather was applied to the book.

Decoration: Edging, gilding etc were applied.

Bookbinding had used the long stitch technique for sewing together the sections of a book. There were various forms but the characteristic of them all was that they were glueless, although from the 1800s there were methods that did in fact utilise glue. This sewing method created a staggered line pattern visible on the spine.

A hardbound book had rigid covers and was stitched in the spine. The book consisted of a number of 'signatures' (folding of paper into 8, 16 or 32) bound together. Throughout the book, binding threads were visible at the centre of each signature contained within. Signatures of hardcover books were typically octavo, a single sheet folded three times, though they may also have been folio and/or quarto. Often the larger and heavier books, if of good quality, were wire bound.

A variation of the hardcover which is more durable is the calf-binding or more simply known as leather bound where the cover is either half or fully bound in leather from a calf, hence its name.

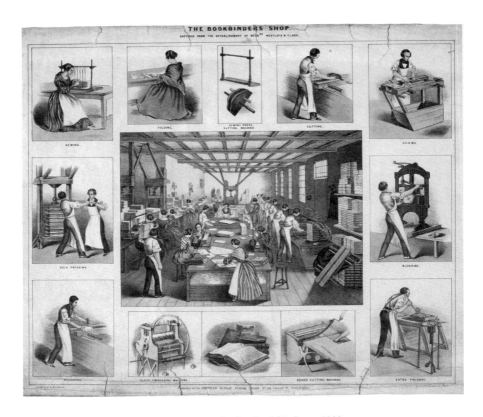

115. Processes in leather book binding c.1800.

There were a number of methods used to bind leather covered and hard bound books and this is the first stage that a bookbinder would have undertaken.

The signatures of the book are clamped together and small vertical holes are punched through the edge of each signature, and then they are sewn together with lock-stitches forming the text block. This method known as over sewing is a very strong method of binding and was used on books up to five inches thick. However, the margins of over sewn books are reduced and the pages will not lie flat when opened, often referred to as tight binding. This sometimes presents a problem to family historians when the writing in the close margin is hidden in the seam when thick books are opened.

The Smyth sewn method was where the signatures of the book were folded and stitched through the fold. The signatures were then sewn together at the spine to form a text block. In contrast to the over sewing method, Smyth sewn books had wide margins and could open completely flat. However, the text block of such books was not very secure, which could cause some signatures to become loose over time. This is why many of the books associated with ships' musters and some railway records we see at the National Archives are falling apart. Many different stitches exist, from basic links to complex decorative stitches, often a mark of an individual bookbinder.

A more modern system of binding evolved in the mid-1800s which involved gluing. Double-fan adhesive binding involved two signatures which were run over a roller to apply a thin layer of glue to each page edge. Then the two signatures were perfectly aligned to form a text block and the glue edges of the text block were attached to a piece of cloth lining to form the spine. Double-fan adhesive bound books could open completely flat and had a wide margin.

Once the stitching had been completed the bookbinder then set about binding the book with hard covers of card or wood, and a leather covering. There were various methods which he would have used.

Leather was the finest bookbinding material. Nothing really compares to the feel and appearance of a good quality leather book.

Goatskins and calf skins were used for the majority of work. Calf was the traditional choice for older English and European books. Goatskin (sometimes referred to as 'Morocco') was used for post 1900 work and was considered the most durable of all leathers.

Quarter leather binding

A quarter bound book had leather on the spine only. The rest of the book was covered in a matching cloth or decorative paper. As with all fine bindings, the spine was solid and had a hand sewn silk headband at the top and bottom. The edges were left plain or gilt. The spine was either smooth or had raised bands. A quarter bound book was considered to be a more economical way of binding a book as it used a small amount of leather, yet still looked its part when shelved.

Half leather binding

A half bound book had leather on the spine and the corners with the rest of the book covered in a matching cloth or decorative paper. The spine was again solid and had a hand sewn silk headband at the top and bottom. The spine could be smooth or have raised bands, and it could be lettered or decorated as desired. A half leather binding provided extra protection to the corners of the book, and was more suitable for larger books.

Full leather binding

A fully bound leather book was completely covered in leather again and had a hand sewn silk headband at the top and bottom. A full leather binding was luxurious and strong. Full leather books were usually titled and decorated in gold leaf.

Lettering was applied to the bindings using heated brass tools and alphabets. Bookbinders were often asked to make a special block for styles of lettering, motifs and crests.

Many bookbinders who operated using leather were also involved in the conservation process. Leather deteriorated over time and needed treatment of its surface to remain tactile. Conservation was necessary to repair damage to an existing book. The purpose of conservation was to slow the book's decay and restore it to a usable state while altering its physical properties as little as possible.

How your bookbinding ancestor would have operated depended upon the period as book styles changed over time. In the Medieval period books were generally large and heavy but around 1500 smaller and lighter books began to be created. The pages of 16th century bindings were made from linen or cotton paper with sheets of vellum or paper strengtheners sewn onto the first and last signatures. Books bound in the 16th century were the first to have decorative end sheets The sewing techniques used for 16th century binding were raised sewing on two to five sewing supports including both thongs and cords that were inset into the boards. The cords were usually made from hemp and linen. The boards were constructed from paper leaves pasted together, pasteboard, or pulp board, but were sometimes made of wood, usually beech. In the 16th century, bindings used boards that extended beyond the pages. The style is still used in modern books. The boards were then covered with leather.

Binding techniques used in the 17th and 18th centuries were generally similar to those used in the 16th century. The invention of the paper-making machine at the end of the 1700s increased the speed of manufacture and also made for an abundant supply of paper. The boards used in 17th century and 18th century bindings were not made of wood but were almost exclusively pasteboard or pulp board.

The 19th century saw the advent of case binding in which the pages and cover were prepared separately. The pages of 19th century books were made of poor-quality paper whose acidity gave rise to the brittle book crisis. Many books bound during the 19th century particularly from the early 1880s onward were machine sewn. The edges of pages of 19th century books were often brightly coloured some of which faded and changed colour because of incompatible dye pigments. Like modern bindings, the spines of 19th century bindings were rounded and lined first with cloth extending past the spine onto the boards and then with paper. The boards were again constructed from paperboard or pulp board with decorated covers. Cloth as opposed to skins was widely used for 19th century covers but paper and card became an increasingly popular material during the Victorian era. Elaborate decorative and illustrative cover designs also emerged during the Victorian period.

Case binding is a modern bookbinding technique dating from the 1820s that continues to be popularly used in the 21st century and effectively did away with all but few leather bound books.

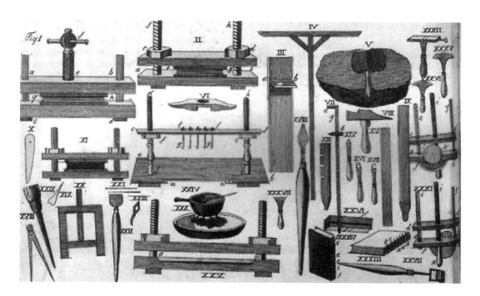

116. Tools typically used by our bookbinder ancestors.

Family bibles

Books with thick bevelled wooden boards became the model for the popular 19th century Family Bible which may well exist within your family archive and could be quite large and cumbersome.

The Family Bible became commonplace in most families and during the Victorian period was made in all shapes and sizes but most had some form of leather or skin covering. Unfortunately the design of most Family Bibles may have looked good when new, but the inferior materials used in the binding and the design of the Bibles produced mainly for home and family use were governed by the economic conditions of the Victorian era. In an attempt to keep costs to a minimum most Family Bibles were covered in thin sheepskin leather which did not have the characteristics to support the heavy boards hence they would often disintegrate with the boards becoming detached.

Records of bookbinders

As your bookbinder ancestor would have invariably worked independently or for a small bookbinding company the records of their service could well be available in local archives. Many would have belonged to trade unions or associations particularly from the mid-1800s. The Modern Records Centre at the University of Warwick holds the following records which are likely to provide some genealogical information:

National Union of Bookbinders and Machine Rulers

The National Union of Bookbinders and Machine Rulers originated when the mainly small local societies joined forces in 1835 to become the Bookbinders' Consolidated Relief Fund. This later developed into the Bookbinders' Consolidated Union which formed branches throughout the United Kingdom. However London retained its own societies despite the Union forming a branch there in 1857. The title of the union was changed in 1872 to the Bookbinders and Machine Rulers' Consolidated Union. In 1911 the various London societies and the Bookbinders and Machine Rulers' Consolidated Union amalgamated to become the National Union of Bookbinders and Machine Rulers. The Union continued until 1921 when it became the National Union of Printing, Bookbinding, Machine Ruling and Paper Workers having then joined forces with the National Union of Printing and Paper Workers.

Trade circulars and reports, 1848-1908 - contain information on union members including obituaries but it is necessary to have the full name of the member and the date of death in order to find relevant information.

London Branch Women Membership Register, 1917-1919 - for which the full name and time of application is needed. This is a register during the First World War when women replaced men in the job and could be extremely useful.

London Bookbinders Sick Benefit Society

Annual reports, 1910-1954 - Information on the benefits paid to members and in some cases deaths are annotated in the lists. In order to find details some idea of the period of sickness or death is needed - most are chronological.

Bookbinders and Machine Rulers Consolidated Union

In 1835, a number of local bookbinders' societies came together to form the Bookbinders' Consolidated Relief Fund and they formally amalgamated as the Bookbinders' Consolidated Union in 1840 later changing its name to the Bookbinders and Machine Rulers' Consolidated Union. In 1911, it further amalgamated with the Vellum Binders Trade Society, the London Consolidated Society of Journeymen Bookbinders and the Society of Day-working Bookbinders of London and Westminster becoming part of the National Union. This Union had branches throughout the country known initially as 'stations' and a full list of these is shown within the catalogue of the Modern Records Centre. The records can be quite comprehensive and of value to family historians detailing:

Lists of Members - Members whose dues were not in arrears are listed for every year by station from 1851. It also indicates those who were travelling around for work as well as those at a fixed employment base, those unemployed or those who were sick. After 1859 their joining date is shown.

Member Obituaries - are listed from 1849 including name, age, date of death and in some cases the cause of death. The death information about some members' wives is also shown. There is an alphabetical index to the obituaries for each volume.

National Union of Printing, Bookbinding and Paper Workers

The National Union of Printing, Bookbinding and Paper Workers arose out of a series of union amalgamations. The Vellum Binders Society founded in 1823, the Bookbinders Consolidated Union and the London Consolidated Lodge of Journeymen Bookbinders founded in 1840, merged to form the National Union of Bookbinders and Machine Rulers in 1911. The National Amalgamated Society of Printers' Warehousemen and Cutters formed in 1900, and the National Union of Printing and Paper Workers in 1914 merged with the National Union of Bookbinders to become the National Union of Printing, Bookbinding, Machine Ruling and Paper Workers in 1921. This became the National Union of Printing, Bookbinding and Paper Workers in 1928. In 1972 all these became SOGAT the Society of Graphical and Allied Trades which is today the Graphical, Paper and Media Union.

For many of the constituent unions there are also national and branch minute books, financial records, benevolent applications and other miscellaneous papers.

Leather bookbinders

Friendly Society of Journeymen Bookbinders of London and Westminster

1820-1832 The Journeymen Bookbinders of London were founded in 1786, becoming known as the London Consolidated Lodge of Journeymen Bookbinders in 1840. The Society was instituted to promote:

> 'a good understanding harmony & unanimity amongst the Journeymen Bookbinders of London & its vicinity, & to prevent any encroachments in their rights & privileges.'

The articles here listed to which members subscribed concern the organisation of the society, the duties of officers and the conduct of members.

Records include a volume of printed material, two manuscript items, audit of the Society's accounts, [1832]. Records are held at Senate House in London.

London bookbinders and paperworkers unions

Constituent Unions included 1866-1965 Bookbinders Consolidated Union, Shop Secretaries Association, London Consolidated Lodge of Journeymen Bookbinders, Vellum Binders Society, National Union of Bookbinders and Machine Rulers, National Union of Printing, Bookbinding, Machine Ruling and Paper Workers, National Union of Printing, Bookbinding and Paper Workers.

Records exist of these various unions from 1867 and include branch meeting reports, committee minutes, financial ledgers, correspondence on varying subjects, and miscellaneous papers.

Parchment and vellum maker

A Parchment or Vellum Maker was a skilled job. Many tanners turned their hand to this (and vice-versa) as the processes were similar to tanning leather. Parchment was produced from the skins of sheep once the grained surface had been scraped off and was commonly used as a writing material particularly for the legal documents such as leases, deeds, court records etc. because of its surface quality, all of which we will be familiar with as family historians. It was also frequently used by educational establishments for the production of diplomas and today we buy the chamois or 'wash leather'.

Vellum which was much tougher was produced from calf skin and used for bookbinding and by the military for drum skins.

The skins used for parchment and vellum did not undergo any form of tanning process but were cleaned, degreased and dried. Skins were suspended on a stretching frame and final removal of unwanted material was undertaken with a filling knife. Your ancestor would also have thrown hot water at the skins periodically in order to expedite the process of removing unwanted materials. A shaving knife was then used to make the skins of uniform thickness.

After this the skins were 'painted' with a thick cream which contained washing soda and were placed in a heated drying room. The soda dissolved any grease that may have been on the skins and acted like blotting paper for the grease.

Once the skins were dry they were washed and then smoothed with a pumice stone. They were then ready to be removed from the frame and could be used for manuscripts or other writing surfaces.

Bellows maker

Very often fancy goods makers and even harness makers also produced bellows for both industrial and personal use. In rural areas the blacksmith would have used bellows in his forge and the churches used bellows to power the organ. Bellows also had many industrial uses such as blowing dust from clocks and piano parts or other delicate and scientific instruments. Large bellows were used in forge shops and by manufacturers of steel items and as such it is possible that our ancestors would have been 'bellowers' or bellows makers. Not all the parts were made from leather and in some cases the loriner would have produced the metal parts, hence the connection to the harness trade.

Essentially, irrespective of their size the bellows were pear shaped boards joined by flexible concertinaed leather sides. Generally bellows were anything from 12 inches to 60 inches in length. The bellow type would govern upon whether the leather was stuck with glue or riveted. Most blacksmith's bellows were riveted because of the durability required during use.

Boat maker

The coracle was a small, lightweight boat traditionally used in Wales and in parts of western and south western England, Ireland particularly the Boyne River and around the River Spey in Scotland. The British also introduced the coracle to India. The word coracle is of Welsh origin coming from cwrwgl and is synonymous with the Gaelic word currach both originating in the early 16th century.

Some of our ancestors may well have been coracle makers. A coracle would have been built by locals as a 'cottage industry' and used for transport across rivers and for fishing. It is more or less oval in shape and looked similar to half a walnut shell. It was made using a framework of split and interwoven willow strips formed to give a shape of a hull and tied together with willow bark. The outer layer was originally made of either horse or cow-hide covered with a thin layer of tar to waterproof it. Because they were all hand made by local craftsmen and made to withstand local river conditions each coracle was unique in design. In general there was one style for each river but of course there were exceptions to the rule.

A currach is a sea-going craft. Again it is keel-less and may be propelled by sail or by oars used in conjunction with a sail. Currachs are still in use in the west of Ireland today and are still made by local craftsmen. The 'modern' constructional materials (as with coracles) are laths for the framework covered with a tarred calico cloth 'skin'.

Sea-going skin boats are known to have been in use around the British Isles centuries ago and records show that some had sixteen oars and may well have been over 25 feet in length.

Coracles have been in use in the British Isles from pre-Roman times. Whilst their prime use was for the purposes of transport and fishing, it has been recorded that they had been used by the military. There was clear evidence that the army used them in India during the Mutiny and other uprisings.

Coracle use in Scotland has significantly declined over the last 150 years but they were in use in Ireland until the late 1940s. They are, however, principally to be found nowadays around the rivers Teifi, Towy and Taf in Wales where they are primarily used for net fishing, with the net being held between two coracles which drifted downstream with the current.

117. Examples of Coracles typically used on the Welsh rivers.

228

All these coracles had to be licensed. Before licensing was introduced in the latter part of the 19th century, many households would have used a coracle to catch fish in order to feed the family.

At any given time, there would have been a few coracle makers making many coracle frames each season. The raw materials required were usually gathered by the fisherman and his family, who then covered the finished frames.

In 1863, the introduction of the expensive licence fee greatly reduced the number of coracles made and used on the rivers particularly in west Wales. In the 1850s it was estimated that there were over 300 coracles fishing the River Teifi at any one time and these were made by around forty coracle makers. Although the licence fee discouraged many from fishing, the great number of salmon returning to rivers in west Wales meant that the coracle fishermen who continued could earn a fair living. They shipped fish to the main markets in Cardiff and London by rail so there was a continued need for coracles which only had a useful life of about two years.

The introduction of licences also increased the volume of fish removed by illegal methods, which became a full time occupation for some families, resulting in many stories about local poachers and water bailiffs. Water bailiffs and police also used coracles and the Glamorgan Constabulary had its own coracle maker.

118. Coracle making was a skilled rural craft often undertaken by families.

There remained traditional coracle builders on the Severn at Ironbridge and Shrewsbury. In its hey-day, towards the end of the last century, there were more coracle builders on the River Severn than on any other river in the British Isles. Coracles were well used at Ironbridge as a ferry because there were very few bridges over that river in the area and the locals resented having to pay a toll to use the Ironbridge. At Shrewsbury coracles were used principally for rod and line fishing. There was also a tradition of coracles in north Wales and they existed on the River Dee around Llangollen until the early 1950s.

Coracles are distinguished from other river craft by their weight. They weighed between 25 and 40 pounds and they could be carried on the shoulders of the coracle man. They were propelled with a single paddle held in two hands over the bow, executing a figure of eight movement. The Coracle Society today preserves the tradition of old coracle makers and users. The making of coracles in the traditional way is a dying art.

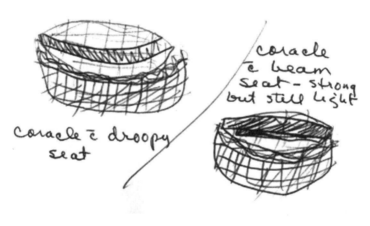

119. Example of a coracle makers journal c.1910.

The currach represents one of two traditions of boat and shipbuilding in Ireland: the skin-covered vessel and the wooden vessel.

The currach is referred to in *Navigatio sancti Brendani abbatis*. which contains an account of the building of an ocean-going boat: using iron tools, where the monks made a thin-sided and wooden-ribbed vessel *sicut mos est in illis partibus* covering it with hides cured with oak bark. Tar was used to seal the places where the skins joined. A mast was then erected in the middle of the vessel and an animal skin sail supplied. Usually the vessel was between 10 and 20 feet long although it was not unusual to see smaller vessels, it possessed a keel and a rudder, and had a wickerwork hull, strengthened by ribs and had a mast. The craft was constructed from the bottom up and a covering of animal hides added when the vessel was complete.

The aim of this design was to produce a sturdy, but lightweight vessel. Often men sailing between Islands, would carry their currach on their backs, and hide them out of sight for safe keeping.

120. Currach making was a coastal industry in Ireland.

Currachs which were covered in cow hide were still a common sight in the 1840s above Lough Ree in County Mayo.

There are still a few full time currach builders in Ireland. It is still not unusual to see the old country farmers with a currach on their land although most of them are in poor repair, or have been broken down altogether. Many fishermen still believe that currachs are far superior to the vessels that they use today. Because of the original shape, believed to be round or oval, they are known to sail a wave very effectively, something which a heavier, larger vessel cannot do.

Wang and sporran makers

Sporran is the Gaelic for purse. The origin of the sporran goes hand in hand with the traditional highland kilt. The functionality has survived from the European medieval pouch that was worn on a belt and illustrations of individuals at the time suggest admirably that it was in place of pockets. A sporran became common attire after 1745 but had been used much earlier in the Highlands of Scotland. As Highland attire did not come with the convenience of pockets, a leather pouch became a useful means of keeping together items such as money, food and at the height of clan skirmishes musket balls and the teeth of any unsuspecting rival clansmen.

The original sporrans were just circles of leather with holes around the circumference through which was threaded a leather thong which drew the neck of the pouch closed.

Deerskin was the obvious material for the early sporrans but in Victorian times when they became less functional and more dressy, the fashion was for goat-hair sporrans that all but covered the front of the kilt.

The sporran conventionally worn on the front of the kilt, was suspended by narrow leather belts, commonly called a wang, fed through loops that fasten in the pit of the back. It always hung a couple of inches below the belt buckle to avoid looking comical.

Conventionally, leather sporrans were of three types - simple daywear/utility pouches with no ornamentation except leather tooling; semidress sporrans with pewter, chrome or silver cantle (the hinged metal jaw at the top of the sporran that acted as a purse clasp) and the elaborate dress versions for formal functions or for use with military uniforms of the Scottish and Irish regiments. Hair sporrans were most often seen in pipe bands. Most sporrans carried some identifier such as the clan crest, or even the regimental emblem.

Sporrans were initially made by makers operating a croft based craft (cottage industry) and many of the clans would have their own sporran makers. Even today most sporran makers are individuals practicing their craft. Industrial production of sporrans did not really take off until after the First World War.

APPENDICES

Appendix 1 - Information held by the National Archives, Kew, relating to the leather industry

The following is a list of records collected from the Ministry of Labour, the Board of Trade, Board of Education and similar departments which can provide additional information particularly in regard to regulations, wage controls etc and should be researched as background information and to enhance research undertaken about individuals and companies.

The manufacture of leather goods and leather gloves, 1948, LAB44/38.
Leather belt maufacture, 1923-1967, LAB83/1391.
Leather manufacture, workers of skins, leather and furs, 1918-1965 LAB83/1409.
Footwear and leather goods manufacture, 1971, LAB44/95.
Leather Goods and Saddlery manufacture, 1945, ED46/610 and 1953, ED46/611.
Duty on leather used in manufacture of boots and shoes, 1937, CUST49/2185.
Manufacture of fur lined leather gloves, 1928, LAB11/768.
Leather Goods and Saddlery Manufacturers Association, 1951, CUST49/3694.
Weightman Bros leather book-binding registered design, 1894, BT51/75/228929.
Leather Splitting & Mfg Co. Ltd dissolved, 1903-1916, BT31/10280/77211.
Banbury Leather Manufacturing Co. Ltd dissolved 1907-1916, BT31/12095/94681 and J13/4702.
Charles Springbett, Golders Green, Leather goods mfg Conscription appeal 1915-1922 MH47/31/38.
Kingsthorpe Leather Mfg Co. Ltd dissolved, 1918-1932, BT31/24087/150691.
Saddlery, Harness and General Leather Goods Manufacturers Association dissolved, 1919-1932 BT31/24325/152549.
Leather Manufacturers Association Ltd dissolved, 1892-1932, BT31/15261/37290.
Manufacture of leather coats, 1929-1930, LAB11/857.
National Association of Manufacturers of Leather Board, Friendly Society, 1942-1950, FS12/418.

Memorial of William Blake manufacturer of Morocco Leather, 1780, T1/562/114 and 115.

Footwear Industry and the supply to armed forces, 1954-1955, BT258/428.

Leather import Policy, 1940-1957, BT258 (various items).

Surgical Boots and associated footwear factory manufacture, 1925-1926, LAB11/345.

Kingswood College of Boot & Shoe Manufacture, 1946-1952, ED168/474 and 475.

Boot and Shoe manufacture in Manchester and Salford, 1921-1930, LAB83/1568.

Boot and Shoe Manufacture, Leicestershire and Rutland, 1920-1939, LAB83/1613.

Boot and Shoe Manufacture, Street, Somerset, 1925-1943, LAB83/1583.

Boot and Shoe Manufacture, Birmingham, 1899-1927, LAB83/1605.

Rushden School of Boot and Shoe Manufacture, 1927-1941, ED82/285 and ED82/95.

Kettering County Boot & Shoe School, 1935, ED41/637.

Boot and Shoe manufacture, Northampton, 191901953, LAB83/1572.

Boot and Shoe Manufacture, Norwich, 1920-1939, LAB83/1570.

Rushden Shoe Manufacturers Ltd winding up, 1937, J13/15424.

Cash book of John Hilditch, Nantwich, 1833-1838, ASSI63/5.

Joseph Kilsby, Roade, shoe maker bankruptcy, 1842, B3/2900.

Northampton Mutual Shoe Manufacturing Industrial Society Ltd Friendly Society, 1861-1865, FS8/19/676.

Act regulating the manufacture of shoes, 1464-1465, C/49/35/20.

The above is not definitive and other records relating to such items as design registration, industrial relations and wills of shoe makers can be located using Discovery either by specific name or using generic terms such as shoe makers, leather manufacturers etc.

Appendix 2 - Auctioneers and trade catalogues

There is huge value in trying to locate both trade and auction catalogues relating to premises that you ancestor may have occupied in pursuance of his trade or craft.

121. Early Auction notice 1833.

Appendix 3 - Walsall leather trades

The following is a listing of manufacturers from the Leather Trades Directory for the early 20th century.

Leather Case Makers

W Guest & Co Ltd, Brace Street.

J H Hawkins & Co, Station Street.

Lavender & Ward Ltd, Bott Lane.

Moss, Stone & Co Ltd, Butts Road.

Patterson & Stone, Frederick Street.

D Power & Sons Ltd, Long Street.

Curriers

A T Arnold & Co, Holtshill Lane.

Beebee & Son, Queen Street.

H Beebee & Co, Park Street.

Boak Currying Co Ltd, Station Street (also Leather Tanners).

Bonser & Jones, Corporation Street.

Sidney Boyd & Co, Duncalfe Street.

J Clare, Lower Forster Street.

Levi Darby, Bradford Lane.

Eldon Currying Works, Eldon Street.

C E Fletcher, Walhouse Road.

Handford Greatrex & Co Ltd, Whittimere Street (also leather tanners).

E T Holden & Son Ltd, Park Street (also leather tanners).

H Hubble, Selborne Street.

H Hucker & Co, Short Acre.

C J Insley & Co, Wisemore.

Leamore Currying Co, Leamore Lane.

J Leckie & Co Ltd, Marsh Street.

Freer Street Leather Dressing Co, Freer Street.

D Mason & Sons Ltd, Marsh Street.

W Nisbet & Sons, Britannia Works, Stafford Street.

E Platt & Co, Portland Street.

E Price Ltd, South Street.

J P Rowbotham, Ablewell Street.

W H Russell, Bridgeman Street.

Smith & Riley, Orlando Street.

J Smith Ltd, Hill Street.

Stokes & Company, Hatherton, Street (also leather tanners).

J Taylor John Street.

J T Underwood Ltd, Cecil Street.

Walsall Leather Dressing Co, Frederick Street.

A Webster, Portland Street.

Fancy Leather Goods Makers

J Allderidge Ltd, Portland Street.

E Arrowsmith Samuel Street.

H R Aulton & Co, Warwick Works, Upper Forster Street.

Bennett Wilmot, Midland Road.

Birchfield's (Leather Goods) Ltd, Bradford Street.

Brace, Windle, Blyth & Co Ltd, Goodall Street.

F W Bromwich, Street Paul's Street.

W Brookes & Sons Ltd, Leicester Street.

H Butcher Wisemore.

Butler & Heath Ltd, Wisemore & School Street.

Claremont Fancy Leather Goods Manufacturers, Stafford Street.

W & L Cockayne Littleton Street.

Cope & Partners, Cecil Street.

Benjamin Cope & Sons Ltd, Leamore Lane.

Daines & Hatherway, Marsh Street.

J T Dance, Lichfield Street.

Frederick Stanley Co, Wolverhampton Road.

E J Gee, Lichfield Street.

Guest & Company Ltd, Brace Street.

Harvey Matthew & Co Ltd, Bath Street.

Harwood & Sons, Glebe Street.

F C Hathaway Ltd, Station Street.

G W Hathaway, Bradford Lane.

E Hawley & Co, Hill Street.

Heath, Machin & Co, Teddesley Street.

J Hodgkins, Mount Street.

J Homer, Mill Lane.

R Hucker (Walsall) Ltd, Spring Hill Road.

E Hulme, Frederick Street.

Ideal Leather Case Co, Sandwell Street.

S J Jackson, Littleton Street.

E Jefferies & Sons Ltd, Mountrath Street.

R T Johansen, Bradford Street.

J E Jupp, Hatherton Street.

Knight Leather Manufacturing Co, Ltd Goodall Street.

John Leckie & Co, Ltd Marsh Street.

W Leech, Lower Hall Lane.

Mark Cross Ltd, Warewell Street.

C B Mole, Littleton Street.

Moore & Butler, Caldmore Road.

John More & Company Ltd, Wolverhampton Street.
Moss Stone & Company Ltd, Butts Road.
C Mountford, Dudley Street.
J P Neville & Son, Persehouse Street.
Oak Leather Goods Co Ltd, School Terrace.
Overton & Co, Ablewell Street.
J Parfield & Co, Walsingham Street.
Patterson & Stone, Frederick Street.
S Peace & Co, Whittimere Street.
J S Pennell, Hart Street.
Philpot & Sons, Vicarage Street.
E C Poppleton, Chuckery Road.
Rhodes & Co, Lichfield Street.
S Richardson & Co, Station Street.
Ross & Son, Bloxwich Road.
S Russell & Sons Ltd, Wednesbury Road.
E F Sharp, Freer Street.
Sheldon & Sons Ltd, Corporation Street.
H Simmons, Revival Street.
S Smallwood, Bath Road.
Specialities (Leather) Ltd, Stafford Street.
Spence & Co, Whittimere Street.
S J Spiers, Cecil Street.
B Stanley, Lichfield Street.
G H Taylor, Wedge Street.
H S Thacker, Green Lane.
Arthur Thomas, Blue Lane West.
Walsall Super Fancy Leather Goods Manufacturers, Castle Works, Bath Road.
W T Wedge & Co, Intown Row.
Whitehouse & Hartley, Lion Works, Navigation Street.
E M Williams, Teddesley Street.
Wilson & Tilt, Upper Bridge Street.
Wincer & Plant Ltd, Glebe Street.
A Wood, Bridgeman Street.

Horse Collar Makers
A George, Bath Street.
M Joynes & Co, Bath Road.
E Stubbs, Lime Street.
Walsall Horse Collar Co, Wisemore.

Leather Belt Makers

Seldon & Co, Bank Street.
Walsall Leather Co Ltd, Stafford Street.

Leather Dealers & Merchants

A T Arnold & Co, Holtshill Lane.
H Beebee & Co, Park Street.
Boak Currying Co, Ltd Station Street.
Bonser & Jones, Corporation Street.
S Boyd & Co, Reliance Works, Duncalfe Street.
Bridge Leather Works, Vicarage Place.
J Clare, Lower Forster Street.
Darby & Son, West Bromwich Street.
C E Fletcher, Walhouse Road.
Handford Greatrex & Co Ltd, Whittimere Street.
T E Holden & Son Ltd, Park Street.
H Hucker & Co, Short Acre and Long Acre Street.
C J Insley & Co, Wisemore.
F McKinstry, Vicarage Street.
Morgan Leather Products Ltd, Queen Street.
Oak Tanning Company Ltd, Hatherton Street.
R T Palmer, Lower Hall Lane.
E Price Ltd, South Street.
J Share, George Street.
Smith & Riley, Orlando Street.
Stokes & Co (Tanners) Ltd, Hatherton Street.
S Swindley Ltd, Lower Rushall Street.
W Thompson, Hall Street.
B B Voss & Son, Marsh Street.
Walsall Leather Company Limited, Stafford Street.
Walsall Leather Dressing Company, Frederick Street.

Saddle & Harness Makers

A George, Bath Street.
J A Barnsby & Sons, Globe Works, Lower Forster Street.
T S Bathurst, Portland Street.
Beebee & Sons Limited, Persehouse Street.
J H Benton, Lower Forster Street.
Brace, Windle, Blythe & Co Ltd, Goodall Street.
W Brookes & Sons Ltd, Leicester Street.
Butler Bros, Park Street.

Jabez Cliff & Co, Globe Works, Lower Forster Street.
William Christie, Station Street.
English Saddle Co, Eldon Street.
W M Gilchrist, Bath Street.
J H Hateley, Teddesley Street.
J H Hawkins & Co, Station Street.
T Holt Station Street.
Jones & Rowley, Algernon Street.
M Joynes & Co, Bath Road.
John Leckie & Co Ltd, Marsh Street.
G A Marlow, Bath Street.
D McDonald, Milton Street.
T Marshall, Upper Forster Street.
D Mason & Son Ltd, Marsh Street.
F Moseley Ltd, Bath Street.
Moss Stone & Co Ltd, Butts Road.
G Nicklin & Son, Persehouse Street.
E & A Noirit, Hatherton Street.
Overton & Co, Ablewell Street.
Pardow & Co, Freer Street.
J Pedley, Wolverhampton Street.
Frank Ringrose, Midland Road.
F W Short, Upper Forster Street.
Stone & Roberts, Wednesbury Road.
H S Thacker, Green Lane.
Whitehouse, Cox & Co, Marsh Street.
H Whitehouse & Co, Green Lane.
Harry Willis, Stafford Street.
Wilmot Bennett, Midland Road.

Tanners
Oak Tanning Co Ltd, Hatherton Street.

Appendix 4 - Northampton Museum, Boot and Shoe Collection

The Boot and Shoe collection is one of the most extensive collections of its kind in the world. Roman and Medieval footwear to the work of modern designers is included and thus provides a comprehensive history of Northampton and its valuable shoe trade. The collection includes much that would interest family historians (see below) and upwards of 5,000 items of leather.

The Shoe Resources Centre holds the following:

Shoemaking tools, machines and components including lasts.
Retail trade material including shop furniture and fittings and advertising material.
Archive material including trade journals, company catalogues, books and photographs.
Fine art including paintings and prints depicting shoes and shoemaking.
Index of shoemakers and shoemaking firms from the Roman period onwards.
Specialist Reference Library.

BIBLIOGRAPHY

Bevington & Sons Bermondsey 1795 - 1950 - The history of a south London tannery, Geoffrey Bevington. Privately published 1993.

Rural Industries of England & Wales, Anna M Jones. ISBN: 0715812564.

Curriers of the City of London, Edward Mayer, Worshipful Company of Curriers 1968.

Tanners, L E Fuller, published by Franklin Walls 1966, ISBN: 0531010384.

Boot and Shoe Manufacture, Frank Plunkett 1931, published by Pitman, ISBN: B000885858.

Boot and Shoe Making, P J Batten 2006, Karnack Publishing, ISBN: 1904891276

The Sweated Trades, Duncan Bythell 1978, Harper Collins, ISBN: 0713412593. Contains information on outworkers in the shoe trade.

The Saddler, Sidney A Davis 1980, Shire Publications, ISBN: 0852635237.

The Working Saddlers Handbook, Keith Savory, J A Allen, ISBN: 0851318061.

Glove making at a glance, Isabel M Edwards 1926, Cope Press, ISBN: 1444699032

A Guide to making Leather Gloves A collection of historical articles on methods and materials, Various Authors, ISBN: 1447424948.

INDEXES

Compiled by Nicholas Newington-Irving FSG

Please note that these indexes refer solely to people and organisations mentioned in this book and are but a very small sample of those involved in the leather trade.

BARRATT (a Rushden bankrupt) 151
BARRETT Arthur 115
BARROW (a tanner & currier) 54
BATA Tomas 113
BATES Herbet Ernest 92, 98, 112
BATHURST T. S. 238
BATTEN P. J. 241
BAZELEY W. 11
BEALE Alfred 150
BEAUMONT Joseph 59
BEEBEE family 235, 238
BEEBEE H. 235, 238
BEEBEE (a currier) 235
BEEBEE (a leather dealer & merchant) 238
BEENSTOCK Fred 149
BELCHER Fred 208
BELEC Jerome 115
BENNET Thomas 197
BENNETT (a fancy leather goods maker)
 236
BENNETT (a saddle & harness maker) 239
BENNION (a shoe machinery manufacturer)
 146
BENSON (a tanner) 58
BENTON J. H. 238
BERRY Arthur Ernest 179
BETSON James 150
BEVINGTON family 54, 241
BEVINGTON Alfred 29
BEVINGTON Geoffrey 241
BIDE William 203
BIGHAM John 5
BILK Acker 130
BING Emily 115
BIRCHFIELD (a fancy leather goods maker)
 236
BIRD John 123
BLACKBURN (a linings producer) 116
BLAKE family 203
BLAKE H. 203
BLAKE William 234
BLAKE (a sole-sewing machine inventor)
 83, 107, 145
BLAND family 55
BLOOR Richard 115
BLYTH (a fancy leather goods maker) 236

BLYTHE (a saddle & harness maker) 238
BOAK (a currier & leather tanner) 235
BOGART Humphrey 144
BOND James 148
BONSER (a currier) 235
BONSER (a leather dealer & merchant) 238
BOORMAN F. 208
BOOT (a surname derived from the leather
 trades) 11
BOOTH Alfred 38
BOOTH Bramwell (Mrs) 136
BOOTH Charles 38-39
BOSTOCK family 155
BOSTOCK Edwin 90, 155-156
BOSTOCK Frederick 155
BOSTOCK Thomas 155
BOSTOCK Thomas senior 155
BOYD Sidney 235, 238
BRACE (a fancy leather goods maker) 236
BRACE (a saddle & harness maker) 238
BRACEGIRDLE (a surname derived from
 the leather trades) 11
BRADD Dennis 115
BRADFORD Thomas 188
BRADLEY L. E. 11
BRANDON Henry 115
BRIGHAM Thomas 181
BRIGHOUSE Henry 149
BROMWICH F. W. 236
BROOKES family 236, 238
BROOKES W. 236, 238
BROOKS (a bootmaker) 158
BROWETT Louisa 5
BROWN George F. 151
BRUCE William 152
BUCKINGHAM family 204
BUCKLER (a surname derived from the
 leather trades) 12
BULLOCK family 54-55
BURCH George 115
BURRELL George 150
BURRELL (a surname derived from the
 leather trades) 11
BUTCHER H. 236
BUTLER Brothers 238
BUTLER (a fancy leather goods maker) 236

BUTLER (a surname derived from the leather trades) 11
BUTTERWORTH Joshua 27
BYTHELL Duncan 241
CAMPBELL Isaac 132
CANN (of Northampton) 152
CARTER John 69
CASE Charles 55
CASWELL (of Kettering) 152
CHAMBERS (a Madras leather trader) 23
CHAPLIN Charles (Sir) 144
CHAPLIN George 115
CHATER (of Northampton) 152
CHAUCER (a surname derived from the leather trades) 12
CHAWNER (a saddler) 187
CHRISTIE William 239
CHURCH (a shoemaker) 148
CLARE J. 235, 238
CLARK family 154, 204
CLARK Catherine 84
CLARK C. 154
CLARK Elizabeth 84
CLARK J. 154
CLARK William 84
CLARK William junior 84
CLARK (a glover) 204
CLARK (an adhesive sole inventor) 91
CLARK (of Rushden) 153
CLAYSON Charles 150
CLERMONT: see DeCLERMONT
CLIFF Jabez 239
COBB Thomas 75
COCKAYNE L. 236
COCKAYNE W. 236
COCKERELL C. E. 208
COLE John 115
COLFE Abraham (Rev) 41-42
COLSON (a Rushden bankrupt) 151
COMBER Amelia 84
COMBER Caroline 84
COMBER Susannah 84
COMBER Thomas 84
COMBER Walter 84
CONNOLLY (a Wimbledon currier) 50
COOKE Richard 69

COOKE (Mrs) 69
COOPER Gary 144
COOPER William 133
COPE family 236
COPE Benjamin 236
COPE (a fancy leather goods maker) 236
CORNISH Robert 75
CORY Violet Winifred 11
COTTLE (a Calcutta tannery operator) 22
COTTON Richard (Sir) 177
COUVES William 115
COX John 29, 150
COX (a saddle & harness maker) 239
COXON John 5
CRAWLEY Elizabeth 63
CRICK Thomas 90
CROKE John 18-19
CROMWELL Oliver 134
CROOKENDEN Caleb 28
CROOKS Leonard 115
CROOKS Stanley 115
CROSS Mark 236
CURRES (a surname derived from the leather trades) 12
CURRIER (a surname derived from the leather trades) 12
CUTHBERTSON (a Calcutta tannery operator) 22
CUTTER Daniel 5
DAINES (a fancy leather goods maker) 236
DANCE J. T. 236
DARBY family 238
DARBY Levi 235
DARBY (a leather dealer & merchant) 238
DARLOW (a Rushden bankrupt) 151
DARNELL A. J. 148
DARWEN family 163
DARWEN J. 163
DAVID (London representatives of an Indian leather trader) 23
DAVIS Sidney A. 241
DAVY Humphrey (Sir) 14
DAWES (a benefactor) 33
DAWSON Ronald 115
DAYEYNE Thomas 27
DE FULFORD Thomas 118

DE ROTHSCHILD Guy 145
DEB S. 23
DeCLERMONT (a Bermondsey leather
  trader) 27, 55
DENMAN J. 56
DENT (a glover) 203
DERBYSHIRE (a linings producer) 116
DODDINGTON Frederick Thomas 5
DONNER (a Bermondsey leather trader) 27,
  55
DONOVAN family 11
DONOVAN D. J. 11
DONOVAN Esther 11
DONOVAN Mary 11
DOOLITTLE Alfred 215
DOOLITTLE Eliza 215
DORRELL Stanley 115
DOULTON Henry (Sir) 117
DUKE Timothy 207
DUKE (a sports ball maker) 206
DUNMORE Edward 150
DYSON Horace 156
DYSTER (a hide, skin & horn broker) 55
EDAKEY George 5
EDAKEY John 5
EDEN Anthony (Sir) 145
EDEN (a Rushden bankrupt) 151
EDWARDS Isabel M. 241
ELLIOTT Samuel 75
EVANS Ewart 164
FAIRCHILD Herbert 115
FAIREY Caroline 84
FAIREY Emma I. 84
FAIREY George 84
FAIREY Joseph 84
FAIREY Sarah 84
FARAWAY Arthur 115
FAULKNER William 150
FAUNTLEROY Charles 29
FERBRAS Robert 40
FISHER George 75
FISHER John 117
FLAWN (a Rushden bankrupt) 151
FLEMMING John 55
FLETCHER C. E. 235, 238
FOLEY William 115

FORD Henry 145
FORSTNER John 23
FOSTER Arnold 131
FOUNTAIN family 68-70
FOUNTAIN John 68-69
FOUNTAIN John III 69
FOUNTAIN John junior 69
FOUNTAIN Mary 69
FOWNES Brothers 203
FRANCIS J. C. 71
FREAK C. 11
FROST John 115
FROST William 115
FULFORD: see DE FULFORD
FULLER L. E. 241
GALE (a tanner & currier) 54
GAME George 115
GANT (a surname derived from the leather
  trades) 12
GARDINER Leslie 115
GARNER James 144
GARRARD Eric 115
GEATREX (a currier & leather tanner) 235
GEE Arthur 165
GEE E. J. 236
GENT John Andrew 150
GEORGE A. 237-238
GIBSON family 157
GILCHRIST W. M. 239
GILES Les 115
GILL Harry 185
GLASTONBURY (a glover) 204
GLOVER (a surname derived from the
  leather trades) 12
GODDEN Josiah Nutt 204
GOOCH John 75
GOODING Samuel 75
GOODYEAR (a welt-sewing machine
  inventor) 145
GOTCH Thomas 81
GOULDING Robert 115
GRANT Cary 144
GRAVE Joseph 5
GRAYSTONES Richard 75
GREATREX (a leather dealer & merchant)
  238

GREEN Charles A. 84
GREEN Edward 103
GREEN G. F. 125
GREEN Jane 84
GREEN Walter 84
GREEN William 84
GRIBBLE James 131
GRIGGS R. 152
GUEST W . 235
GUEST (a fancy leather goods maker) 236
GUNN (a sports ball maker) 207
HACKSLEY John 150
HALL family 153
HALSTEAD Robert 5
HAMMOND James 5
HAMPTON Brothers 116
HANDFORD (a leather dealer & merchant) 235, 238
HARDIE Kier 132
HARGREAVES Charles 5
HARGREAVES Michael 5
HARMONIAUX Gordon 115
HARPER (a Calcutta tannery operator) 22
HARRISON John 58, 75
HARRISON Rex 144
HARTLEY (a fancy leather goods maker) 237
HARVEY John 115, 199
HARWOOD family 210, 236
HARWOOD (a fancy leather goods maker) 210, 236
HASLEDEN (a Rushden bankrupt) 151
HASLEWOOD John 40
HATELEY J. H. 239
HATHAWAY F. C. 236
HATHAWAY G. W. 236
HATHERWAY (a fancy leather goods maker) 236
HAWKINS George 115
HAWKINS G. T. 152
HAWKINS J. H. 239, 235
HAWLEY E. 236
HAWORTH John 5
HAY William 75
HAYES Reginald 115
HAYNES (of Northampton) 152

HEARN F. 57
HEATH H. M. 208
HEATH (a fancy leather goods maker) 236
HEINZ Howard 145
HEPBURN (a Bermondsey leather trader) 27
HEPBURN (a tanner & currier) 54
HEPWORTH (Mrs) 149
HERST Norbert 56
HERST (a leather trade merchant) 56
HEYGATE Jas 151
HILDITCH John 234
HOBDAY (a saddler & harness maker) 175
HOBSON Alice 149
HOBSON Henry 149
HOBSON Maggie 149
HOBSON Vicky 149
HOCKLEY Leslie 115
HODGKIN John Mason 152
HODGKINS J. 236
HOLDEN family 235, 238
HOLDEN Edward Thomas (Sir) 39, 235
HOLDEN T. E. 238
HOLLINGTON Horace 115
HOLT T. 239
HOMER J. 236
HOMER (ancient Greek writer) 13
HONDA Henry 144
HORNIDGE W. B. 11
HOWE Elias 193
HOWLETT James 157
HOWLETT John Geoffrey 157
HOWLETT (a leather currier) 157
HOYLE William 4
HUBBLE H. 235
HUCKER H. 235, 238
HUCKER R. 236
HUGHE Samuel 84
HUGHE Syncosh 84
HUGHES Joseph 115
HUGHES Ronald 115
HUGHES Thomas 150
HULME E. 236
HUSSEY John 123
INSKIP William 11, 125
INSLEY C. J. 235, 238
IRVING: see NEWINGTON-IRVING

IVENSON John 75
IVES T. 206
JACKMAN Peter 115
JACKSON S. J. 236
JACKSON (a benefactor) 33
JACKSON (a Bolton mill owner) 59
JAMES Brothers 180
JAQUES (of Rushden) 153
JEFFRIES Cheater 203
JEFFRIES E. 236
JEFFRIES (a saddlers) 188
JESSOP George 5
JOHANSEN R. T. 236
JONES Anna M. 241
JONES E. F. 11
JONES William George 115
JONES (a currier) 235
JONES (a leather dealer & merchant) 238
JONES (a saddle & harness maker) 239
JONES (a shoe manufacturer) 103
JOSLIN (a shoe mercer) 57
JOYNES M. 237, 239
JUPP J. E. 236
KARLOFF Boris 144
KELLER Thomas 150
KEMPSTER John 115
KENNEDY John Fitzgerald 145
KENT William 28
KEYSER S. A. 27
KIDD W. J. 58
KILSBY Joseph 234
KING Peter 115
KIRBY family 186
KIRBY David 150
KIRBY T. 186
KNIGHT (a fancy leather goods maker) 236
LAMB Alexander 28
LANE family 204
LANE Richard 204
LAVENDER (a leather case maker) 235
LAWRENCE Joseph 71
LAWRENCE (a shoemaker) 131
LEARMONTH (a Bermondsey leather
  trader) 27
LECKIE John 236, 239
LECKIE J. 235

LEECH Herbert James 180
LEECH William James 180
LEECH W. 236
LEGG Henry 115
LETCH Arthur 115
LILLEY Harold 204
LINDSELL Francis 115
LOAKE Brothers 153
LOGSDON Edward 5
LORINER (a surname derived from the
  leather trades) 12
LORNE David 75
LOVEDAY Frederick 84
LOVERIDGE George 11
LOWE W. H. 11
LUPTON James 5
LYNCH James 115
M'MURDO Edward 29
MACHIN (a fancy leather goods maker) 236
MACKAY: see BLAKE (a sole-sewing
  machine inventor)
MACKENZIE Eneas 122
MACRAE James 27
MAIDLOW Charles 5
MANBY William 41
MANFIELD family 153
MANSFIELD Sydney 115
MARLOW G. A. 239
MARSDEN William (Dr) 117
MARSHALL T. 239
MARTIN Dean 145
MARTIN Thomas 205
MARX Karl 145
MASKEW Thomas 29
MASON family 235, 239
MASON D. 235, 239
MATTHEW Harvey 236
MAW family 55
MAYER Edward 241
MAYHEW F. W. 175
McDONALD D. 239
McKINSTRY F. 238
McLEARY Thomas 115
McQUEEN Steve 144
MENUHIN Yehudi 145
MEREDITH Frederick 115

WATTS William 75
WATTS (a Calcutta tannery operator) 22
WATTS (London representatives of an Indian leather trader) 23
WEBB family 59, 153
WEBB Alan 115
WEBB Cliff 182
WEBB George 153
WEBSTER A. 235
WEBSTER Gabriel 5
WEDGE W. T. 237
WEIGHTMAN Brothers 233
WELLER James 115
WELLS Frederick 208
WEST John Richard 5
WEST (a Rushden bankrupt) 151
WESTLEY (of Burton Latimer) 154
WHITE George (Sir) 157
WHITE John 137, 153
WHITEHOUSE H. 239
WHITEHOUSE (a fancy leather goods maker) 237
WHITEHOUSE (a saddle & harness maker) 239
WHITNEY (of Burton Latimer) 154
WHITTINGTON Richard ('Dick') 40, 56
WILD family 51
WILD Charles 51
WILD Edward 51
WILD Elizabeth 51
WILD Jane 51
WILD Sarah 51
WILD Sarah junior 51
WILD Thomas 51
WILD Thomas junior 51
WILD Wade 51
WILD William 133-134
WILKES Marjorie 204
WILLIAMS E. M. 237
WILLIAMS J. 71
WILLIAMS (Mrs) 11
WILLIAMSON Henry 50
WILLIAMSON John 50
WILLIAMSON John James 50
WILLIAMSON Maurice 115
WILLIAMSON Stephen 50

WILLIAMSON Stephen junior 50
WILLIAMSON Susannah: see ROW Susannah
WILLIS Harry 239
WILMOT (a fancy leather goods maker) 236
WILSON T. K. 234
WILSON (a fancy leather goods maker) 237
WINCER (a fancy leather goods maker) 237
WINDLE (a fancy leather goods maker) 236
WINDLE (a saddle & harness maker) 238
WINDLEY Frederick 115
WINTER James 192-193
WISDEN (a sports ball maker) 206
WOOD A. 237
WOOD William 11
WOOLSTON John 136
WRIGHT Arthur 115
WRIGHT John 115
WRIGHT Joseph 150
WRIGHT William 75
YOUNG Alfred 150
YOUNG (a Calcutta Tannery operator) 22

INDEX OF CORPORATIONS, ORGANIZATIONE, etc

see also the Index of Names for sole traders

Aberdeen Hand-Sewn Boot & Shoe Makers Union 130
Ainge & Hasleden 151
Alfred Booth & Co. 38
Alfred Gillett Charitable Trust 154-155
Alfred Reader & Co. 205, 207-209
Allen & Caswell 152
Allsop Bros. Ltd. 54
Amalgamated Association of Boot & Shoe Makers 125, 128, 130
Amalgamated Cordwainers Association 125, 127
Amalgamated Society of Boot & Shoe Makers 127, 130
Amalgamated Society of Boot & Shoe Makers of Ireland 127
Amalgamated Society of Boot & Shoe Makers & Repairers 130

Stewart Adams & Sons 203
Stokes & Co. 235
Stokes & Co. (Tanners) Ltd. 238
Stone & Roberts 239
Sun Fire Office 28
Surridge 206
Sweated Trade Commission 44, 176
S. Boyd & Co. 238
S. Deb & Co. 23
S. Peace & Co. 237
S. Richardson & Co. 237
S. Russell & Sons Ltd. 237
S. Swindley Ltd. 238
S.A. Keyser 27
S.E. Norris & Co. Ltd. 58
Tebbutt & Hall Bros. 153
Tecnic Boot Co. Ltd. 113, 153
Teston Independent Society of Cricket Ball
    Makers 208-209
Tonbridge Sports Industries 206
True-form 113
Turney Bros. Ltd. 59
Tworts 206
T. E. Holden & Son Ltd. 238
T. Ives & Son, Ltd. 206
T. Kirby & Sons 186
Union of Clickers & Rough-stuff Cutters 125
United Shoe Machinery Co. 146
United Society of Boot & Shoe Makers 130
United Tanners Federation 57
Vellum Binders Society 225-226
Vellum Binders Trade Society 225
Walker & Aldridge 188
Walsall Horse Collar Co. Ltd. 237
Walsall Leather Co. Ltd. 238
Walsall Leather Dressing Co. Ltd. 235, 238
Walsall Science & Art Institute 39
Walsall Super Fancy Leather Goods
    Manufacturers 237
Walsall & District Amalgamated Leather
    Trades Union 130
Watts & Co. 22-23
Webb & Son 59
Weightman Bros. 233
Wellingborough Boot & Shoe Manufacturing
    Co. Ltd. 153

West Ham United Football Club 114
Western District Ladies Hand-Sewn Boot &
    Shoe Makers 129
Whitehouse & Hartley 237
Whitehouse, Cox & Co. 239
Whitney & Westley Ltd. 154
Wild Tannery 51
William Axtell & Son 27
William Paul Ltd. 58-59
William Sutton, Ltd. 58
William Walker & Sons Ltd. 58
Wilson & Tilt 237
Wincer & Plant Ltd. 237
Wisden 206
Worcestershire Association of Glover
    Manufacturers 204
Working Men's Club & Institute Union 138
Worshipful Company of Coach & Coach
    Harness Makers 180-182
Worshipful Company of Cordwainers 118,
    140
Worshipful Company of Curriers 24, 31-33,
    186, 241
Worshipful Company of Glovers 191, 195-
    196
Worshipful Company of Glovers & Pursers
    196
Worshipful Company of Horners 213-214
Worshipful Company of Leather Dressers 186
Worshipful Company of Leathersellers 39-
    43, 140, 196
Worshipful Company of Loriners 182, 184-
    186
Worshipful Company of Pattenmakers 159
Worshipful Company of Saddlers 176-177
Worshipful Company of Upholders 181
W. Barratt & Co. Ltd. 152
W. Brookes & Sons Ltd. 236, 238
W. Guest & Co. Ltd. 235
W. Nisbet & Sons 235
W.J. Kidd Ltd. 58
W.J. Turney & Co. Ltd. 59
W.T. Wedges & Co. 237
Young & Co. 22
Youngents Ltd. 152

About the SOCIETY OF GENEALOGISTS

Founded in 1911 the Society of Genealogists (SoG) is Britain's premier family history organisation. The Society maintains a splendid genealogical library and education centre in Clerkenwell.

The Society's collections are particularly valuable for research before the start of civil registration of births marriages and deaths in 1837 but there is plenty for the beginner too. Anyone starting their family history can use the online census indexes or look for entries in birth, death and marriage online indexes in the free open community access area.

The Library contains Britain's largest collection of parish register copies, indexes and transcripts and many nonconformist registers. Most cover the period from the 16th century to 1837. Along with registers, the library holds local histories, copies of churchyard gravestone inscriptions, poll books, trade directories, census indexes and a wealth of information about the parishes where our ancestors lived.

Unique indexes include Boyd's Marriage Index with more than seven million names compiled from 4300 churches between 1538-1837 and the Bernau Index with references to 4.5 million names in Chancery and other court proceedings. Also available are indexes of wills and marriage licences, and of apprentices and masters (1710-1774). Over the years the Society has rescued and made available records discarded by government departments and institutions but of great interest to family historians. These include records from the Bank of England, Trinity House and information on teachers and civil servants.

Boyd's and other unique databases are published online on **www.findmypast.com** and on the Society's own website **www.sog.org.uk**. There is free access to these and many other genealogical sites within the Library's Internet suite.

The Society is the ideal place to discover if a family history has already been researched with its huge collection of unique manuscript notes, extensive collections of past research and printed and unpublished family histories. If you expect to be carrying out family history research in the British Isles then membership is very worthwhile although non-members can use the library for a small search fee.

The Society of Genealogists is an educational charity. It holds study days, lectures, tutorials and evening classes and speakers from the Society regularly speak to groups around the country. The SoG runs workshops demonstrating computer programs of use to family historians. A diary of events and booking forms are available from the Society on 020 7553 3290 or on the website **www.sog.org.uk**.

Members enjoy free access to the Library, certain borrowing rights, free copies of the quarterly *Genealogists' Magazine* and various discounts of publications, courses, postal searches along with free access to data on the members' area of our website.

More details about the Society can be found on its extensive website at **www.sog.org.uk**

For a free Membership Pack contact the Society at:

14 Charterhouse Buildings,
Goswell Road,
London EC1M 7BA.
Telephone: 020 7553 3291
Fax: 020 7250 1800

The Society is always happy to help with enquiries and the following contacts may be of assistance.

Library & shop hours:

Monday	Closed
Tuesday	10am - 6pm
Wednesday	10am - 6pm
Thursday	10am - 8pm
Friday	Closed
Saturday	10am - 6pm
Sunday	Closed

Contacts:

Membership
Tel: 020 7553 3291
Email: membership@sog.org.uk

Lectures & courses
Tel: 020 7553 3290
Email: events@sog.org.uk

Family history advice line
Tel: 020 7490 8911
See website for availability